Why Viet Nam?

CHINA

Kochiu Mengtzu Wenshan Paise

Lan Toui Hok ou Lao Cai Ha Giang Chinghsi
Lai Chau P'inghsiang

Boun Neva NORTH VIET-NAM
Dien Bien Phu Thai
Muong Sai Mai Son Nguyen
Son Tay Bac Ninh Haiphong
LAOS Samneva Hoa Binh HANOI Hai Hon Gai
Hoa Binh Duong Kien An
LUANG PRABANG Nam Dinh Thai Binh
Plain of Jars Khang Ninh Binh Lang Son
Xieng Khouang Khai Ke Bon Thanh Hoa

Gulf of Tonkin

VIENTIANE Vinh
Nong Khai Bung Kan Ha Tinh

Nakhon HAINAN
Phanom
Sakon Nakhon Thakhek Chang Hoa
Dong Hoi
Kuchinaral Seno Chap Le
Kalasin Savannakhet Sepone Le Thuy
Maha Sarakham Ben Vinh Linh
Roi Et Lao Quang CEASE FIRE LINE
THAILAND Yasothon Bao Dong Ha
Huong Quang Tri
Hoa
Sisaket Ubon Hue
Ratchathani Saravane Phu Bay Da Nang
Pakse
Attopeu

Quang Ngai

Kontum
Pleiku
CAMBODIA SOUTH Qui Nhon
Kompong Thom Song Cau
Kompong Baray Buon Brieng VIET Tuy Hoa
Chhang Prek Kak Kratie
Kompong Cham Ban Me Thuot NAM Nha Trang
PHNOM PENH Loc Ninh Da Lat
Tay Ninh Thu Dau Mot Duc Phong Cam Ranh
Chant Rea Phu Cuong
Moc Hoa Bien Hoa Phan Rang
Ha Tien SAIGON Gia
Long Xuyen Tan An Dinh
Sa Dec My Binh Gia Phan Thiet
Rach Gia Vinh Tho Go Cong Vung Tau
Can Tho Long Truc Giang
Phu Vinh
Khanh South China Sea
Hung
Ca Mau Bac Lieu

MILES
0   100   Con Son Is.

BOUNDARIES
ROADS
RAILROADS

The Washington Post

Why Viet Nam?

FRANK N. TRAGER

FREDERICK A. PRAEGER, Publishers
New York • Washington • London

FREDERICK A. PRAEGER, PUBLISHERS
111 Fourth Avenue, New York, N.Y. 10003, U.S.A.
77-79 Charlotte Street, London, W.1, England

Published in the United States of America in 1966
by Frederick A. Praeger, Inc., Publishers

© 1966 by Frederick A. Praeger, Inc.

Library of Congress Catalog Card Number: 66–14508

Printed in the United States of America

Contents

PART I
Viet Nam Before the Geneva Agreements of 1954

Introduction: Southeast Asia and the United States   3

1. THE VIET PEOPLE: WHO, WHEN, AND WHERE   16
   - *The Indochinese Peninsula*   21
   - *The French Intrusion and Conquest*   24

2. VIET NAM FIGHTS FOR INDEPENDENCE AGAINST THE FRENCH   33
   - *French Rule and the Rise and Early Struggles of Vietnamese Nationalism, 1885–1926*   33
   - *The Struggle Continues—To the Proclamation of the Democratic Republic of Viet Nam*   51
   - *On Warfare Against a Colonial Power Before World War II: Some Conclusions*   59

PART II
The End of Hostilities? And Geneva 1954

3. THE WAR AGAINST THE FRENCH: TO DIEN BIEN PHU   67

4. THE GENEVA CONFERENCE OF 1954—AND ITS RESULTS   81
   - *Background to Geneva*   81
   - *The Geneva Agreements*   88

PART III
The Republic of Viet Nam—The Diem Regime

5. THE WAR BETWEEN THE STATES BEGINS   105
      The Advent of Ngo Dinh Diem   107
      *"The Red Tide of Communism Overflowed into
           Viet Nam"*   115
6. THE SEARCH FOR SECURITY, STABILITY, AND IMPROVE-
      MENT IN THE CONDITIONS OF LIVING, 1955–63   122
      Survival with Progress   126
7. THE UNITED STATES AND THE DIEM REGIME   140
      *To Aid the Republic of Viet Nam: A Commit-
           ment of Three Presidents*   141
      Aid to Viet Nam   144
      The Attempted Coup of November, 1960   157
8. THE PROTRACTED CONFLICT, OR LONG WAR, SHORT
      CAMPAIGN   163
      Communist Strategy After 1956   164
      The End of Diem   171
      The United States Commitment Stands   179

PART IV
What Is at Stake in Viet Nam?

9. TO GUARANTEE THE INDEPENDENCE OF THE REPUBLIC
      OF VIET NAM   187
      The Strike Against the North   187
      Reaction at Home   194
10. CONCLUSION: FOR A FREE VIET NAM   206
      What Price Wars of National Liberation?   206
      The Honolulu Meeting   210
      *The Stakes in Viet Nam: Freedom for the Repub-
           lic of Viet Nam*   211
EPILOGUE   217
APPENDIX   221
NOTES   227
INDEX   233

part one

*Viet Nam Before the
Geneva Agreements of 1954*

Introduction: *Southeast Asia and the United States*

The term Southeast Asia came into general usage during World War II, when the Allies created a Southeast Asia Command, under Lord Louis Mountbatten, with headquarters in Ceylon. Today, Southeast Asia is the generally accepted designation for the area south of the eastern Himalayan ranges, stretching from the Pacific Ocean to the Bay of Bengal. It comprises nine independent states—the Philippines, Indonesia, Malaysia, the Republic of Viet Nam (South), Cambodia, Laos, Thailand, Burma, and the city-state of Singapore; the (Communist) Democratic Republic of Viet Nam; the eastern portion of the island of New Guinea under Australian trusteeship; the partially dependent Sultanate of Brunei, and the smaller half of the island of Timor, a Portuguese colony. This vast area, with a population of some 230 million, has been the object of Chinese, Japanese, and Western imperialism.

In one sense, Southeast Asia represents a confluence of two great civilizations, the Indian and the Chinese. For the most part, the people of Southeast Asia are racial cousins of the Chinese, and their art, religion, and literature have been heavily influenced by India. It would be a mistake, however, to regard Southeast Asian cultures as imitations or mere copies of these traditional influences. Southeast Asians, over the millenniums, have selectively adapted and developed their borrowings: Buddhism, which originated in India but has virtually disappeared from there, has triumphed in Burma, Thailand, Laos, Cambodia, and, to some extent, in Viet Nam, having superseded or absorbed earlier Hinduized and animist elements; Islam, making its way across the Indian Ocean and overland from India, has captured the loyalty of the overwhelming majority of the peoples in Malaya and the Indonesian archipelago. (Only in the Philippines have missionary efforts succeeded in making Christianity the majority religion.) When the Europeans came to Southeast Asia beginning in the sixteenth century, they encountered flourishing civilizations of a high level. The magnificent cultural legacies of Pagan (Burma), Angkor Thom (Cambodia), and Borodbudhur (Indonesia) bear witness to this past. Pride in this past has been vigorously revived under the impulse of contemporary nationalism in Southeast Asia.

The countries of Southeast Asia share a number of characteristics:

1. They are all old nations with long histories and rich, though diverse, cultures.

2. With the exception of Thailand, they all lost their independence in modern times to old-style Western imperialism, and, for the most part, regained their independence after World War II by adopting old-style Western nationalism.

3. They are rich in resources, which are still largely underdeveloped. Southeast Asia supplies 90 per cent of the world's natural rubber and 60 per cent of its tin ore. The region is the rice bowl of Asia, capable even in today's turbulent times of exporting 4.5–5 million tons of rice. It is rich in hardwoods, fibers, oil, and other natural products. With the exception of the island of Java in Indonesia, and the Red River valley in North Viet Nam, the region is underpopulated with respect to its resource base, having an average density of about 100 persons per square mile.

4. On attaining independence, the governments of the various countries began to engage in the task of nationbuilding and in the search for stability, law and order, security, and improvement in the conditions of living.

5. At the beginning of their search for these goals, each

nation in Southeast Asia became the victim of some form of Communist insurrectionary activity, which started in most areas about the time that the Cominform was organized in Warsaw—in September, 1947—at the direction and under the control of Moscow.

6. The states of the Southeast Asian region are of strategic value; they dominate the sea lanes of the eastern Indian Ocean and the South China Sea. This has made the region a target of China's imperialist "march to the tropics," which, begun many centuries ago, has continued with even more emphasis and effect since the People's Republic of China was established as the Communist government of mainland China.

Despite these shared characteristics, Southeast Asia is diverse in religion, culture, language, and ethnic composition. The leaders of Southeast Asian independence were more at home in dealing with their former metropolitan powers in London, Paris, The Hague, and Washington than in dealing with each other. Past wars, e.g., between the Theravada Buddhist Burmese and the Theravada Buddhist Thai (there were fourteen such wars between the fifteenth and the eighteenth centuries), between the Thai and the Theravada Cambodians, between the Cambodians and the Confucian–Mahayana Buddhist Vietnamese, and between the Muslim peoples of the Malayo-Indonesian archipelago, have inhibited intraregional cooperation. In fact, most of these states had had "imperialist" periods of their own before the European conquests, something they now prefer to forget or to ignore.

Early attempts at regional unity were promoted by Prime Minister Nehru of India in New Delhi in 1947 and in 1949, and by the Colombo Powers (India, Pakistan, Ceylon, Burma, and Indonesia) in Bandung in 1955, but little came of these. More recent examples of regional cooperation have included collaboration between Burma and Thailand; by Malaya, Thailand, and the Philippines in the 1961 Association of Southeast Asia—revived in March, 1966; within the U.N. Economic Commission for Asia and the Far East; by the member countries of the Colombo Plan; by the four riparian states of the Mekong basin; and the Southeast Asia Treaty Organization (SEATO). But these modest gains have been offset in part by the more recent losses: the damaged Federation of Malaysia, the abortive Maphilindo, and Indonesia's "confrontation" policy toward Malaysia.

Those proposals that call for Indian moral leadership, an Indian "Monroe Doctrine," or an Indo-Japanese security anchorage for the defense of Southeast Asia reveal an abysmal ignorance of Southeast Asian attitudes toward Indians and the Japanese. Regional cooperation cannot be imposed on Southeast Asia from the outside; it may be encouraged, but if it is to survive it must develop from its own indigenous roots. This lack of regional cohesiveness means that the U.S. and its allies must approach each independent sovereignty in Southeast Asia on an individual basis. Only by recognizing and treating the particularities of each nation do we have a chance of building friendly relations with these countries, and of helping them to solve their domestic and external problems.

The colonial experience deepened the divisions among the various peoples of Southeast Asia, frequently even among the ethnic groups within each country, and fostered a "plural society"—a term of disapprobation in Southeast Asia. Colonialism, with its pluses and minuses, has left considerable suspicion of the Westerner among the Southeast Asian states. Though a diminishing factor, it is still one to be reckoned with in dealing with the ardent nationalisms in this area, and one that is continuously exploited by the Soviet Union and China, whose own imperialism (in Eastern Europe and in the Sino-Soviet Asian lands) has not been directly experienced by the present generation of Southeast Asian leaders.

All the independent states of Southeast Asia, with the exception of South Viet Nam, have joined the United Nations. This, coupled with their exuberant nationalism at home, has given them a chance to play a role on the world's stage. Each state has done this, whether "neutralist," committed to collective security arrangements with Western powers, or committed to joint policies with Moscow or Peking or both, but the terms and content of their international policies are varied and disparate. It might be said that in many respects they have found it easier to be ardent nationalists and to play a role in foreign affairs than to build and administer stable and viable institutions at home.

It is true that, in Southeast Asia, suspicion of the West is waning. Except in Portuguese Timor, old-style Western imperialism no longer exists. The former colonials of Southeast Asia, now acting at the United Nations as elder brothers to the Africans, are today much less rabid on the colonial issue than they once were. But the problem of colonialism persists because the memory of it colors so much of the thinking, propaganda, and the general frame of reference of the people who are presently in power in Southeast Asia. While those in the West think of the advent of the Europeans in Southeast Asia primarily in terms of exploration, the Southeast Asians think about it primarily in terms of exploitation. Westerners think of the Europeans as having exercised political sovereignty while encouraging the development of the area. The Southeast Asians think in terms of the repressiveness of the political sovereignty once exercised by the colonial power, and of the economic residue that still remains after political control has departed, the so-called colonial economy. Each country is concerned with ridding itself of the kind of extractive economy which is a legacy from colonial times. These were the countries that had primarily one-product economies—producing rice or tin or rubber—and where the controls and profits were in the hands of Europeans, Indians, and Chinese. Dependence upon such a primary-products economy is in the eyes of most Southeast Asians an unwelcome remnant of colonialism. For the most part, these countries had no indigenous middle class at the time of independence. They were hostile to imported Indian or Chinese capital and labor and suspicious of Western capital. Consequently, they proposed and initiated many forms of economic planning and of government intervention to develop their economies and make them more balanced, and to transfer ownership to local hands.

Anticolonialism and nationalism have always been strongly supported by certain indigenous cultural elements. Thus, Buddhism was the matrix for nationalism in Burma. Between 1904 and 1906, the Young Men's Buddhist Association was organized in Rangoon. The name was designed to show contempt for the colonial power's support for the YMCA and the missionaries. From the 1890's through the 1920's (when Buddhist organizations came together to form the General Council of Burmese Associations), Buddhism served as the first front of nationalism in Burma. As a consequence, the nationalist elite that has been in power since 1948 has had to consider how to give respect to their cultural past, how to raise the status of Buddhism in the country, and how to reconcile the conflicting claims of religion and polity.

Islam played the same role in Indonesia that Buddhism served in Burma. Sarekat Islam, an organization of Indonesian batik handicraft workers, which was formed some time around 1911, was a major fount of Indonesian nationalism. The organization grew during the World War I period, and gave substance to the more politically oriented nationalist organizations founded in the 1920's. Though the movement was split by the Indonesian Communists after the second meeting of the Comintern in 1920, Islam, in one guise or another, has been a force in Indonesian politics to be reckoned with to this day. Its strength was evident in October, 1965, when it supported the military's counterattack on what was the strongest Communist Party outside the bloc countries.

Similarly, the Mandarin-led secret societies of Viet Nam, the sects in later years, and the Buddhist organizations today, played active roles against the French, the Japanese, and even their own government.

These religio-cultural traditions in Southeast Asia have been turned into an asset by some governments; their persistence has also tended to restrict the actions of these governments. The ruling elites have had to recognize and accommodate traditional or customary law with statute law; they have had to devise ways to introduce some form of administrative modernization program into the villages without severely disrupting normal village life.

These three elements—regional cohesion and security, the colonial residue, and nationalism in its religio-cultural context —are components of a fourth issue—nation-building. Each of these Southeast Asian countries—with the exception of Thailand which was never a Western colony—has had the enormous task of converting the negative aspects of the struggle against colonialism into the positive actions that are needed to build a national state. The fight against colonialism, economic exploitation, and prejudice served to hold the nationalist elites together—in most part, they were able to stay together until they achieved independence. After that, some of the centrifugal forces that normally operate in any political group began to split them or to change them. It is much easier to unite against an outside opponent than to build solidly and jointly from within.

Though these nationalists were always anticolonial, at independence they adopted, for the most part, Westerns forms of government—at least superficially. The "compliment" has not stood the test of time too well. These village-based societies— their population is still at least 80 per cent rural—do not readily coalesce into a national state. Local and representative administration by the devolution of power from the center has not yet become rooted. The institutions necessary for nation-building have not easily materialized, and where they have materialized, they have not survived too well. The trained administrators have yet to appear; where they have appeared, they have all too often been hampered by their fear of, or actual, political interference. The scientific and technological skills required to run a modern society are hard to come by—and, when they do appear, they are not always well used. Education has been

broadened but also thinned, and the college generation, inadequately equipped with the specialized skills needed for modernization, is frequently more interested in using its education
for its own political advantage than in the country's service.

The task of nation-building has been complicated further
by the fact that the nationalist elites, now getting old, have not
adequately made provisions for their own replacement.

Integral to the task of nation-building is the status that is
achieved and the role played by the nonindigenous minorities
—the Indians in Burma and Malaya, the Chinese throughout
the whole region. The Chinese are feared, envied, and mis-
trusted. As these countries, especially those of mainland Southeast Asia, recover their sense of history, they single out with
great pride the dates that are connected with victories over
the Chinese: in Burma, the years of successful defensive warfare in 1765–69; in Viet Nam, the ousting of the Chinese in
939 A.D. after almost a thousand years of subjugation. The Indians, on the other hand, were neither liked nor respected, and
the Burmese were happy to get rid of about 500,000 of them
after World War II; they have not allowed the money-lending
chettyar caste back into Burma, and they were not displeased
by the recent departure of another 100,000 Indians. About
500,000 Indians are left in Burma and about 725,000 in Malaya,
where they are largely estate workers or unskilled workers. A
few Indians have attained high rank in the extraordinary alliance that Tungku Abdul Rahman has forged in Malaysia, but
the Indians do not really count as a force either there or in
Burma. The overseas Chinese, who total perhaps as many as
14 million throughout Southeast Asia, do matter in each country, if only through the sheer weight of their numbers. Moreover, they are also numerically preponderant in some of the
skilled trades, in commerce, in the ownership of pawnshops,
and in lending institutions. Their loyalty is almost always suspect in the eyes of the indigenous peoples.

In addition to the nonindigenous minorities, each of these

countries also has indigenous minorities. Part of the problem in Laos is the fact that the Lao people make up probably little more than one-half of the total population of 3 million, and the non-Lao peoples in provinces such as Sam Neua and Phong Saly, resenting what they consider to be neglect from the center, have been amenable to the influence of the Pathet Lao. The aggrieved indigenous minorities in the northeast area of Thailand, in the northeast area of Laos, in the Karen, Shan, and Kachin areas of Burma, and in the "Moi" and Meo areas of Viet Nam, have at various times expressed their resentment. (The Karen insurrection, begun in 1949, only ended in 1964.) The northeast Lao-related peoples in Thailand, and their counterparts in the plateau area of Viet Nam, have been susceptible to Communist provocation. In all of mainland Southeast Asia, tension exists between the indigenous majority, customarily lowland farmers, and the ethnically and linguistically different hill peoples, who are frequently seminomadic. In Indonesia, the Sudanese in West Java are restive under the rule of the majority Javanese; the Sumatrans, the Sulawesians (in Celebes), and the Madurese, among others, regard the Javanese as being, in effect, cultural imperialists within Indonesia. Their dissatisfaction with their treatment by the central government was one of the contributing reasons for the rebellion in 1958. Similar rifts are endemic in the Philippines.

The difficulties in integrating these various societies and consolidating the states have been vastly compounded by the difficulties of establishing order, extending the writ of law, and coping with Communist and ethnic insurrections, all in a terrain with primitive roads and inadequate communications.

The United States entered the arena in Southeast Asia only after 1898, when it defeated Spain and seized the Philippines. After some three decades of self-doubt, the United States enacted legislation in 1934 that set out a ten-year timetable for the eventual independence of the colony. World War II intervened, and the Philippines finally gained independence in

1946. Apart from the Philippines, U.S. interests in Southeast Asia were minimal.

During the years immediately following World War II, the United States was content to let England, France, and Holland take the lead in establishing relationships with the former colonies. There was satisfaction in official and unofficial quarters in the United States over the peaceful, and ultimately friendly, withdrawal of the British from their Asian colonies—India, Pakistan, Ceylon, and Burma—in 1947–48; it was expected that a similar withdrawal would take place in Malaya and Singapore once the "emergency" caused by Communist insurrection was terminated. The United States expressed considerable annoyance and, finally, placed political and financial pressure on the Dutch to quit Indonesia (1948–49). But with incredible inconsistency and with complete lack of regard for the reality of the situation within Viet Nam, the United States supported the French effort to remain in their colonial territory—to remain, that is, until the French were defeated, in 1954, at Dien Bien Phu. Under both Presidents Truman and Eisenhower, the United States accepted the French position that they were fighting the Communists, and ignored the fact that they were also fighting against bona fide nationalists; accepted the French promise of self-government for the states of Indochina within a French Union, and ignored the reality that denied to the Indochinese any true measure of self-government. The French, it was argued, were our allies and we wished them well; more specifically, we wished to see them firmly entrenched within a European Defense Community or Western European Union. On all scores, United States reliance on French policies, including those pursued at Geneva in 1954, was a disaster.

However, the events of 1949–50 changed all this. If the Communists had not taken over China by 1949 and invaded South Korea (and Tibet) in 1950, U.S. interests in Southeast Asia would probably have remained at a low key, even though the Communist insurrections had begun in Southeast Asia in 1947. In early 1950, shortly after the fall of China to the Communists, there began a re-examination of U.S. Asian policy, which led to more intensive involvement in free Asia. We have been involved there ever since.

This involvement took the form of aid agreements, which were negotiated with every nation in Southeast Asia; bilateral treaties, including security and political arrangements with Korea, Japan, Nationalist China (Taiwan), the Philippines and, to a very real degree, with Thailand, though with Thailand there is no formal bilateral treaty to that effect; regional agreements, such as those with Australia and New Zealand (ANZUS); and the Southeast Asia Treaty Organization (SEATO), created by the Manila Treaty of 1954. In short, between Secretary of State Dean Acheson's "Crisis in Asia" speech of January, 1950, and the 1954 Manila Treaty, the United States established a clear policy with respect to its involvement in Southeast Asian affairs. It was based on a determination to contain further Communist advances in Southeast Asia while assisting the independent states to retain their freedom and to build up, or to rebuild, their economies.

In October, 1952, shortly before the death of Stalin, and again after the triumph of Khrushchev, there was a shift in Communist policy to the so-called soft line. This created an illusion of relative safety among many people in Southeast Asia, as elsewhere. This was the period in which Chou En-lai, Nehru, and Burmese Premier U Nu agreed upon the Five Principles of Peaceful Coexistence. It was the period of the Bulganin and Khrushchev visit to Asia, and of the 1955 Bandung Conference in Indonesia, with its promotion of the "Bandung spirit" of peaceful coexistence in the area. It was also the period in which the Sino-Soviet bloc initiated its very considerable aid and trade programs with many of the "neutralist" Southeast Asian nations. Since then, Burma has received a total of $93 million, Cambodia over $60 million, and Indonesia over $1 billion for military and economic aid.

The direct support given by Communist bloc governments to the governments of Southeast Asian countries was coun-

tered by the continuing Communist policy of subversion and
infiltration, leading to the instigation and support of insurrections in the various countries—even the "neutralist" ones. The
Chinese Communists, through the use of propaganda and covert subventions, attempted to affect the course of national
elections in Burma. With the approval of their Soviet allies,
they also backed Kachin, Shan, and Thai autonomous movements in Yunan (the first two aimed at minorities in Burma,
the third, at minorities in Thailand), and set up camps or
schools at Kunming and other places for the training of Southeast Asian nationals for infiltration purposes.

The main test in mainland Southeast Asia was over Laos and
Viet Nam. After 1949, the Chinese Communists gave considerable backing to the Viet Minh effort to conquer the former French Indochinese states. The Geneva Agreements of
1954, which were supposed to end the hostilities between the
Viet Minh and the French (and which the United States did
not sign), settled nothing. They simply made it possible for
the Communists to continue to apply their revolutionary line,
the promotion of "wars of national liberation," in mainland
Southeast Asia.

The Communists in Hanoi, Peking, and elsewhere were
willing to support Premier Souvanna Phouma's policy calling
for the withdrawal from Laos of the International Control
Commission created at Geneva, when he attempted to form a
coalition government with his Communist half brother Souphanouvong and the Pathet Lao in 1957. However, when a
majority vote in the Laotian parliament brought down the
Souvanna Phouma government in late 1957, the Communists
stepped up their campaign of subversion in Laos. Subject only
to the exigencies of the Communist aggression in Viet Nam,
this campaign has continued ceaselessly, even after the Geneva
Conference of 1962. The latter agreement—which the United
States signed—has not preserved the peace in Laos. The feasi-
bility, in a weak and unstable country, of a coalition government that includes the Communists has not been demonstrated.

Since 1962, the "troika" foisted on Laos has enabled the Pathet Lao (Communist) forces legally to entrench themselves in the northeast provinces of Laos abutting onto Communist China and North Viet Nam and, from that vantage point, to conduct almost continuous guerrilla-type warfare against the central government of Laos. It has also required the United States to shore up militarily the government of Souvanna Phouma, who governs a country that is de facto partitioned and still infested with Communist insurrectionists.

In South Viet Nam, Communist aggression has been open and continuous since 1955, and was stepped up considerably in 1959. The response to this was, for too long, essentially defensive. Only since February, 1965, have the Vietnamese, the United States, and their allies who have committed themselves to the defense of South Viet Nam embarked on the long overdue policy of attacking the attackers in their base in North Viet Nam. When the Communists finally realize that their military probes, their wars-by-proxy, their "wars of national liberation," and their other forms of aggression no longer pay, the opportunity will have been created to restore, rebuild, and reconstruct the political and social base for the process of nation-building in the independent nations of Southeast Asia.

That political and social reform is necessary in the region is almost universally accepted. Such political and social reconstruction, however, is possible only when a country is reasonably secure and when law and order obtain—and only under such conditions can the process be sustained.

1. *The Viet People: Who, When, and Where*

The Viet people, the majority population of the Democratic Republic of Viet Nam (Communist North Viet Nam) and of the Republic of Viet Nam (South Viet Nam) belong to the Mongoloid race. They are the descendants of a people who originated in what is now China, migrated southward, and by conquest and intermarriage absorbed and displaced an aboriginal group, which was probably Melanoid, and the Malayo-Indonesian groups which apparently preceded them on the Indochinese peninsula. Together they gave rise, some time before 300 B.C., to a Bronze Age culture, called Dong Son after a village in Central Viet Nam.

The name Viet is a reading of two Chinese characters (pronounced You-eh), probably given originally to lands "beyond," or "far away" from, the ancient seat of power in China, i.e., lands somewhat south of the Yangtze River. Certain local rulers in this general area, who owed fealty to Chinese Emperor Shih Huang-ti (246–10), appear to have reached the northern borders of what is now Viet Nam, perhaps advancing as far south as the Red River. One such ruler, known as General Trieu-Da, emerged as a Chinese king over a land called Nam Yue, or Nam Viet, but this kingdom, whose capital is believed to have been near Canton, is generally *not* regarded as part of what is Viet Nam today. It is possible that Trieu-Da's successors extended its borders into North Viet Nam before his dynasty was eventually overthrown by the Han Chinese Emperor Wu-ti (about the year 111 B.C.). In any event, the Han Chinese did so and named the province Giao-Chi, i.e., "meeting (or splayed) toes." Giao-Chi under the Han Chinese comprised Hainan Island and what is now North Viet Nam and part of Central Viet Nam. The name Viet Nam (or Nam Viet) disappears until the end of the period of Chinese domination, in the tenth century.

The Viet peoples, struggling throughout the first millenium A.D. against their Chinese overlords, have created legends around the efforts of those who, however temporarily, succeeded in throwing off Chinese imperialist rule. Among their heroes are the Trung Sisters, Trung Trac and Trung Nhi, who, as generals and queens, led the revolt from 39 A.D. until their defeat in 43 A.D. They were subsequently honored and worshipped annually on the sixth day of the second lunar month. Similarly honored was a group of heroes of the Early Ly dynasty, sometimes taken as the first Vietnamese dynasty, that extended its rule over what is today North Viet Nam and the northern part of central Viet Nam. The founder of the dynasty, who ruled as Ly Nam De from 544 to 548, had been known as Ly Bon, or Ly Bi, when he led the successful revolt against the Chinese. These patriots, too, as others before and after them, were put down by their Chinese masters.

In the middle of the tenth century—about the year 939—the Vietnamese, taking advantage of the declining power of the T'ang dynasty, were successful in finally throwing off Chinese rule, though there were later, successful, struggles against each Chinese power that felt itself strong enough to attack their land. Prince Tran Hung Dao, one of the great Viet heroes, is still celebrated for defeating the invading Mongol armies of Kublai Khan at the end of the thirteenth century. Other wars were fought against the Ming and the Manchus. Always, the Viet people were fighting to retain their independence.

The Chinese, after suppressing the Early Ly revolt, had called the territory Annam, "Pacified South." This name, considered to be disparaging by the Vietnamese, was later applied by Westerners to Central Viet Nam, but it has never

been employed by the Vietnamese themselves. They called
their country Dai Co Viet (Great Viet State), or Dai Viet
(Viet Nation-State), and, following an official proclamation
in 1802, Viet Nam.

It may be said that in the tenth century, when the Dai Viet
or Viet Nam state emerged from Chinese imperialist rule, the
Viet people had clearly broken political ties with their puta-
tive ancestral land. Throughout the poorly recorded history
of the previous thousand years, they had displayed a determination to be free from foreign or distant domination. One
might say, with some truth, that the struggles were largely revolts by feudal chieftains against a more distant, more powerful group of feudal lords for personal gain and power. Such a
reading, however, does not take into account all the known
facts and many of the probable factors in the early history of
the people.

The facts are easy: here is a people who derive in the main
from what is now called China; who, until the seventeenth
century, used Chinese characters to write their language (*chu
nom*, a popular form of Chinese calligraphy is still in use today for certain types of scholarly writing); who followed
Chinese Confucian, Mahayana Buddhist, and Taoist traditions
—and to a great extent still do so; who still honor the memory
of at least two first-century Chinese governors, Tich Quang
and Nham Dien, who are recorded as having taught them
"morals and ritual" (i.e., Confucian ethics) and the "use of
farm implements"; and who, in comparison with the two
other great migrations southward into the Indochinese peninsula (by the Tibeto-Burman and Shan–Thai–Lao peoples),
remain today the most sinicized of all Southeast Asian members of the Mongoloid race. As one close student of Viet Nam
has written, "Chinese influence permeated all levels of Vietnamese society."[1]

The racial and cultural affinity between the Viets and the
Chinese should not blind us to the real and tangible differences
between them. The various Mongoloid peoples who inhabit

such a vast geographical area in Asia have been, and still are, as varied, as friendly or unfriendly, as peaceful or warlike toward their neighbors as are peoples in the rest of the world. The variations within the great Mongoloid areas are at least as significant as the similarities. The Han Chinese, the great instigators of the Chinese imperialist system of tributary states, emulated in this sense by the Mongol, Ming, Ching, Republican, and Communist Chinese after them, did not hesitate when strong to seek to impose their rule on their non-Han neighbors and ethnic cousins. The Viet people, though absorbing what they valued from their more powerful kin, nonetheless made it clear in the course of their history that they wished to be free of their powerful neighbors.

The use of the terms "nationalism" or "zeal for independence" with reference to events of the distant past may be debatable. Loyalty to one's countryside, however, is a fact in human experience, and we are justified in seeing in this loyalty an explanation of the fact that one particular Sinitic people, the Viets, took repeated action for at least ten centuries to establish an independent, distinct regime. And, though they were to succumb once more to foreign domination, they once again found the instruments and the institutions to throw it off.

The name Viet Nam largely disappeared in Western usage with the beginning of the European explorations in the East. The name that came to stand for North Viet Nam, Tonkin (or Tongking), was the Chinese name for the city of Hanoi ("Capital of the East" in Vietnamese). The name Tonkin, according to at least one authority, had not even existed in the Vietnamese language before the twentieth century. Annam, as indicated, was used by non-Viets for Central Viet Nam, the area roughly between the 16th and 19th parallels, where Hué, the imperial capital of Viet Nam, was situated. The South was called Cochinchina (or Cochin China), a name of obscure, possibly Portuguese, origin. The Vietnamese seldom, if ever, used these Westernisms. For them, the parts of the country are simply Bac, Trung, and Nam (North, Center, South), with

the words *Ky* or *Bo* (domain or region) added. The central
mountains, designated on the maps as the Annamite Chain,
are called Trong Son by the Vietnamese.

The Viet people, today numbering about 32 million—a little
over half of them in North Viet Nam—make up between 85
and 90 per cent of the population of all Viet Nam. By no
reading of history can they be called a docile, peaceful people.
As they moved southward they came into contact with earlier
arrivals, whom they successively conquered, displaced, or absorbed as they imposed their rule.[2] After centuries of intermittent warfare, they had, by the fifteenth century, conquered
the Chams, one of the Malayo-Indonesian peoples who then
occupied central Viet Nam and who had represented, for at
least a millennium, the most Hinduized of those Southeast
Asian states that had been influenced by India. Today, the remnants of the Chams—now largely converted to Islam—still live
in central Viet Nam. They number some 35,000, and are divided into several subtribal groups.

During their drive to the south, the Viets also drove into the
uplands the earlier Malayo-Indonesian peoples whom they
stigmatized as the "Moi" ("savages"), whose number is estimated today at between 800,000 and 1 million. These are the
peoples today called *montagnards* (mountaineers). By the
mid-eighteenth century, the Viets had conquered the Khmers
(Cambodians), whose empire, which at one time extended
from the China Sea to the Bay of Bengal, had long since
passed its peak. There remain today in South Viet Nam perhaps as many as 400,000 "Cambodians." The people of Cambodia have not forgotten the truly great glory of their past
and still harbor resentment, if not enmity, toward the Viets
on their east and toward the Thai on their west, whose parallel movement southward also contributed to the Khmer decline.

By the mid-eighteenth century, the Viet people dominated
the land called Viet Nam from the China border to the southeastern tip of the Camau peninsula.

The Indochinese Peninsula

The ancient Greeks, as recorded by Pliny the Elder, had a word for this area: they called it the *Chryse Chersonese*, the Golden Peninsula. This vast area, which extends from the eastern rim of the Himalayas southward to the Indian Ocean and the South China Sea, came to include, at the time of European penetration, the independent kingdoms or empires of Burma, Thailand, Cambodia, Laos, and Viet Nam, and, in the "tail" of the Indochinese "kite," the Malayan sultanates. There is some historical logic in calling this peninsula Indochina, for it represents the confluence and further evolution of two great cultural strains from India and China. While noting this, it is important to realize that the evolution of these cultures has resulted in genuine indigenous or naturalized adaptations in each of the states of Indochina.

Viet Nam occupies the eastern edge of this peninsula, forming an S-shaped curve. Its north-south axis extends for about 1,000 miles; it narrows at the "waist" to an average of 40 miles, and extends at its greatest width, in the valleys of the Red River in the north and the Mekong in the south, to almost 300 miles. These two valleys, with their fertile deltas, form the rice baskets of North and South Viet Nam. Between these two rice-producing areas stretch, in the west, the long central mountainous chain whose peaks, near Dalat, reach to about 6,500 feet; and, in the east, a narrow, heavily populated coastal plain divided by massifs and hilly spurs.

These four major geographical regions, the two river deltas, the central mountainous spine inland, and the coastal plain, have conditioned the lives and fortunes of the Vietnamese for 2,000 years. With 126,000 square miles, their land is slightly larger than New Mexico. It receives the southwest and northeast monsoons, which bring rainfall of from 50 to 120 inches per year and which create the two main tropical seasons, hot-dry (October–May) and hot-wet. The Viets are essentially a lowland people. Their economy, based on wet-rice cultivation and fishing; the still persistent remnants of their animistic myths and superstitions, which cause them to fear the hills and mountains; and their cautious respect for the highlands (where malaria has been endemic), have combined to keep them a lowland people—inhabitants of the deltas and the coastal plains. The uplands, plateaus, and mountains are the homes of the minorities—the earlier inhabitants who were displaced and downgraded in the southward march of the Viets, and the later arrivals, like the Muongs, the Man, the Meo, and the Thai. One other major group of late arrivals is the Chinese, numbering perhaps as many as a million, who live mainly in the urban areas. For the most part, they have remained, as elsewhere in Southeast Asia, a self-separated group.

The Red River valley and delta of the North is one of the most densely populated areas in Southeast Asia; its density of 1,500 persons per square mile is exceeded only by Java. The Mekong basin in the South supports with ease a population that averages 250 persons per square mile. The mountainous central region, which constitutes about 90 per cent of the total area of Viet Nam, contains less than 10 per cent of its population. Here the tribal and non-Viet peoples tend to practice nomadic "shifting," in contrast to the sedentary agriculture of the lowland majority.

The Viet people who entered and ultimately conquered part of the peninsula found Hinduized and Buddhist kingdoms and societies which they assimilated with their own Sinicized cultural patterns, including the practice of the northern Mahayana variety of Buddhism. The mixture has given rise to such Buddhist groups, in the South, as the current General Association of Vietnamese Buddhists, which claims 1 million members, and the Buddhist-influenced sects known as the Cao Dai and Hoa Hao, which claim as many as 3.5 million members.

The original Chinese influence came into the country with the Viets and was further reinforced by the thousand years of Chinese suzerainty. Vietnamese emperors, as those of China, ruled their kingdoms by a "mandate from Heaven." Ancestor worship is still practiced almost everywhere in Viet Nam, even by Buddhists and, to some extent, Roman Catholics. Vietnamese was written in Chinese characters until it was romanized by French missionaries in the seventeenth century. The civil service was organized on the Chinese mandarinate system, with promotions and appointments based, in principle, solely on education and examination.

Both the Chinese and the Buddhist cultural patterns strongly emphasized the central role of the hierarchal family and of the communalized and autonomous village system, with its elements of prescribed ceremony, respect for authority, and cooperative effort. It was accompanied by general indifference to, if not actual antagonism toward, the central government—the source of power, taxes, and other forms of levies, and by the restraints and inhibitions of the calendar-governed, relatively self-sufficient life of the villages.

When the French arrived in Indochina, Viet Nam was an integrated society which had assimilated Confucian, Buddhist, and Vietnamese elements. There was domestic conflict, to be sure—especially between powerful northern and southern Viet families seeking supreme power, and at one time a dividing wall was actually built at the 19th parallel. Certain cultural differences, including dialect, pronunciation, and even dress, have persisted between North and South Viet Nam to this day. However, the society as a whole, prior to the final French conquest in the second half of the nineteenth century, represented a convergence of political and religious power, vested in a sovereign emperor or ruler assisted by a mandarin bureaucracy and dependent upon Buddhist monks for religious sanction. All these were related intimately to an ancestral family system, the village commune or cooperative, and an autonomous village structure. The totality of this power had "magical" properties which were not to be lightly violated; it provided minutely for every aspect of individual life, which was always subordinate to the group, the family, the clan, or the tribe.

The French Intrusion and Conquest

The French were the last European power in Southeast Asia to arrive and to found an empire. Like other Europeans, they came in search of treasure and trade and to save "heathen souls." French missionaries were originally under the jurisdiction of the Roman Catholic archbishops of Lisbon and Goa, for the Portuguese (and the Spaniards) had preceded the French to the East Indies. In the seventeenth century, France initiated its own missionary movement, spurred on by the labors of Father Alexander de Rhodes, a French Jesuit.

The activities of the Jesuits in Asia, which gained impetus after 1549 when Saint Francis Xavier established his mission in Japan, earned them respect throughout Eastern Asia. The closing of the Japanese mission at the beginning of the seventeenth century made several distinguished Jesuits available for other missions. Beginning in 1615, Viet Nam attracted a number of them, among whom Father Alexander de Rhodes appears to have been the most gifted. It was he who translated the catechism into Vietnamese and who perfected the efforts of his predecessors in converting the written language from an ideographic Chinese script into a romanized alphabet, Quoc Ngu, which is still in use today. He persuaded the Vatican and the French Crown to engage more seriously and effectively in missionary labors in Viet Nam. His plan for training indigenous priests and for replacing Portuguese control of the missionary activities by French control was sanctioned, both in Rome and in Paris, shortly before his death in 1660. (Viet Nam—Annam in particular—had been assigned to the Portuguese Society for the Propagation of the Faith by Pope Alexander VI, who in 1493, had divided the world between Portuguese and Spanish interests.)

Thus, in the second half of the seventeenth century, France began its own missionary movement aimed at replacing the waning Portuguese religious and political influence. Simultaneously, the French sought to limit the control of the Jesuit order in countries outside of France. In 1659, the French founded the Société des Missions Etrangères, which a few years later began to send missionaries into Cambodia and the three regions of Viet Nam—Tonkin, Annam, and Cochinchina—from its field base in Ayuthia, the capital of Siam. With the setting up of the French Compagnie des Indes Orientales in 1664, the stage was set for a fertile combination of religious and mercantile expansion in the Indochinese peninsula.

These events coincided with one of the weak periods in Vietnamese history. The reigning Le dynasty had been "permitted to exist as a semicorpse but not allowed to die." Actual power rested in the hands of two powerful families, the Trinh in the North (Tonkin) and the Nguyen in the Center-South (Annam). Their struggle for power punctuates the history of the seventeenth and eighteenth centuries.

Most students of Southeast Asian history are agreed that European commercial relations with Viet Nam began with the establishment of missionary influence. Religion, trade, and political interest remained closely allied, despite a ruling by French King Louis XIV that missionary activity was not to be carried out for such ends. French bishops and apostolic vicars who succeeded Alexander de Rhodes, especially François Pallu and Pierre de la Motte, advanced the cause of the Société des Missions Etrangères "in all questions which from near or far touch on the advancement of the missions and on the progress of French influence."[3]

But this "double current of ideas" did not fulfill, in the eighteenth century, the optimistic beginnings of the seventeenth century. Conflict between the missionary orders, at least before the suppression of the Jesuits in France in 1774; the anticlericalism of the French Revolution, which affected the roles of the Church and its missions; the debilitating effects of the eighteenth-century wars with England; and the subsequent defeat of the French in India—all contributed to the decline of French fortunes in Indochina.

The decline coincided with the renewal of hostilities between the Trinh and the Nguyen families and their associates, and, more particularly, with rebellion known in Vietnamese history by the area of its origin, Tay Son in central Annam. Three brothers, Nhac, Lu, and Hué, led a successful revolt in the early 1770's against the Nguyen family, the leaders of the Center and South, driving them and their supporters to the area of Saigon and the Camau peninsula. The Tay Son brothers were able to consolidate their power in the vicinity of Ankhe and Quinhon. The Trinh of the North seized the opportunity to invade and capture the city of Hué in 1775. For over a decade, civil war marked the course of Viet Nam's history. Gradually, the Tay Son brothers, under the leadership of the youngest, Hué—who has been described as "a military genius of Napoleonic stature"—exploited their advantage against both the Trinh at Hanoi and the remnants of the Nguyen at Saigon. They won; by 1789, they had defeated not only these rival claimants to power, but also a Chinese (Manchu) army that had invaded Viet Nam to assist these tributary princes. Hué married a daughter of the Le dynasty, nominal occupiers of the throne, and proclaimed himself the emperor of a unified Viet Nam. At his death, in 1792, he was succeeded by his son Nguyen Quan Toan.

The cause of the displaced Nguyen family had meanwhile come under the leadership of one of its scions, Nguyen Anh, who had retreated before the Tay Son brothers, first to the Camau peninsula and then to Poulo Condore Island off the coast of Cochinchina. In his quest for support, he met the French apostolic vicar to Cochinchina, Monsignor Pigneau de Béhaine, titular Bishop of Adran, one of the great French missionary-political figures.

Pigneau was one of the colorful and effective individuals

in that troublesome time. In 1765, he had been sent to Cambodia as a missionary of the Société. In 1782, he decided to risk his political future on an alliance with Nguyen Anh. For the next five years, he endeavored to get the French authorities, first in Pondicherry (India) and, having failed there, in Paris, to back the young pretender who styled himself King of Cochinchina. In late 1787, he secured a treaty of alliance between Paris and Nguyen Anh whereby France was to supply arms and men to help win the throne for its ally, in return for which France would enjoy certain trading, territorial, and other privileges to the exclusion of other Europeans. The French aid was to have been delivered by way of the French base in Pondicherry, but the authorities there, acting either on their own or under instructions from Paris, refused to honor the treaty. Pigneau thereupon proceeded on his own to raise a small military force and a fleet. In 1789, he came to the aid of Nguyen Anh, who had returned to the mainland. Together they waged war against the Tay Son. Ten years later, Pigneau was killed while leading an assault. But Nguyen Anh went on, and by 1802 he had succeeded in defeating the Tay Son, the remnants of the Trinh, and all other opposition. In that year he proclaimed himself Emperor Gia Long. From his capital at Hué he ruled over Bac, Trung, and Nam, once more united into a single state, Viet Nam. Gia Long, founder of the Nguyen dynasty, was recognized by the Chinese Emperor T'sing, and received the seal of office as a tributary prince in 1804.

There are various historical interpretations of the Tay Son rebellion and its reversal with the accession of Gia Long to the throne. Some regard the Tay Son brothers as bandits and Gia Long as a national hero who reunited the kingdom under the legitimate royal government. Others see the Tay Son brothers as the archetype of the leaders of those peasant rebellions whose main object was to secure some measure of relief for the peasants from the burdens that were imposed as a result of the ceaseless quarrels of warring nobles and their mandarins. These regard Hué, the youngest of the Tay Son brothers who defeated the feudal families and the Chinese, as their true hero; Gia Long, in their view, was not rightfully entitled to the throne; furthermore, he committed the fatal mistake of inviting in the French—a mistake with dire consequences, as later events proved. Whatever view is held of the Tay Son brothers, Gia Long is still celebrated today as a national hero in both North and South Viet Nam.

The French Government had not honored the treaty of 1787. During the subsequent years of turmoil at home, it was neither willing nor able to involve itself in the affairs of Viet Nam. Gia Long, therefore, had little if any difficulty in fending off the few official trading ventures proposed during the time of Napoleon and his successor, Louis XVIII. The Vietnamese emperor apparently wished to avoid becoming embroiled in the war between the French and the English. He turned his considerable energies to the repair and restoration of his own war-torn kingdom. The large landholdings of the noble class were broken up and villages were no longer allowed to be held as tax-fiefs. Dikes were built in Tonkin; a road was completed from Hanoi to Saigon, a distance of 1,300 miles; fortifications in the manner of French outposts were constructed at strategic centers throughout the land. And, probably to honor the Bishop of Adran, Catholicism was liberally tolerated. At his death, in 1820, Gia Long recommended to his designated heir, a son by his first concubine—who ruled as the Emperor Ming Mang—that the three principal religions of the realm, Confucianism, Buddhism, and Catholicism, be equally protected. But this was not to be.

At the time of Gia Long's death,

after almost two centuries of desultory activity on the part of French missionaries, traders, diplomats, and adventurers in the Far East, France had very little to show in the way of tangible achievement. . . . British naval and commercial hegemony . . . based on India, was unchallengeable, so that any move which France might contemplate within the area would have to fall

within the bounds of British consent. . . . There were nevertheless two factors on the positive side of the French ledger.
One was the vigorous religious revival, centering on France,
which swept Catholic Europe following the downfall of Napoleon. The other was the well-nigh desperate concern on the part
of the Orleanist and Napoleonic dynasties, which ruled France
from 1830 to 1870, to recover at least a measure of the international prestige that had so long been associated with the name of
France. These two elements united to revive the imperialist
tradition of France in the Orient during the mid-century decades.[4]

The piecemeal conquest of Viet Nam and of the revived
kingdoms of Laos and Cambodia were the fruits of this
imperialist foray. The area as a whole came to be known as
French Indochina.

The conquest grew in the first instance out of the antimissionary, anti-Catholic policies, aimed at the "European
barbarians," which were gradually adopted by the Vietnamese
emperors Ming Mang (1820–41), Thieu Tri (1841–47), and
Tu Duc (1847–83). In 1825, Ming Mang limited the freedom
of the missionaries; in 1833 an edict of death was issued against
several, one of whom, Father Francis Isadore Gagelin, lost his
life. In 1836, proselytization was prohibited and all ports,
save one, were closed to Europeans. In 1848, it was decreed
that European priests, if found, were "to be thrown into the
sea with rocks tied to their necks"; native Christians were to
recant or be banished. The martyrdom of some European
Christians spurred new missionaries to enter the country il-
licitly.

The antimissionary activities of the Vietnamese emperors
were a consequence, and not the cause, of French activity.
Ming Mang continued the policies of his able father. He
improved the central administration, lightened and reorganized the tax system, instituted a scale of salaries and perquisites
for the civil service instead of assigning to them feudatory
villages, and generally tried to improve the conditions of his

kingdom. Le Thanh Khoi calls him "one of the most remarkable legislators Viet Nam has known."[5] But, unlike his
father, he had no personal reason to be especially partial to
the French. He refused to them and to the British the
exclusive trading privileges or monopolistic treaties they desired. "Commerce was free for all nations under the conditions of Vietnamese law." His sympathies were Confucianist
and traditional, based on the three fundamental relations:
that of prince to subject, of father to son, and of husband to
wife.[6] His sympathies were clearly not with the missionaries
and the other Europeans. Nevertheless, even after the pro-
scriptions, the Europeans persisted in following their own
pursuits within Viet Nam. This persistence brought about a
series of clashes and ultimately led to the persecution and
martyrdom of the Europeans.

The Vietnamese view of the matter was that certain for-
eigners (who happened to be French missionaries) were in-
sisting on rights of entry into the kingdom, contrary to the
decrees of the emperor, for the privilege of seeking converts
—they were persisting, in short, in acting contrary to the laws
and customs of the land. Initially, the French missionaries had
been granted a privilege—they had been given the opportunity to make converts. They refused to accept the emperor's
right to withdraw that privilege.

Ming Mang thus became anti-Christian, not because he
was antireligious but because the foreign Christians who had
been allowed into his kingdom flouted its rule and ruler. His
decrees were certainly not unjustifiable and could be defended
under the European custom *eius regio, cuius religio*, which
placed the sanction of religion in the authority of the ruler.
A year before his death, he attempted, unsuccessfully, to negotiate commercial trading terms with the French in order
to mitigate the restraints he had placed on French missionaries.
The mission that he sent to the court of Louis Philippe was refused an audience because of pressure exerted by the Société
des Missions Etrangères, which insisted it should have un-

conditional rights of entry in Viet Nam and unconditional rights to perform its missionary activities.

In the succeeding reigns of Thieu Tri and Tu Duc, matters went from bad to worse. Imprisonment of missionaries who had illegally entered Viet Nam led to bold efforts on the part of the French Navy to release them. In 1843, 1845, and 1847, French armed vessels secured the freedom of such prisoners. In 1847, Captain Rigault de Genouilly destroyed a Vietnamese fleet and harbor forts at Tourane. The emperors responded by offering rewards for the death of Europeans found within the kingdom; they "decreed the end of all Christianizing efforts."

During the transition from the end of the Orleanist dynasty in France to the advent of Louis Napoleon, there was a temporary respite both in the demands within France for action in Viet Nam and in the persecution of Christians and missionaries. But the respite was short-lived. By the mid-1850's, the French Government was ready to take measures in response to the appeals of the missionaries and the Société. In 1855, it dispatched a mission headed by Louis Charles de Montigny, and sent two naval vessels to rendezvous with him at Tourane. The vessels got there first, inflicted damage on the port, and then withdrew. De Montigny arrived in January, 1857, and left within a fortnight, after issuing the following ultimatum to the Emperor:

if, from this date [February 6, 1857] on, religious persecutions do not cease, and if there should be new executions for the mere fact of practising the religion of France . . . the acts of hostility will naturally place the Government of His Imperial Majesty in the obligation of taking more energetic measures.[7]

Napoleon III was now prepared to act. In 1856, he had joined with Britain in the war against China to avenge the death of a French missionary killed in February of that year. A similar excuse existed in the case of Viet Nam. In 1857, Napoleon III informed the world that "the ruthless persecu-

tions of missionaries have brought our warships, on more than
one occasion, to the coast of the Annamite kingdom, but their
efforts to enter into relations with the government have been
futile. The government of the [French] Emperor cannot
allow its overtures to be spurned. Therefore, an expedition
has been planned."

In the ensuing three decades, France, initially helped by
Spain, established its power over Indochina. By 1885, under
a variety of administrations—from protectorates to outright
colonies—French rule was firmly established over the states of
Cambodia, Cochinchina, Annam, and Tonkin; the final "pacifi-
cation" campaigns in Tonkin took another thirteen years.[8]
(Laos was added to these by 1895.)

Thus France acquired its eastern empire, subjugating in
the process an old and highly developed civilization, subduing
—in Viet Nam as in other states—a people fully desirous of
pursuing their own culture and their own way of life. In so
doing, France was only doing—belatedly—what other nations,
Asian as well as European, had been·doing for a long time.

2. *Viet Nam Fights for Independence Against the French*

French Rule and the Rise and Early Struggles of
Vietnamese Nationalism, 1885–1926

The French conquest of Viet Nam was accompanied by, and in part accomplished through, a series of treaties. The first, signed in 1862, permitted the French to establish direct colonial rule over Cochinchina (South Viet Nam). Subsequent treaties with China in 1884–85, by which China relinquished her "tributary rights," established protectorates over Annam (Central Viet Nam) and Tonkin (North Viet Nam). The name of the country, Viet Nam, was officially abolished. In similar fashion, involving conflict with Siam, the French also established protectorates over Cambodia (1863) and Laos (1893–95). By 1897, the French had complete mastery over all these territories, but had not secured peace among the inhabitants. The inhabitants of Central Viet Nam—Annamites, as they were called by the Europeans—began their protracted resistance against French rule in 1885, when the regents and mandarins (also called Scholars), who supported the twelve-year-old Emperor Ham Nghi at Hué, attacked the French. They were repulsed and fled to the mountainous area of Ha Tinh province, where for three years they successfully eluded capture. (A similar resistance to French power, led by Prince Si Vattha, took place in Cambodia in 1885–86.) The desperate Revolt of the Scholars was only the first of a series of resistance efforts.

Though it is customary to classify colonial rule as "direct" or "indirect," these terms do not reveal the substance of French administration in Indochina. Cochinchina, the first part of the peninsula to become a French colony, was under military rule—the so-called Rule of the Admirals—until 1879–80, when a civil governor and a subordinate Colonial Council were named. The council was represented in the French Chamber of Deputies, but the members of the council were elected primarily by French civil servants and residents in Cochinchina. Tonkin was treated in the same way. In the protectorate of Annam, as in Cambodia and Laos, the semblance of emperor and of kingly rule was allowed to remain, but control and effective power resided in France and in the resident French appointees. Responsibility for Indochina alternated between the Ministry of Marine and the Ministry of Commerce, which competed for that prize. In 1893, the affairs of Indochina were placed under the authority of the newly created Ministry of Colonies. Until World War II, this ministry and its successors had jurisdiction over the Governor-General of Indochina. He, in turn, governed through a series of chief residents, who were in charge of local administration in the colony of Cochinchina (which also had a direct governor) and in the protectorates (where the emperor or king was the nominal head). All mandarins (local civil servants) were subordinate to the chief residents and to the French-dominated local councils.[1]

The resistance to and rebellions against French rule began almost immediately after the imposition of full French power and administration. Four years after the suppression of the Revolt of the Scholars, a more serious one was organized by De Tham, the "Tiger of Yen The," who continued to prove troublesome to the French throughout the first decade of the twentieth century. De Tham withdrew to a rugged section of northern Tonkin, where he became an almost legendary hero because of his ability to hold off the French. In Viet Nam, nationalism as we speak of it today certainly originated in the waning years of the nineteenth century. Some of the

movements were organized by the deposed or slighted Vietnamese emperors, some by the mandarians who were loyal to
them, some by other patriotic Vietnamese who were willing to
fight against French colonialism and its destruction or denigra-
tion of traditional Vietnamese society. How much popular
support these movements acquired is debatable, but they
certainly had the support of the educated elite, which inspired,
organized, and animated them.

The French were willing to use the mandarins and other
Vietnamese as intermediaries between themselves and the
general public, but they were always placed in positions inferior to those held by the French, and they were always regarded as untrustworthy. The French were determined to
introduce their own form of administration, their own brand
of civilization, their own laws and customs—all superior, by
definition and by decree, to the indigenous variety. In this
way they alienated those who might have helped them build
the multiracial, egalitarian society which, in theory, they
espoused. They further deepened the antagonism of the more
ardent patriots, who could not accept the avowed purpose
of French colonial policy, the "civilizing mission" of France.

Sixty-five years after the first Revolt of the Scholars, Doan
Quan Tan, a Vietnamese who was not unfriendly to the
French, spoke to the Alliance Française of Indochina. Even
then (April 16, 1949) he could say:

But here and now the people of our country are jostled and bul-
lied; rights are claimed and satisfaction is given; the French administrator, the French colonial, the French shop-keeper, all have
to do with an all-powerful French administration inclined to fa-
vour them. "It's only human," say the French, indulgently. "It's
inhuman," is the opinion of the Vietnamian, the butt of this unequal treatment, ill-used in their own land, by strangers whom
they consider as guests. In short, some speak of rights, but only
for themselves, the lot of duty falls on other shoulders. On one
side are all the civic and political rights, and the liberties that en-
sue. On the other side, nothing. Not even the right to justice or to

equity. However intelligent, all their lives the Vietnamians have been relegated to inferior posts; they had never the right to administrate a province; except for a few rare exceptions, they could never become the judges of their own countrymen; though fulfilling the same office and doing the same work, they never got but ten-seventeenths of their French colleague's salary. Not a few high-up civil servants of the Viet-Nam earned less than a French gendarme. But why, you will probably ask me, did the Vietnamians never protest instead of waiting, instead of putting up with the injustices, the blunders and humiliations, instead of shutting themselves up in their silence; only to burst out all of a sudden? How could they protest? We hadn't the right to vote, the Cochinchinese deputy was elected by the French and the Hindus, which latter were, as we have explained, French citizens, imported for the purpose of the elections and royally rewarded from funds . . . acquired in Indo-China.

And this is the explanation, in brutal terms, of our present conflict.[2]

As we shall see, Doan Quan Tan was a good analyst of the ailment; but he failed to give due credit to the protests that were made repeatedly, and, just as repeatedly, suppressed.

Following the Rule of the Admirals (1861–79), a number of governors-general were dispatched to Indochina. Of these, only Paul Bert, who died soon after he took office, had any sympathetic understanding of the plight of the Vietnamese. Sporadic armed resistance continued through the end of the nineteenth century. By 1900, a year unmarred by any serious rebel activity, the bloody struggle of conquest was considered ended.

In 1897, with victory assured, the French dispatched Paul Doumer as governor-general, with the avowed purpose of making the colony economically self-sufficient. Doumer, an able administrator and financial expert who later became President of France (1931–32), was eminently equipped for this task. He set up an irreversible pattern by which Indochina was to develop, not according to her own needs but in accordance with the nineteenth-century colonial concept, i.e., in a functional relationship to France. In 1898, he unified the administration of the five territories with a central budget and with centralized services, all responsible directly to the governor-general. The local budgets of the separate states were financed through direct taxation. The general budget, financed through indirect taxation, was devised to support an ambitious program of long-term development projects—including mines, roads, bridges, railroads, and harbors—which were to provide the infrastructure for the newly reorganized colony.

In his zeal for a purely organizational approach, Doumer imposed many hardships on the local population that brought them, as individuals, no tangible benefits. His most unpopular measures were government salt and alcohol monopolies, which touched the daily lives of the peasants: many depended upon salt production and marketing for their livelihood; all used alcohol in their traditional rites. During his five-year term, he did little, if anything, to develop a policy that would involve the Vietnamese in the colonial government. He was indifferent to popular demands for education; discontent spread among the educated at his policy of employing French personnel even on the lowest administrative levels of government. The cornerstone of his administration was the nineteenth-century French policy of assimilation, which had the long-range goal of turning Vietnamese into Frenchmen. To quote Virginia Thompson:

The political and cultural assimilation of a colony was favored by an overwhelming majority in the late 19th Century. This involved the destruction of existing native institutions, and their replacement by those prevalent in France, with an inevitable substitution of language. It was believed that the mere knowledge of French would bring an insatiable thirst for French ideas and manufactures.[3]

By the end of Doumer's term, the destructive aspect of the policy had succeeded admirably, but no efforts had been made to create new Vietnamese institutions to fill the void.

It was Doumer's successor, Governor-General Paul Beau (1902–07), who fell heir to the problem of the "moral conquest" of the Vietnamese people. His genuine concern for the indigenous population was manifested in the creation of some local medical facilities, in the abolition of corporal punishment, and in the enunciation of a "revolutionary" educational policy—revolutionary only in that it was the first step taken by the French in the field. Beau appointed a director of public education, created a French-Vietnamese curriculum, started sending gifted students to France, and cautiously opened some lower-rank administrative jobs to the Vietnamese. His reforms were too late and too superficial. Three years of bad harvests and fundamental discontent with high taxes, corrupt tax collectors, and monopolies further aggravated peasant misery.

The factors that gave rise to Vietnamese nationalism and then, later, to Communism, are easy to see and to diagnose. Primarily, the Vietnamese did not want to be dominated by the French any more than they had, in previous centuries, accepted domination by the Chinese. Nationalism in a colonial country always begins as a revolt against the alien power, whether the domination is political, racial, cultural, economic, or religious.

The pre-European, pre-French economy of Indochina—like the economies of most of mainland Southeast Asia—was based primarily on subsistence production by the indigenous population. Rice and other food products, edible oils from kernels, fruit, fish, woods, weaving, semiprecious and precious minerals, and ores constituted the staples of the empire. Rice was seldom exported. But fish, nuts, ebony, ivory, turtleshells, and lacquers were exchanged in coastal trade.

The arrival of the French as empire-builders in the 1860's, the opening of the Suez Canal, and the use of imported Chinese labor and capital transformed this subsistence economy into an extractive one, owned and managed by the

French. Rice and rubber became the major items of export for the world market; raw silk, pepper, tobacco, and other products were sent to France for domestic consumption. There is no doubt that the French improved the quantity and the quality of rice production; before World War II, Indochina became the world's third largest exporter of rice, after Burma and Thailand. The French also developed the rubber plantations and the extensive coal mines at Hongay and elsewhere in Tonkin. Tonkin became the industrial section, while the South became the granary for the whole country. (This situation still prevailed at the time of the 1954 Geneva Agreements.)

The French built a variety of roads connecting the two parts of the country and the two poles of the economy; like other imperialist powers at the beginning of the twentieth century, they initiated public-works, public-health, and sanitation programs, primarily in the major cities, where the majority of French administrative and managerial personnel lived. They introduced new and better crops, improved irrigation and canals, and generally helped both production and marketing.

The changeover from a subsistence to a commercial economy brought undesirable changes in the countryside. Wealthy landlords gradually won control of the major crop-producing areas—to the extent that when the French departed, they and the Chinese moneylenders, constituting less than 3 per cent of the population, owned about 50 per cent of the Mekong delta rice lands. The peasant farmers, who formerly had use-title to their land, became debt-ridden tenant farmers, or farm laborers, or a displaced, urban-drawn "lumpen-proletariat." Rural Vietnamese, who made up 80 per cent of the indigenous population and were the mainstay of the country, tended less and less to remain peasants rooted in the soil. The benefits of their land and of their labor went to the foreigner—the French and the Chinese.

France had invested heavily in Indochina and, although

the investment proved to be profitable, it benefited primarily France and the French. Only a thin top layer of the Vietnamese acquired French culture, French citizenship, and a share in the new money economy that had been grafted onto the subsistence economy of the rural masses. As Furnivall pointed out in his classic work on Burma[4] (where the conditions were the same as in Indochina), the rural masses paid taxes, had little if any say in the government, gradually lost their rights to the land, and found their traditional, commune-autonomous village system disrupted by foreign economic, legal, and sociocultural modes. They were thus prepared to back nationalist leaders who fought to get rid of the French.

There was seldom a time during the period of French domination when nationalist-minded and patriotic Vietnamese leaders could not rally to their banner both educated Vietnamese and more or less illiterate followers in the countryside. Even the French-educated Vietnamese elites found few opportunities to participate in the French regime in Viet Nam, except in positions of inferior power with inferior pay. Progressive self-government was not France's aim for the colony. French colonial administration amounted to rule by French officials in Paris, Hanoi, and Saigon. Though some Vietnamese were grudgingly appointed to the so-called consultative bodies in the colony, these were limited to a docile minority, beneficiaries of French benevolence.

In this atmosphere of deprivation, Vietnamese nationalism flourished. As in other Southeast Asian colonies, especially Burma and the Dutch East Indies, the indigenous patriotism, which was almost always underestimated by the colonial power, was strengthened by the Japanese victory over Russia, by the Chinese Republican victory of Sun Yat-sen, by the Russian Revolution, and, above all, by Western-derived ideas of democratic and Marxist-revolutionary education—in this case, transmitted through the French themselves.

During Governor-General Beau's term of office, an event occurred that was to give nationalist sentiment a new direction and new courage: the Japanese victory over Russia in 1905. Up to this point, the French had studiously ignored all counsel against their policy of repression and exploitation, seeing their military victory as a sufficient mandate to proceed with colonization without fear of serious opposition. The earliest opposition, which derived from the high-ranking members of the mandarinate, who had most to lose by French conquest, and from those who sought to preserve the monarchy and the traditional Confucian ideals and systems, consisted of small armed bands with little organization and little sense of national purpose. At the turn of the century, however, the Western ideas that came to Viet Nam through the French, and, indirectly, through Viet Nam's traditional teacher, China, inspired a new form of resistance. The new nationalist leaders, drawn from the educated elite, or *lettrés*, were animated by more than the simple desire to depose the French; a strong emphasis was placed on the need for modernizing Vietnamese society. Some of the leaders chose exile in southern China, principally the Canton area, which became a center for Vietnamese nationalism and, later, Communism. Others went to Japan, where they received both overt and covert support, especially after 1905.

With the victory of Japan over a European power, Vietnamese students began to study in Japanese schools, from where they sent letters and pamphlets back home. These, in the words of one student, were intended to show how Japan had "been able to conquer the impotent Europeans" and were designed to enlist other Vietnamese students to come to Japan to join forces with the "six hundred" already there, whose "only aim" was to "prepare the population [in Viet Nam] for the future." A prominent student leader was Phan Boi Chau, who earlier had been a supporter of Phan Dinh Phung, one of those who had fought for an imperial restoration after the defeat of Emperor Ham Nghi and his Scholars in 1888.

Phan Boi Chau had been organizing bands of Vietnamese

youths against the French since 1900. His first defiant political pamphlet, "Letters Written in Blood from Overseas," was published in 1903 in a traditional Chinese literary form, with allusions that could be understood only by the educated elite. He was a major link in the chain of nationalist leaders that spread from Viet Nam to Japan and back. By 1905, he had come to the conclusion that Japan would lead the colonial Asian nations out of bondage. He returned from Tokyo with the firm belief in a society built on modern, rational and scientific concepts; his faith in the restoration of the monarchy —also based on the Japanese example—was reinforced. He was convinced that Japan would aid his cause. In 1906, he issued a pamphlet, "Advice to the Young to Study Abroad," in which he exhorted his countrymen to organize societies to help send young students to Japan. A popular song of the period extolled the Japanese emperor as a wise prince who had reformed his country and inspired it with the sentiment of national solidarity; the Vietnamese emperor was, by comparison, described as "a wooden statue." The song further accused the French of keeping the Vietnamese in darkness.

Chau attracted a great following among the young. He organized a secret revolutionary society known as the Viet Nam Duy Tan Hoi (Viet Nam Modernization League), and he encouraged one of the great early nationalist figures, Prince Nguyen Cuong De, to accept exile in Japan, supporting him while there. In 1908, Chau formed the League of East Asians "to contest Western imperialism and defend the genius of the East."

The most effective spokesman and leader of those educated Vietnamese who were hoping to achieve modernization, and eventual independence, through collaboration with the French was Phan Chau Trinh. Like Phan Boi Chau, he had been traveling up and down his country calling for the awakening of national energies and deriding the corrupt mandarins. In August, 1906, he addressed a memorandum to Governor-General Beau in which he protested the evils of the French administration. The memorandum is of particular significance in that it marked the first documented rejection by an educated Vietnamese of the antiquated monarchical system.[5] Trinh's memorandum signaled the birth of the reformist movement; it set up a new republican ideal in place of the traditional monarchial one, called for participation by the masses in government and in all walks of life, and demanded modernization of the economy. Trinh made a sincere offer to collaborate with the French in working toward a "Vietnamese Democracy."

In 1907, several educational societies and schools were founded under the general leadership of the Free School of Tonkin. This school, inspired by the ideals of Phan Chau Trinh, quickly attracted more than a thousand students. It offered a free education in French, Chinese, and Vietnamese, with a curriculum devoted to traditional culture, to political economy, and to the exact sciences. The Society for Encouragement of Secondary, Superior, and Professional Education, whose aim was to send students abroad, was founded about the same time. The French, seemingly unaware that the goal of the Society was to send its students for study in France, assumed that it was Japan-oriented; as a result, the Society was suppressed. The Free School originally had the support of the French, but the French closed its doors only nine months after the school opened, when it began to print nationalist propaganda on its printing presses. Its leaders were imprisoned on Poulo Condore Island, which the French had transformed into a prison camp for political offenders.

In 1908, the French, dissatisfied with the new emperor Thanh Thai, who seemed open to current ideas for reform, deposed him and banished him to the island of Reunion, declaring him insane. There was unrest among the peasants; this was generally attributed to discontent with taxation and to the inflammatory influence of the students who had studied in Japan. The peasants, who were cutting off their queues as a symbol of their desire for modernization, did not directly challenge French authority, but directed most of their ire against the mandarins. Phan Chau Trinh had earlier published a pamplet in which he blamed the mandarins for the misery and ignorance of the Vietnamese people.[6] He charged that the mandarins, in whom too much authority had been vested by the French, were, in their own interests, perpetuating the misunderstanding between the French and the "natives." He also criticized the French for their contempt of the Vietnamese. Phan Chau Trinh was assumed to be behind the peasant disorders. Though he announced that he was not hostile to France, provided it modernized the country, he was seized by the French and condemned to death. The sentence was commuted in 1908, and he was imprisoned at Paulo Condore. In 1911, he was exiled to France, where he became teacher to young Vietnamese who had been exiled or had left home for further education—among his pupils was Nguyen Ai Quoc, later to become famous as Ho Chi Minh.

On June 27, 1908, the French discovered a plot, ten months in preparation, to poison their garrison in Hanoi. Behind it was the "Tiger of Yen The," De Tham, who for almost two decades had been leading his rebel bands in Yen The province, where he controlled what was virtually an independent principality. Legends had grown around his exploits; the French were disturbed by his popularity. He was a national hero, backed by the Japan-centered group and its leaders, Phan Boi Chau and Prince Cuong De. The latter was now recognized as king by De Tham and Phan Boi Chau.

Preparation for the plot was carried out through an "education" society in which the native soldiers in the Hanoi garrison were enrolled. De Tham subsequently recruited these soldiers for a secret army he was setting up, ostensibly on behalf of exiled "King" Cuong De. He led the soldiers to believe that Chau and Cuong had written that the war was to take place that year. Elaborate rites and rituals were organized for the soldiers. The plotters encouraged the masses to think that the Japanese would come to their aid once the revolt was under way. The poison plot itself was a fiasco. Few Vietnamese troops were actually involved. The French exposed it, sentenced the ringleaders to death, and crushed De Tham's followers—though De Tham once again managed to escape.

In the subsequent trials, the links between the various nationalist groups became apparent. There was an air of hysteria among the French in Viet Nam, which resulted in the closing of the newly opened University of Hanoi and many other local educational institutions. Such reactions were strongly criticized in *Asie Française,* the publication of the Comité de l'Asie Française. The Comité had been founded in 1901 to express the views of moderate Frenchmen of the Center parties on Middle Eastern and Asian problems; its first president was Eugene Etienne, a senator and later a member of the French Cabinet. The announced goal of the Comité was to form "a unifying center for economic, diplomatic, ethnic, social, and religious information, which is needed for reasoned action in face of the problems of the Levant and the Far East."

Asie Française provides a valuable chronicle of events in Viet Nam from the paper's founding in April, 1901, until its demise in 1940, especially in the absence of an independent, uncensored press in that country. Its policy, based in part on concern for the subject peoples, was also prompted by the fear that the ferment in China might endanger French interests in Asia. This was revealed in the first issue: "The time has come for France to have a definite Asian policy, conscious of herself. The Chinese crisis, just begun, will not fail to change profoundly, for better or for worse, the situation of people with interests in Asia." The Comité saw a strengthened China as a threat to French rule in Indochina, and urged consistently that Indochina be made *"un organisme animé d'une vie propre,"* able to survive by itself without being a drain on the metropole.[7]

A series of "Lettres de l'Indochine," usually unsigned, which appeared in its pages shortly after the Japanese victory

over Russia, pointed to a growing political consciousness
among the peasants and a declining respect for the monarchy
at Hué, which the peasants regarded as a mere French puppet
and an unnecessary expense. Commenting on this, *Asie Française* suggested that one important effect of French domination was the transformation of the structure of Viet Nam's
society. During the early stages of the conquest, the French
had tried to preserve and work through some of the local
institutions and the mandarinate. But the mandarinate was corrupt and self-seeking; faced with foreign domination, some
mandarins had turned to armed resistance, but many more had
abandoned their moral and educative role in the society and
had either fled or collaborated with the French, thereby dis-
crediting themselves in the eyes of the people. The monarchy
had not escaped degradation either; by one method or another,
the French had always assured themselves of a cooperative
sovereign. Thus, with all the traditional sources of authority
in their society discredited, the Vietnamese were susceptible to
new ideas and institutions.

A letter published in *Asie Française* in June, 1906, described the discontent among the peasantry. The great economic changes in the country, the letter charged, had not
affected the masses; railroads were being built, but hunger was
rife; the cost of living had skyrocketed. The major objects of
bitterness were the alcohol and salt monopolies and taxation,
which hit the peasants hardest. A Tonkinese observed that the
peasant was not thinking of revolt, since he was used to
domination, but that he would as willingly accept Japanese
domination as French. It was emphasized that France could
not count on the Vietnamese to prevent Japan from taking
over their country, if such an attempt were made.

An article in the issue of July, 1906, was devoted to the
plight of the educated Vietnamese, both those who had been
educated in the classical Vietnamese manner and those who
had received a Western education. The French, it was pointed
out, were creating among the latter a dangerous class of up-

rooted intellectuals who had high aspirations but whose achievements had not been recognized by the administration. Vietnamese society, too, failed to give them the respect traditionally accorded classical scholars. The French had encouraged many youths to be educated in France, where they had been exposed to a democratic society; yet on their return these Vietnamese had been treated with contempt by French officials and colonists. An indication of the hunger for Western ideas—and the way in which it was being met by Japan and China—was the popularity in Viet Nam of Chinese translations of works by Rousseau, Voltaire, and other Europeans. Another potential source of discontent mentioned by *Asie Française* was the children of native women and French fathers, who had no place in either society.

Along with this growing feeling of national and individual frustration, secret societies, with close ties to similar Chinese societies, were attracting growing numbers. Their actions were marked by brutality toward those who refused to join, or refused to abide by their orders. The societies were a haven for nationalist agitators—many of whom were influenced more by the Japanese than by the Chinese.

The editors of *Asie Française* attempted to foster the policy of *association*, by which was meant the retention and modernization of all that was valuable in the Vietnamese culture and its incorporation into the culture that the French had brought; this contrasted with the official policy of *assimilation*, with all that it implied for the destruction of the indigenous culture. A letter from a group of Annamites expressed their resentment of French official policies: "For fifty years we have suffered under a policy of domination which has created a gulf between masters and subjects which grows bigger every day, inciting hatred and leading to bloodshed." They added that France understood this, and begged it to work for our "physical and moral uplifting, like the Americans in the Philippines. . . . We do not intend to be slaves forever. We want to be treated like men."

The French administration in Indochina refused to heed the
warnings. The unrests of 1908, culminating in the abortive
poison plot, were the result. Suppression by force was a pallia-
tive; the closing of Hanoi University and other schools
hardly helped to remove or alleviate the underlying causes.
"Phobias dominate our colonial policy," *Asie Française* com-
mented, pointing out that the leaders of the revolt were of
the traditional school and that revolutionary ideas were enter-
ing the country in a thousand ways besides French-language
schools, and that closing the schools would not prevent the
growth of anti-French feelings. The French authorities had
hinted that Japanese influence had been behind the events,
even though Japan had signed a treaty with France, in 1907,
promising not to interfere with France's interests in Asia.
"We must stop seeing an evil Japanese fairy behind Indochinese agitation," *Asie Française* counseled.

The next few years were fairly quiet ones in Indochina.
Phan Boi Chau and Prince Cuong De remained in Japan until
French pressure forced their expulsion in 1910, when they
went to China. The outbreak, in 1911, of the Chinese Revolution, headed by Sun Yat-sen and others who had previously
found refuge and support among the Vietnamese in Hanoi,
had its echoes in acts of violence that broke out in Viet Nam.
Phan Boi Chau, now in Canton, organized what became the
fountainhead of successful nationalist organizations, the Viet
Nam Quang Phuc Hoi (Viet Nam Restoration League), and
proclaimed a Provisional Government of the Republic of
Annam. (Even he used the alien name for his country.) The
violence within Viet Nam remained in a low key until April
26, 1913, when nationalists exploded a bomb in Hanoi. It was
to have been the first of a series of attempts to kill all important civil and military leaders and those loyal to France. It was
apparently well organized; its ultimate aim was to drive out
the French from the whole country—an army of revolutionaries from Annam was to have poured into Tonkin on the
successful completion of the plot.

The French saw in the incident, as in the 1908 plot, the work of Phan Boi Chau and Prince Cuong De. French colonists, who attributed the unrest to the "misguided" humanitarianism and liberalism of Governor-General Albert Sarraut, just as they had blamed the events of 1908 on the policies of Governor-General Beau, urged the administration to impose "severe" justice. The ensuing military measures ended with the suppression of all resistance, the sentencing of eighty-five ringleaders, and the killing of De Tham, the legendary resistance fighter who had been eluding the French since 1897.

Phan Chau Trinh, who was in Paris, voiced his concern. Writing in a Paris newspaper, he stated that earlier he had warned Sarraut and M. Messimy, Minister of Colonies, of the consequences of French policies:

I told them that if they did not give the people of Annam the reforms they promised, there would be much to fear. That was twenty months ago. Since then they have done some small things for the Annamites, but their efforts were like giving candy to a baby to erase the sting of blows he had received; the alcohol monopoly was renewed, although they promised it would not be; the patriots imprisoned in Poulo Condore perished though they were promised pardon; the education we call for is always refused; the contempt in which we are held is ever increased, and now they add new faults to these old ones: they violate the sacred tomb of Tu Duc for money. The people of Annam want to learn, to be respected. . . . they want little by little to emancipate themselves. On this point, do you not think it is to France's interest to come to an understanding with the Annamites? On the day on which the people of Annam, having been taught by France, obtain their autonomy from her, France, which will have prepared us for the liberty which it gives us, will have preserved all her interests with us; we will love her as friends and as allies.

This comment by the moderate, exiled nationalist Trinh was as unacceptable to the French as the views of the more extreme, revolutionary-minded nationalists. Both, then, were to fail against the recalcitrance of French policy. They failed

also because they did not fully understand the importance of
social and economic change; instead, they heightened their
own hatred of the French. Their strictly politically oriented
program, aimed primarily at creating educational opportunities and political reforms, offered little that was of tangible
value to the mass of the people; it represented only the desires of the educated elements of the society and of the
new bourgeoisie. To the end, they never realized the necessity
of attracting broad peasant support in furthering their nationalist cause.

As World War I approached, the Germans apparently
tried to exploit the difficulties of the French in Indochina.
German schools in Canton were attracting Vietnamese students from 1912 on. In 1914, Prince Cuong De made a trip to
Berlin to seek funds; it was estimated that Vietnamese nationalists received some 500,000 French francs from the Germans in the next few years. German propaganda made certain
inroads in the nationalist movement in the early war period,
but it was unsuccessful in seriously sabotaging the French war
effort in Indochina. The entry of Japan into the war against
Germany, and against German interests in neutral China, and
the Japanese victory at Tsingtao in the fall of 1914 frustrated
German efforts to instigate revolts against the French. Though
sporadic incidents did occur, the Vietnamese revolutionaries,
a few hundred strong, could elicit no support either from the
masses or from their own class for their program of revolt.
Dependent for their support on foreign handouts, some joined
bandit groups, while the majority made their way to Siam,
to wait for a more opportune time. In May, 1916, the young
king of Annam, Duy Tan, was involved, with some of the
old-style monarchist supporters, in an abortive plot; he was
deposed in favor of Khai Dinh and exiled. Relative quiet was
then maintained for a few years. An attempted bomb plot in
Tonkin, in late 1920, similar to that of 1913, was foiled; an
attempt was made to assassinate Martial Merlin, the reactionary governor-general, while he was visiting Canton.

The first period of Vietnamese nationalism, which for forty years had been trying to find some way of reasserting the individuality of Vietnamese life, may be said to have come to an end in the mid-1920's. Phan Boi Chau was arrested by the French in June, 1925, after a series of student demonstrations; he was sentenced to death, but the sentence was commuted to house imprisonment for life (he died in 1940), effectively removing him from all nationalist activity. Phan Chau Trinh, the moderate who had so earnestly sought for an accommodation with France and for modernization of the traditional structure of his country, died in 1926. Their paths diverged in method, not in goal. Each, in the short run, failed—but only in the short run. What is impressive in their lifelong labors is the caliber of their dedication to Vietnamese freedom. Their sons and grandsons share this devotion, which is one of the basic values in their culture. The new nationalist era, under the second generation of nationalist leaders, fell under new influences. The first generation had seen its inspiration in part in a Japan that had defeated Czarist Russia; the second generation was influenced, directly and indirectly, by the Russia that had staged the Bolshevik Revolution and by the revolution in China.

The Struggle Continues—To the Proclamation of the Democratic Republic of Viet Nam

The efforts of the early nationalists were, in the main, directed to the restoration of an independent modernized monarchy, or to reforms within the framework of French rule. The moderates—typified by spokesmen like Phan Chau Trinh —who were influenced by the kind of thinking expressed in *Asie Française*, formed a Constitutionalist Party, in 1923, to work toward transforming the consultative colonial councils into full legislative bodies. They achieved a measure of success, particularly in Cochinchina, where they were led by Bui Quang Chieu, a government official and agricultural engineer who, in 1917, had founded the newspaper *La Tribune Indi-gène;* by Nguyen Phan Long, a former civil servant and jour-nalist; and by Duong Van Giao, a prominent Saigon lawyer. Through cooperation with the French, the moderates had be-come members of a prosperous professional middle class. A bloc of candidates from their party won seats on the Saigon city council in 1925, but they failed to effect any lasting re-forms. There seemed to be a better climate for constitutional reform in the 1930's, but again they were disappointed. The party broke up shortly before World War II; some of its members joined the Cao Dai sect, and others joined the more revolutionary independence movements.

Bao Dai, who, in 1925, had ascended the throne of his father, Khai Dinh, remained in France to complete his education, as his father had requested. On his return to Annam in 1932, he pursued a reform policy; he appointed Ngo Dinh Diem as his Minister of the Interior and as head of a commission to re-organize his government on a more democratic basis. The combined efforts of the French and of the conservative man-darinate at Hué thwarted Bao Dai's policies, and Diem resigned in protest.

The more revolutionary elements, the young disciples of Phan Boi Chau, moved in another direction. In 1925, they reorganized in an attempt to seek independence for a modern Viet Nam, free of the monarchy and of the traditional man-darinate. In the period after World War I, Vietnamese youth had been exposed to new doctrines from the Chinese Republic and from Moscow. Revolutionary groups with strong repub-lican views, and others, under Marxist influence, began to emerge in Viet Nam. From the mid-1920's on, two fundamen-tal revolutionary tendencies evolved in Viet Nam. The names of the groups changed continually. Occasionally, the support-ers of these different viewpoints were united; more often, they contested for the leadership of the struggle against the French. Two separate approaches emerged from the two separate groups; and, ultimately, two separate countries—the (Com-

munist) Democratic Republic of Viet Nam and the (nationalist, anti-Communist) Republic of Viet Nam.

In 1927, the nationalists were organized under the name of
Viet Nam Quoc Dan Dang (Viet Nam Nationalist Party). It
has been called the most significant of all non-Communist
revolutionary nationalist organizations; it was modeled on the
Kuomintang and frequently received support from it. The
Communists, under one name or another, such as the Viet
Nam Cach Menh Dong Minh Hoi (Viet Nam Revolutionary
League), and the Indochinese Communist Party (founded in
1930), were led almost from the beginning by the official
Comintern agent Nguyen Ai Quoc (Ho Chi Minh). The
Party (CPIC) was recognized by and accepted in the Com-
intern in 1931.

These two forces, the nationalists (various groups) and the
Communists (Stalinists and Trotskyists), occasionally cooper-
ated in uneasy united fronts, depending upon the current shifts
of Kuomintang and Comintern policies. What has elsewhere
been referred to by this writer as the Nationalist-Marxist
amalgam between the two World Wars[8] runs through the
Vietnamese struggle against the French from the mid-1920's
to the beginnings of the Franco-Vietnamese War of 1946–54.
No anticolonial struggle in Southeast Asia has been as fragmented as that in Viet Nam.[9]

The "front" for the Viet Nam Nationalist Party, VNQDD,
was a publishing business in Hanoi; clandestinely, it enrolled
and trained party members for revolutionary action against
the French authorities. The French security police—a highly
efficient body at that time—uncovered some of the members in
1929, following the assassination of a French labor recruiter.
Their arrest led to plans for an uprising which was to link up
with nationalist-minded Vietnamese troops serving with the
French Army at Lao Kay, near the Tonkin-China border.
The insurrection, led by a young student, Nguyen Thai Hoc,
was scheduled for February 10, 1930. Four companies of
Vietnamese soldiers mutinied that night at Yen Bay, killing

their French officers. Other attacks followed in Phu Tho and Hai Duong provinces; bombs were exploded in Hanoi. The French police and armed forces quickly suppressed the mutineers; Nguyen Thai Hoc and others charged with complicity in the insurrection were executed. The few remaining leaders of the VNQDD fled to Canton and Yunnan where they later and separately reconstituted nationalist parties. Activity by the party within Indochina seemed to have completely halted by 1932.

The Yen Bay nationalist uprising—as it is called—was followed by a Communist effort. In September, 1930, the Viet Nam Communist Party, whose headquarters were at Haiphong, organized a series of demonstrations and strikes; public buildings were sacked; some 6,000 peasants marched on Vinh. Two "soviets" were set up in nearby areas. Landlords were killed in Ha Tinh and Nghe An provinces, and their estates divided among the peasants. The Communists were then operating under the "hard line" revolutionary policy enunciated by the Sixth Comintern Congress of 1928.

The French responded vigorously. Heavily armed French troops, backed by aircraft, quelled the uprising. Ten thousand civilian casualties were reported; another 10,000 were arrested and confined to prisons and penal islands. French security police penetrated the Communist ranks and destroyed their organization. Ho Chi Minh, who had been directing the Vietnamese Communists from Hong Kong—where he was living under an assumed name—was arrested by the British police. In January, 1933, he was allowed to leave the colony; he slipped into China and eventually made his way to Moscow.

During the next few years of relative quiet, nationalist and Communist activities shifted from Tonkin and Hanoi to Cochinchina and Saigon. The underground Indochinese Communist Party resurfaced in 1933, under the leadership of Moscow-trained Tran Van Giau, and formed a united front with the Trotskyists and various unaffiliated nationalists for the municipal elections in Saigon. Their group, La Lutte (The

Struggle), succeeded in electing two members. The Communists also helped to organize a number of rural societies and the Indochinese Democratic Front. In the Saigon municipal elections of 1935 and 1937, four and three representatives, respectively, of the Lutte group were elected. From the start of La Lutte, Ta Thu Thau, the Cochinchinese leader of the Trotskyists' Fourth International (whom the Stalinists later assassinated), was the outstanding leader of the radical anti-French groups. During the Popular Front period (1935–39), until the Nazi-Soviet Pact was signed (August 23, 1939), the Trotskyists won increasing support. In the April, 1939, elections for the Colonial Council of Cochinchina, Ta Thu Thau and two of his comrades, Tran Van Thach and Phan Van Hum, received 80 per cent of the votes. They defeated two Stalinists, three Constitutionalists, and several independents.

In September, 1939, when World War II broke out, the Communists in France, deferring to the recent Nazi-Soviet Pact, refused to support the French war effort. The Communists in Viet Nam resumed their militant attitude; as a result, Trotskyists and Stalinists were harassed by raids and mass arrests. In related fashion, the French were unwilling to make any concessions to the Vietnamese nationalists even in the face of Japanese armed forces poised in China.

After the fall of Paris, Vichy France submitted to Japanese pressures. In return for Japanese recognition of French sovereignty over Indochina, Japan was given air bases in Tonkin, the right to garrison them, and troop transit rights. Viet Nam's ports on the China Sea were to prove of immense strategic value during the Japanese attack on British and Allied ships. From bases in Viet Nam the Japanese bombed and sank ships, including the *Repulse* and the *Prince of Wales,* and initiated their invasion of Burma and Malaya. At first, the French military forces were not disbanded. In November, 1940, the French Army ruthlessly crushed an uprising organized by the Communists under Tran Van Giau in the Mekong delta area.

The Vichy French regime in Viet Nam—a nasty, cowardly episode—under Governor-General Admiral Jean Decoux (appointed on June 25, 1940, the day France signed the armistice with Germany), lasted until March 9, 1945, when the Japanese surrounded the French garrisons and assumed direct control of the country. Overlooking Prince Nguyen Cuong De, the aging pretender who was still exiled in Japan, the Japanese appointed Bao Dai, the puppet emperor of Annam, as emperor over all of Viet Nam. As a Japanese puppet, Bao Dai was as powerless as he had been under the French. He tried to enlist various nationalists; Ngo Dinh Diem, who was offered an important position, turned him down.

During the war years, Nationalist and Communist leaders found refuge in China. Some members of the old VNQDD continued a party of that name; others formed the Dai Viet QDD (Great Viet Nam Nationalist Party). With the assistance of the Kuomintang, these two formed a nationalist coalition which included the Viet Nam Restoration League, whose members still backed the pretender, Prince Cuong De. This coalition came to be known as the Viet Nam Cach Menh Dong Minh Hoi (the Viet Nam Revolutionary League, or League of Vietnamese Revolutionary Parties). The Communists were also regrouping in China. Because Kuomintang leaders were suspicious of the Indochinese Communist Party, the Communists, in May, 1941, organized another "united front" to include certain independent nationalist elements: the Viet Nam Doc Lap Dong Min Hoi (Revolutionary League for the Independence of Viet Nam), popularly known as the Viet Minh. The first meeting took place in Kwangsi province, close to the Vietnamese city of Cao Bang. Ho Chi Minh was now back in China, heading the Communist effort. This was the time when he shifted from earlier aliases, such as Nguyen Ai Quoc ("Nguyen the Patriot"), and Hong Qui Vit ("Hong Who Lives"), to Ho Chi Minh ("He Who Aspires to Enlightenment"). Nevertheless, the Chinese, suspicious of the Viet Minh, arrested Ho (probably in January, 1942) and kept him im-

prisoned for about a year. In October, 1942, the Dong Minh
Hoi, was organized, under Chinese guidance, to help in the
war effort against the Vichy French and the Japanese in Viet
Nam. Either this League of Revolutionary Parties failed to
satisfy the needs of the Kuomintang or the latter were willing
to make a concession for more assistance. In any event, Ho Chi
Minh effected his release from jail "to make the League work
better." He and his Viet Minh thereupon joined the Dong
Minh Hoi as one of the constituent groups of an enlarged
"united front." Ho became one of its officers.

At Chinese insistence, the Indochinese Communist Party
had been kept out of the League, though the Communists
were able to exert their full influence through their "front,"
the Viet Minh, which was a partner in the League. The Communist Party's organization was meanwhile kept intact under
the leadership of two of Ho's most trusted lieutenants: Vo
Nguyen Giap, who had learned guerrilla tactics under Mao
Tse-tung's followers in Yenan and directed Communist activities in North Viet Nam; and Pham Van Dong, who was responsible for activities in the South.

The Viet Minh, in its pursuance of the war against the
Vichy regime in Viet Nam and against the Japanese, received
aid from the Allies, including the United States, in return for
which it performed intelligence work behind Japanese lines.
In March, 1944, a government-in-exile was set up in Liuchow
under the aegis of the Chinese, in which Ho Chi Minh held a
minsterial post. These arrangements enabled Ho Chi Minh
gradually to acquire a leading role among Viet Nam's nationalists. Viet Minh forces—then called a "People's Army" for
"national liberation"—were fighting in the Cao Bang—Lang Son
area, adjacent to China; this was referred to as the "liberated
zone" of Viet Nam. Allied help given to the Viet Minh forces
in that area helped Ho win some degree of recognition of its
legitimacy. The Viet Minh's criticism of the Bao Dai regime as
a Japanese puppet government found support, in early 1945,
among those Vietnamese who had understandably lost respect

for the emperor during the years in which he had been a French puppet. Hence the drive by Ho and the Viet Minh Communists for a takeover of Viet Nam was facilitated by the aspirations of many Vietnamese. They wished to end their dependence on outside masters, whether French, Japanese, or any other.[10]

The Chinese under Chiang Kai-shek, with the help of the Communist-controlled Viet Minh and of the nationalist-controlled League of Revolutionary Parties, were militarily in control of Viet Nam down to the 16th parallel at the end of the war. It was agreed at the Potsdam Conference that the British were to assist the Free French Forces south of this line. The Chinese, in their area, and the Anglo-French forces, in theirs, were to help in disarming the Japanese and in restoring law and order. These military arrangements were rapidly converted into political ones. On August 19, 1945, the Viet Minh, with some assistance from the Japanese, took over Hanoi; they failed in a similar effort in Saigon. On August 29, Ho Chi Minh formed the Provisional Government of the Democratic Republic of Viet Nam with himself as President. Emperor Bao Dai, who had handed over his Grand Seal to the forces of Tran Van Giau five days earlier, accepted the post of Supreme Political Advisor to the Viet Minh regime and bestowed on it the trappings of legitimacy. On September 2, the Democratic Republic of Viet Nam was officially proclaimed in Hanoi.

The Viet Minh, of course—like the Chinese, although for different reasons—did not want the French back. Vietnamese nationalists in the North as in the South were decidedly against the French. They had been beaten, suppressed, and imprisoned by Vichy troops during the war whenever they had sought to offer any kind of resistance against the Japanese and the Vichyites. Now, as the Japanese occupation collapsed, in August 1945, they aspired to genuine national freedom.

This was denied them. Fresh French troops, supported by the British, began to arrive in September. Saigon was retaken. In the North, however, the Chinese refused to admit the

French until the end of February, 1946, by which time they had wrung certain concessions from the French; but the delay also enabled the Viet Minh to further entrench themselves in Hanoi as the effective government of North Viet Nam.

On March 6, 1946, the French agreed to recognize the Democratic Republic of Viet Nam (i.e., Tonkin) as a free state within the Indochinese Federation in the framework of the newly formed French Union. They also agreed to conduct a referendum on whether the South (Annam and Cochinchina) would join this Vietnamese free state. Conferences to work out the details of the March agreement were held between the Viet Minh and the French at Dalat in April and at Fontainebleau in July; another conference held at Dalat included representatives of Laos, Cambodia, and the Vietnamese nationalists, but not the Viet Minh. It soon became clear to the Viet Minh that the French had no real intention of carrying out the agreed-upon referendum, which, had it then taken place, would undoubtedly have joined the two parts of Viet Nam. For at that time, the nationalists in Viet Nam were openly critical of the Communists for having agreed with France on *anything* short of complete national recognition.

Hostilities between the French and the Viet Minh, which had been continuing throughout this period, were temporarily halted by a new agreement, the *Modus Vivendi* of September 14–15, 1946. Nevertheless, sporadic clashes continued. On November 23, the French bombed Haiphong; on December 19, the North responded with concerted attacks on French forts in Tonkin and Annam. Thus began the full-scale war which ended—for a time—in 1954, with the partition of Viet Nam at the 17th parallel.

On Warfare Against a Colonial Power Before World War II: Some Conclusions

On the whole, it may be said that the native problem in Indo-China is not really serious. There is little of the open secession that is so obvious in Tunisia or of the passive hate that characterizes

Algeria. In Indo-China the general *reveil* movement of Asiatic
[*sic*] Powers naturally finds an echo, but it is difficult to make
rebels of a prosperous peasantry.

Stephen H. Roberts[11]

In 1930, one year after Roberts made his bold prediction,
four companies of Vietnamese troops mutinied at Yen Bay, as
part of a wider attempt to free Viet Nam from foreign domination. This was only one of many uprisings; it was a small,
outward sign of the general discontent with French rule. The
prosperity that Roberts thought he discerned was not enough
to lull the proud heirs of a thousand-year-old civilization into
passive submission. Nor did the prosperity reach the masses of
the rural inhabitants or the urban workers. Though economic
discontent played a part, it was not the major cause of the ultimate struggle. The Communists finally succeeded in North
Viet Nam because they combined in their strategy the exploitation of purely local grievances with the theory and practice of anti-imperialist, anticapitalist warfare. In this instance,
the French colonial regime fulfilled the theory and became the
target for the practice. Despite the Communists' claim that
they had led the revolution since 1930, what was actually hap-
pening at that time in Viet Nam was essentially a patriotic
anticolonial war that enlisted the support of all bona fide nationalists in Viet Nam. The belated though effective entry of
the Communists into this struggle, immediately after World
War II, alarmed certain circles in the West and aroused misguided support for a reimposition of French colonial rule—a
misfortune for all genuine champions of Vietnamese national
independence.

All Vietnamese—whether monarchist, mandarinal, authoritarian, reformist, republican constitutionalist, or revolutionist—
wanted to be rid of an alien master. The idea of a national
Viet state emerged only slowly and episodically. At various
times, the whole of Viet Nam had been united as one unit under a dynastic empire, but at many other times this empire had

been fragmented by revolts in different provinces. The ties binding the North (Tonkin), the Center (Annam), and the South (Cochinchina) were frequently tenuous; they did not provide a strong historical base for a united nationalist movement until opposition to alien domination, the "cement of the negative," brought them together.

The French were aware of the dissonances among the Viet people, and during the early years of their rule they believed they were completely safe from a general uprising. "There is nothing in common between the various peoples, or their ideas or methods. There is no native public opinion, there probably never will be one. Thus a general uprising is not possible," wrote Roberts.[12] The French believed this. They overlooked the ties that bound the Vietnamese peoples; they could never quite understand the common grievances of the Indochinese states and peoples; they were never able to live up to their role as exponents and practitioners of the libertarian, revolutionary ideas embodied in their "mission."

The Vietnamese, for the most part, essayed what I have called romantic rebellion—looking backward to a past which they attempted to restore. The more far-sighted members of the educated middle class recognized that the progress of their people was shackled by the archaic system of government within the Indochinese protectorates, which the French were committed to perpetuating under French domination and control. Their efforts in the 1920's were directed at attempting to effect reform. Their requests were for the most part modest; their activities were carried out in the open.

But the French were not prepared to loosen their hold on their colony to any significant extent. All Vietnamese attempts at reform were thwarted by the French security service that enjoyed the support of the reactionary French community. To protect the French interests, they restricted travel by the Vietnamese, both within the colony and abroad. They made searches without warrants—they could detain individuals for up to ten years without trial. The security service fomented regional and personal rivalries to break the unity of the nationalist front, and often applied pressure and threats. The frustrations caused by police harassment of all open attempts to reform the system of government eventually forced the nationalists to go underground and engage in conspiratorial agitation—and to be suppressed when discovered.

The security police were backed by military power which the Vietnamese, in the pre-World War II period, could not equal. As far back as 1891, Governor-General de Lanessan had arranged for the military policing of the Tonkin-Chinese frontier region. Each region was under the command of a colonel with both civil and military powers. Eventually Tonkin as a whole was composed of five Military Territories and two Frontier Regions. Annam and the delta area were similarly controlled. To back up the military, armed village police with regular pay and uniforms were organized, and a militia (a higher grade of service under French officers and NCO's) was stationed at fixed posts. Regular troops and the French Foreign Legion were used initially to guard the frontiers between the several states and between French Indochina and China, and to act as a reserve force. By 1931, these three types of forces were supplemented by a *garde indigène* (with French officers) operating in the protectorates; a *garde civile* in Cochinchina, and *partisans* in the Tonkin area. The *garde civile* replaced the former militia, and was subordinate to the French *gendarmerie*. The *partisans* were native units serving as a "trip-wire" border-defense force. Under one name or another, these military and police formations had been largely retained throughout the French period.

All nationalist political agitation could thus be carefully guarded or suppressed, and any nationalist military operations were easily overpowered by the various French forces. Military activities by both nationalists and Communists in the period before World War II were few, poorly planned, and poorly executed. There was then no concerted military theory or practice to counter the French. The models for insurrection were the nineteenth-century ones of terror, assassination, mutiny, bomb-throwing, and other forms of unsustained, uncoordinated violence, followed by withdrawal to remote areas, or foreign exile. Sympathetic though the Kuomintang was, provocative though the Japanese wanted to be, neither the Chinese nor the Japanese invested in training and supplying a Vietnamese guerrilla force capable of sustained and increasing action.

Thus, it can be seen that Vietnamese nationalism was in large measure an expression of opposition to an alien-imposed power. This expression persisted and grew through almost a century of French occupation. It is the same force of nationalism that has sustained the Republic of Viet Nam in its struggle against the efforts of the Communists—in the South and in the North—to impose an alien-oriented dictatorship on the Vietnamese. The people of South Viet Nam rightly recognize that if they were to lose in this struggle, they would become the political chattel of Moscow or of Peking—or of both. The people of Viet Nam remain adamant in struggling against the imposition of *any* alien domination—regardless of its source.

part two

The End of Hostilities?
And Geneva 1954

3. The War Against the French: To Dien Bien Phu

It has been said that the French lost Indochina at the Brazzaville Conference—convened by the Free French under General de Gaulle in January, 1944. There, de Gaulle announced what became future French policy. The recommendations for the Indochinese states were clearly stated:

The aims of the work of civilization which France is accomplishing in her possessions exclude any idea of autonomy and any possibility of development outside the French Empire bloc. The attainment of "self-government" in the colonies, even in the most distant future, must be excluded.

French resistance to *any* progressive development for self-government and independence created the conditions for the ultimate success of the Viet Minh and defeated the possibility of the emergence of a nationalist, anti-Communist front. The unwillingness of the French to prepare the Indochinese states for eventual self-government and independence ensured nationalist support for the Communists; if the nationalists had not given them their support, they would have had to conduct a two-front war—against the French and against the Communists. To this, they were clearly unequal. Since the French were willing to negotiate with the Communist Viet Minh— even if this was only a stalling device—the nationalists were willing to give their support to the Viet Minh in their "August (1945) Revolution."

As Truong Chinh remarked in 1946: "The [Indochinese Communist] Party had correctly seen that the Japanese and

the French would inevitably come into conflict and had decided [1942–44] should this happen, to change its tactics at
once and immediately launch the general insurrection." After
quoting Stalin—"In every revolution, victory does not come
by itself, one must prepare it, win it"—Truong Chinh went on
to detail the "careful preparation" of the Party:

On the one hand, to unify the people's revolutionary forces, to
mobilize manpower and wealth, to stimulate the ardent patriotism
of the people, to adjust the different national salvation organizations, to lead the people in the struggle against white terror and
for the defence of daily rights and interests.

On the other hand, to develop the para-military organizations
such as the self-defence brigades, to train military and political
cadres, to procure arms, to organize the army, to establish the resistance zones, to carry out propaganda among the enemy soldiers,
to train the people for destruction work and the tactics of scorched
earth, etc., to launch guerrilla warfare and seize power in different
localities.[1]

The defeat of the French in Europe and their consequent
loss of face within the colony, the easy Japanese acquisition of
Indochina, and the anarchy that prevailed there after the Japanese surrender in August, 1945, facilitated the Viet Minh takeover in the North. By this time, the Vietnamese Communists
had been trained in methods of guerrilla warfare; originally,
they had learned the techniques and strategies from the Chinese Communists. They had learned how to combine military
and political warfare; how to win, at least for a time, the support of the people in the countryside by making concessions to
their economic interests; how to utilize the terrain, which they
knew better than the French; and how to make effective use
of their sanctuaries in the mountainous jungle area bordering
on China—the Viet Bac area—where the French military could
not easily reach them. General Vo Nguyen Giap claimed that
in 1944 he started with a Viet Nam Liberation Army of "34
men and cadres . . . equipped with 2 revolvers, 17 rifles, 14
flint lock rifles and one light machine gun." Other sources in-

dicate that he had, originally, some "700 anti-Japanese ma-
quis." By the time of the Japanese surrender in August, 1945,
this force had grown, with the aid of the United States, to
some 5,000 men.

It is not without irony that the Declaration of Independence of the newly proclaimed Democratic Republic of Viet
Nam (D.R.V.N.), which President Ho Chi Minh read to a
mass meeting in Hanoi on September 2, 1945, began: "We
hold these truths to be self-evident, that all men are created
equal, that they are endowed by their Creator with certain
unalienable rights, that among these are life, liberty, and the
pursuit of happiness," and ended: "Viet Nam has the right to
be free and independent."

It is reported that the crowd cheered with wild enthusiasm.

There is little doubt that during World War II the United
States favored the idea of eventual independence for the states
of Indochina. Franklin D. Roosevelt repeatedly and openly
had indicated his hopes for these states: "Indochina should not
go back to France but . . . should be administered by an international trusteeship." However, the death of Franklin D.
Roosevelt ended this phase of American policy.

The British, out of concern for their own Asian empire, assisted the Free French to return to Indochina. They dispatched
an Anglo-Indian division under General Douglas Gracey—
they disembarked in Saigon on September 6, 1945—to accept
the surrender of 40,000 Japanese troops. Units of the Kuomintang Army by arrangement with the Allies prepared in
similar fashion to accept the Japanese surrender north of the
16th parallel. Free French divisions under General Leclerc arrived in October, behind the British, and rapidly reimposed
control over most of Cambodia, South Viet Nam, and parts of
Laos. French concessions to the Kuomintang (retrocession of
their extraterritorial rights in China) and their March 6, 1946,
agreement with Ho Chi Minh recognizing the D.R.V.N. as a
"free state . . . belong[ing] to the Indochinese Federation
and to the French Union" (the terms of this agreement were

to be worked out in future meetings) enabled the French to re-enter Haiphong and Hanoi by mid-March; the war began in November.

These months of negotiations were busy ones for both sides. French recognition of Ho Chi Minh improved his political position throughout the century and afforded him the chance to liquidate or politically emasculate the anti-French nationalists who criticized his policy. General Giap also had time to build up his military forces. At the outbreak of the war, there were some 60,000 Viet Minh regular and regional troops in training. The French had brought into Indochina some 63,000 forces that were well armed and well supplied (17,000 were deployed in North Viet Nam). In the initial military exchanges —the French naval attack on Haiphong on November 23, 1946, which was launched after giving the Viet Minh a two-hour ultimatum to withdraw (6,000 Vietnamese were killed), and the Viet Minh attack on the French in Hanoi on December 19—it appeared that the French were in full command of the situation. Throughout 1947, the Viet Minh's poorly equipped army-in-training suffered severe losses. The French controlled the cities, the main highways, and the waterways. There appeared to be some justification for the boast of Paul Coste-Floret, the French Minister of War: "There is no military problem any longer in Indochina. The success of French arms is complete."

The boast was premature. Ho and Giap, recognizing their unreadiness for open warfare, withdrew to the northern mountains and jungles, and to jungles near the coast, south of the Red River delta. There they prepared for the guerrilla war— the long struggle—which lay ahead. In those years before Communist China became the supplier and trainer of the Viet Minh, the latter perfected their own variation of the Leninist-Maoist theory (and practice) of military-political warfare.[2]

At the Second Comintern Congress in 1920, Lenin had clearly foreseen the importance of the "colonial and semicolonial" peoples as temporary united-front allies of the professional revolutionaries (the cadres of the Communist parties). Mao adapted this by his call to place reliance on the peasant masses, to use the countryside as the military-political base of operations, thus being able to surround and defeat the enemy, i.e., the capitalist-imperialists who held the cities. His doctrine of "protracted war," developed in the twenty-two years between the Kuomintang's successful attack on the Communist Party of China in 1927 and the latter's eventual victory in China in 1949, could be summed up by: "The enemy advances, we retreat; the enemy halts, we harass; the enemy tires, we attack; the enemy retreats, we pursue." This military supplement to Lenin's "two steps forward, one step backward" was ideally suited to fit the patterns of guerrilla warfare; it placed the emphasis on men, not weapons, and on the need to win popular support before advancing to ultimate political victory. It has frequently been summarized as a long-term, three-phase struggle.

Phase one is concerned with cadre organization, defensive actions, and survival when the enemy has decisive military superiority; phase two is the period of active guerrilla warfare (great mobility, intelligence work, and the use of surprise attack and dispersal tactics); phase three begins at that stage when the enemy's forces have lost their decisive superiority and the Party's armed forces are sufficiently strong to initiate a general revolutionary offensive. Phase three begins when the Party believes it can go on to win ultimate victory; before it is launched, there must be an accurate appraisal of what the Communists call the "objective conditions," as well as decision-making of the highest quality.

Under the leadership of General Giap, the Viet Minh military—called variously the Viet Nam Army of Liberation, or the People's Army—was organized and trained as a military-political force. It was divided into three major components: the local militia (the farmer-by-day and guerrilla-at-night); the better-trained, better-armed regional troops, which were charged with the defense of the provinces or localities in which they had their homes; and the regular army, the elite corps which had received the most advanced military-political training and the best available weapons. The local militia and regional forces were used for intelligence, security, and logistics work, and in guerrilla actions. The best of them were recruited into the regular army. The militia and regional troops, originally, were armed with some 30,000 Japanese rifles and 2,000 light machine guns which the Viet Minh had bought from the Kuomintang (weapons picked up from the Japanese at the time of their surrender). The regular army received more advanced matériel, mostly French or American weapons acquired during the war against Japan and weapons captured from the French after hostilities had begun.

The training of the Viet Minh Army was based on Mao Tse-tung's "eight reminders" for the behavior of a People's Army soldier. These were:

1. Be polite to the people.
2. Be fair in all dealings with them.
3. Return everything borrowed.
4. Pay for everything damaged.
5. Do not bully the people.
6. Do not damage the crops.
7. Do not flirt with the women.
8. Do not ill-treat prisoners.

To these, Ho Chi Minh added a ninth point: teach the peasant to read. Education, of course, had always been highly respected in Viet Nam; furthermore, literacy made the peasant accessible to written propaganda.

In 1947, the French Expeditionary Corps was expanded. Almost 50,000 African troops and 20,000 Foreign Legionnaires were brought in, doubling the existing strength. Under General Valluy, they had little difficulty in taking and holding the main cities: Hanoi, Haiphong, Hué, Tourane, Dalat, Saigon, and, indeed, wherever they positioned important garrisons. From there, they spread their control through the South, and by March, had re-established control over the main towns and major roads of Tonkin and northern Annam. But Giap and Ho, secure in their Viet Bac stronghold (Ho remained there until 1954)—there were no roads, so that French armored transport and troops could not penetrate, and jungle cover and limestone caves offered protection from air surveillance and attack—began the more serious preparations involved in training the hard-core army, the Chu Luc, for the tasks ahead. Meanwhile, guerrilla activity by the regional troops and local militia was the order of the day; they harrassed the French while supplying intelligence, tax monies, food, and other needed items to their leaders.

The Viet Minh were less effective in the South than in the North. Under Tran Van Giau, and later under Nguyen Binh, they had alienated the Cao Dai sect, whose estimated 2 million members (1954) were dominant in the Tay Ninh area north-west of Saigon. In time, the Cao Dai made an agreement with the French for a degree of autonomy, and for the creation and partial support of a Cao Dai self-defense force. In similar fashion, the Viet Minh "lost" the Hoa Hao sect, estimated at 1.5 million members in 1954, which was predominant in the Can Tho—Bassac River area of the Mekong delta. The Hoa Hao leader Tran Van Soai had also entered into an agreement with the French in March, 1947.

In February, 1947, the "imperious" High Commissioner Admiral D'Argenlieu was removed from office. His successor, Emile Bollaert, an old-time Radical Socialist, was appointed with instructions to carry out a "constructive phase." Bollaert sent the soldier-scholar Paul Mus to negotiate with Ho Chi Minh. At the same time he sought, first indirectly and then directly, to re-enlist the support of former Emperor Bao Dai, who had fled to Hong Kong a year earlier while still officially Ho's "Supreme Advisor." Bao Dai had also been approached by the Viet Minh to negotiate "on its behalf with the French."[3]

All negotiations failed. The Viet Minh would not yield to the French terms, which amounted to virtual surrender; and Bao Dai neither found united support from among his own

followers nor was offered sufficient guarantees for independence by the French to warrant his return.

Concurrent with the negotiations, guerrilla warfare was
stepped up, with sabotage of communications and transport
facilities, ambushes of small French military units, and surprise attacks on lightly guarded French outposts. Despite their
numerical superiority in troops and weapons, the French were
unable to mount an effective counterguerrilla campaign. They
used their armored cars, tanks, artillery pieces, and planes to
protect the cities and the larger garrisons, but they could not
penetrate the roadless mountains and jungles, or the waterways and canals of the Red River and Mekong deltas.

The French continued to pursue what became known as the
Bao Dai formula: they hoped to form a government around
him that would draw nationalist support from Ho Chi Minh.
From December, 1947, to March, 1949, at least three agreements were signed by Bao Dai and the French. Each one, as
Ngo Dinh Diem pointed out to Bao Dai, offered but a façade
of independence to Viet Nam. Each one was so hedged in
with French restraints as to deny the possibility of real independence for Viet Nam within the French Union. The final
agreement, the Elysée Agreement of March 8, 1949, was in
the form of an exchange of letters between French President
Auriol and Bao Dai (as chief of state, not as emperor). On
April 24, Bao Dai returned to Annam from Geneva; the
French Parliament ratified a number of agreements changing
the political status of the component parts of Indochina; and,
on July 1, 1949, Bao Dai formally decreed the establishment
of the State of Viet Nam.

On paper, there were now three independent Associated
States within the French Union—the kingdoms of Cambodia,
Laos, and Viet Nam. In fact, there was no real transfer of
power in Viet Nam. The French military controlled the Vietnamese Army, French colons retained their separate legal status, and French economic interests were still protected. Ngo
Dinh Diem again refused to become Bao Dai's prime minister

under such circumstances, stating that Vietnamese nationalist aspirations would be satisfied only when Viet Nam received a political status similar to that enjoyed by India and Pakistan in the British Commonwealth. The United Kingdom and the United States, in unseemly haste, recognized the Associated States one week after French ratification of the agreements (January, 1950).

Three basic factors served to invalidate these Bao Dai–French agreements. The first stemmed from the fact that bona fide anti-Communist nationalists, although refusing to cooperate with the Viet Minh, also refused to accept anything less than true independence for Viet Nam. Dr. Phan Quang Dan, one of Bao Dai's advisers who broke with him over the agreements, explained this stand:

The Vietnamese people considered Bao Dai's regime as a puppet regime, created and supported by the French for the sole purpose of endorsing French colonial policy and lending it an appearance of legality. Viet Nam had no national assembly and no constitution. Bao Dai's successive governments were all created out of sheer arbitrariness, under French inspiration. And the treaties they negotiated and signed with the French were all for the maintenance of French colonial privileges. The Protocol of the Bay of Along of December 7, 1947, the Élysée Agreements of March 8, 1949, and Conventions of Saigon of December 31, 1949, and the Pau Agreements of December, 1950, claimed repeatedly that Viet Nam was completely independent; but each time it was only sham independence.

Consequently the Communists not only enjoyed the neutrality of the great majority of the Vietnamese population, but had also the active support of many sincere nationalists, who fought along with the Viet Minh against French colonialism.

As a result of the general hostility of the Vietnamese people to French policy, the French found themselves in an increasingly critical situation.[4]

The second factor related to the continuing guerrilla war. Periodically, successive generals—Leclerc, Valluy, Blaizot, Carpentier, de Lattre, Salan, Navarre, Ely, and others—issued announcements that areas were "cleared"; that "mopping-up" operations were successful; and even in certain cases, such as after a French paratroop offensive in the fall of 1947 against a Viet Minh stronghold in the Cao Bang–Lang Son area, that a major victory had been won. However, no final blow was delivered; the guerrillas either withdrew or were replaced, and, somehow, were always there on another day. The terrain—whether mountain, jungle, or paddy field—continued to favor the guerrillas. The French military could not move as freely as the guerrilla in this terrain—they had no helicopters—and the guerrillas continued their harassment by sabotaging and ambushing the French military on roads, waterways, and railways. The Viet Minh local militia and regional forces easily found recruits, porters, intelligence, food, and places for concealment. They became adept at manufacturing explosives, grenades, and ammunition, and in capturing weapons. To the extent that French colonial policy never provided for a viable and independent future for bona fide Vietnamese nationalism, it ensured sociopolitical, psychological, and military support both for the guerrillas who were fighting the French and for the Viet Minh regime in Hanoi that was the symbol of this resistance.

But guerrillas, troublesome as they are—witness the fact that the Burmese Government has been fighting guerrillas since 1948—are essentially a nuisance, not a threat, unless they turn themselves into a real force capable of overturning the government. And this is where the third factor entered: the growing strength of the Viet Minh army. For some time after October, 1949, the Viet Minh were capable of passing over to the third phase of guerrilla warfare. By 1950, the regular army felt strong enough and was trained sufficiently to take to the field. This new state was brought about chiefly by external Communist support given to General Giap's Chu Luc.

The Viet Minh had received diplomatic and material support from the Communist world at least from the time of the establishment of the D.R.V.N. The French Communist Party had exerted political pressure, when it was in the government, for recognition of the new regime; when it was out, it had exerted pressure against the continuation of the war. In factories and at the docks, Communist-controlled unions sabotaged matériel meant for the French forces in Viet Nam. Supplies were sent from the Soviet Union and Czechoslovakia, although the supply route was a long and difficult one.

It was the advent of Communist rule in China, bringing Communist assistance to the very borders of Tonkin, that was probably the decisive factor in determining the final outcome of the struggle. Now there was direct access to the Communist world. War matériel moved directly across the border: recoilless cannons, heavy mortars, anti-aircraft guns, machine guns, tommy guns, bazookas, rifles, trucks, tanks. At the final battle at Dien Bien Phu, the Chinese Communists contributed military leadership and cadres to the Viet Minh.

Giap's Chu Luc, which had been in training since 1950, was now prepared to move out of its protected terrain into what Giap called "the war of movement," or the third phase of operations. In addition to having weapons of Communist manufacture, it also had received American-made equipment that had been captured by the Chinese during the Korean War.

Giap described this turning point of the war: "In effect, 1950 marked the opening of a new phase in the evolution of our Resistance. During the winter, in the frontier campaign, for the first time, we opened a relatively big counter-attack which resulted in the liberation of the provinces of Cao Bang, Lang Son and Lao Cai. Immediately after, we began a series of offensive operations on the [Red River] delta front."[5]

It is difficult to determine, with any degree of accuracy, the size of the opposing forces. However, it does appear that in the period 1950–53, Chu Luc consisted of some 60 battalions of approximately 1,000 men each. These were grouped into divisions of about 12,000 men, with 4 regiments to a division and 3 battalions to a regiment. One of these divisions was sufficiently supplied to constitute an armored or "heavy" division.

By 1953, the French Expeditionary Corps was composed of approximately 175,000 regular army troops (54,000 Frenchmen, 30,000 North Africans, 18,000 Africans, 20,000 Foreign Legionnaires, and 50,000 Vietnamese), and 5,000 navy and 10,000 air force personnel. Ground troops were divided into 90–100 infantry battalions which were, to a considerable extent, tied down to the defense of roads, communications, and population centers. Only a small percentage were available for mobile warfare.[6]

It is clear that after 1950 the Viet Minh were able to escalate the conflict into conventional armed warfare. This was not clearly recognized by the French—an error that contributed considerably to their ultimate defeat. In February, 1950, five Viet Minh battalions overran the French frontier post of Lao Kay. The Viet Minh had a superiority in numbers of five to one, it had mounted a superior force in accordance with Mao's advice. A second, though unsuccessful, large attack (four battalions) was launched at Dong Khe in May. This flexing of the Viet Minh's military muscles before the onset of the monsoon season helped to prepare Giap for an offensive operation that was launched after the end of the rains.

In September, Dong Khe, a key French garrison on the road between Cao Bang and Lang Son, fell under a large-scale assault. Giap had readied some fourteen infantry and three artillery battalions for this campaign. In October, Giap attacked again, and, while the French were withdrawing from Cao Bang, in a series of actions decimated a French garrison force of about 1,500, a reinforcing column of 3,000, and a paratroop relief battalion. This in turn forced a hasty French withdrawal from Lang Son, with the result that the Viet Minh obtained a large stock of military equiment and supplies. The Viet Minh had imposed a considerable defeat on the French and had largely secured northern Tonkin. They now held territory that extended from Lao Kay (at the northwest Red River junction with Communist China) to the east and to the south along the border, and to the area south of Lang Son.

Although General de Lattre de Tassigny, who was appointed military and civilian commander in Viet Nam in December, 1950, was able to halt the decline in the French military position, he was not able to stop the Viet Minh general assault. His firepower and airpower were effective against the Viet Minh's numerical superiority, but he did not have enough power, nor could he use it frequently enough, to gain a lasting victory.

In January, 1952, the Viet Minh launched a three-division assault against a French force of 20,000 men in the Hoa Binh area, forcing them to withdraw. Neither General Salan, who succeeded de Lattre, nor General Navarre, who followed Salan, ever succeeded in modifying the French concept of static defense in any way that enabled them to cope effectively with the strategic offensive of Giap. By May, 1953, the Viet Minh had seven regular divisions, with independent units equivalent to another two divisions, operating against the French Expeditionary Corps, which, according to General Navarre, had less than three divisions available for mobile warfare.[7] Despite this, Navarre decided to hold and defend Dien Bien Phu, thereby hoping to stop the Viet Minh from taking northern Laos and linking it with northern Tonkin and Communist China; Navarre thought he could hold down at least three Viet Minh divisions with his defending force of twelve French battalions.

Dien Bien Phu, a saucer-shaped paddy field twelve miles from north to south and eight miles across, fringed by low but steep and heavily wooded hills, was to become the graveyard for French aspirations in Indochina. For fifty-five days, from March 13, 1954, to May 8, 1954, Giap, his Chinese advisers, and military personnel (backed up by $500-million worth of Soviet bloc military and economic aid), gradually compressed the French, until, on May 7, his 308th Division was able to plant its unit flag on the French Command HQ bunker. The French attempted one final breakout on May 8; it was unsuccessful, and Dien Bien Phu fell to the Viet Minh. The forces under French command (including German Legionnaires and Indochinese soldiers) had lost 7,200 men who were killed or wounded, and 11,000 men who were marched into captivity. Viet Minh casualties were probably three times as great—but it was still a tremendous victory. They had defeated the French Staff and Army in open battle.

Dien Bien Phu rang down the curtain on major military action. France had lost the war; it had, in fact, agreed to negotiate with the Viet Minh even before the battle was over. The French military believed that it would outmaneuver the guerrillas by its strategic defense and tactical superiority. In this, it was tragically mistaken—but then the whole course of French policy in Indochina was based on the mistaken notion that the "work of civilization which France is accomplishing in her possessions exclude[s] any idea of autonomy and any possibility of development outside the French Empire bloc. . . . 'self-government' in the colonies, even in the most distant future, must be excluded."

The disastrous Geneva Agreements of 1954 were the price that was paid for this mistaken policy.

4. The Geneva Conference of 1954—And Its Results

Background to Geneva

As 1954 dawned in Indochina, a century of French domination was drawing to an end. Militarily and psychologically, the French had been worn down by the Viet Minh and the nationalists; the final hour of their dominance was at hand. In a curious way, the French decision to save Laos from a second invasion by General Giap's Viet Minh forces—in October, 1953, the French had recognized the independence of the kingdoms of Cambodia and Laos within the French Union—led to the final, fatal engagement at Dien Bien Phu.

Earlier, in July, 1953, Premier Joseph Laniel had indicated that France was prepared to "perfect" or to "complete" the independence of the Associated States, but only within the French Union. However, he also indicated that he hoped to transform the Union into a "community" of freely associated and independent sovereign states. This approach, comparable to the British Commonwealth idea, was greeted with much enthusiasm by the Eisenhower Administration and led to further U.S. political and military considerations designed to help the French win the war against the Communists. What had been tainted earlier by being a colonial war now became a war against Communism designed to give independence to formerly colonial peoples. Such a cause was capable of winning the support of the United States Congress and the American people.

The United States readily agreed to increase its Mutual

Security grants to France to approximately $750 million per year, in addition to a variety of military supply items. In 1953–54, the United States was bearing between two-thirds and three-fourths of the cost of the war. Even after the battle of Dien Bien Phu had begun, top-level consideration was given to a major United States–sponsored air attack to relieve the besieged area. But this and all other proposed acts of direct U.S. military intervention became bogged down in the intense diplomatic conflict that developed among the three major Western allies.

The diplomatic disarray had come about because Washington, London, and Paris could not agree on a unified course of defensive action in Viet Nam, on the requirements for and the timing of a proposed Southeast Asian regional security pact, or on the terms for and the nature of a proper settlement at the forthcoming Geneva Conference. The Communist delegations at Geneva had no such problems.

Until all classified exchanges and related records are available, sharp debate will continue as to what in fact took place among the allies as represented by the chief negotiators: Secretary of State John Foster Dulles, Foreign Secretary Anthony Eden, Foreign Minister Georges Bidault, and Premier Pierre Mendès-France (who entered the picture in mid-June, 1954). Each of these principals, and his government, has his supporters and detractors. Despite the difficulties in getting at the truth, some well-substantiated data may be cited that reveal the major contours of the conflict.

1. The Big Four (Bidault, Dulles, Eden, and Soviet Foreign Minister Molotov) Berlin Conference, January 25–February 18, 1954, held to discuss German and Austrian questions, produced nothing positive on these issues, but led to a proposal for holding a wider conference in April on "Asian questions," i.e., Korea and Indochina. By "wider" representation, Molotov meant at least the presence of Communist China. This, presumably, would bring Peking into the concert of nations and would force the United States, if it were

to agree to such a meeting, to negotiate with the People's Republic of China in an international gathering. The United States overcame its aversion to a meeting at which its delegation would sit with that of the unrecognized Peking regime because the Administration desired to bring about some kind of permanent settlement in Korea, following the armistice of July 27, 1953.

The United States accepted the inclusion of the Indochina question on the agenda partly because the Laniel-Bidault government was in difficulty at home on this question; two days before the final battle of Dien Bien Phu began, Premier Laniel told the National Assembly that he was prepared for a "negotiated settlement" in Indochina. The United States was also willing to accept "Indochina" on the agenda because this French government supported the French-born idea of the European Defense Community. The latter, calling, among other things, for German rearmament, was a central theme in U.S. diplomacy of the period; it was bitterly opposed by the Russians and by the Gaullists and the French Communists. Hence to assist Laniel-Bidault on the Indochina issue lightened its burdens at home. If that government fell, the next one might be less favorably disposed to EDC; this later proved to be the case. EDC was defeated in the French Assembly on August 30, on a trick-motion of the Gaullists, under the government of Premier Mendès-France, who also opposed it.

2. Though the idea of a Geneva Conference had been accepted, Secretary Dulles had no intention of remaining idle until it opened. On March 29, 1954, after some weeks of intense diplomatic activity, he made a major address before the Overseas Press Club in New York. There he called for "united action" by the allies and the employment of "whatever means" were required to meet the threat of Communism in Southeast Asia. "This might," he said, "involve serious risks, but these risks are far less than would face us a few years from now if we are not resolute today." By "today," he meant

the immediate present. That Dulles was prepared to recommend U.S. involvement in the Indochina War, provided there was political agreement among the major Western allies for united action to defeat the Communist enemy, seems certain. He had already taken steps to bring into being a defense pact group to preserve the newly independent countries and what were to become the ex-colonial Indochinese countries of Southeast Asia. Neither his friends nor his critics deny this. It is relevant to note that on April 7, President Eisenhower remarked that the loss of Indochina could be compared to falling dominoes. He said, "You have a row of dominoes set up, and you knocked over the first one, and what would happen to the last one was the certainty that it would go over very quickly."[1] The Dulles approach was in part designed to avoid only the *unilateral* character of a major American air strike to relieve the defenders of Dien Bien Phu (proposed in the very earnest discussions and negotiations between Admiral Arthur W. Radford, Chairman of the United States Joint Chiefs of State, and his opposite French number, General Paul Ely). It was also designed to form a vigorous defense organization capable and willing of acting promptly not only in Indochina, but in all of Southeast Asia; and the whole was premised on the final fullness of French decision to grant *complete* independence to the Indochinese states. It was in such a context that Dulles' outlook of anti-Communism and anticolonialism found fulfillment.

3. President Eisenhower wrote to Prime Minister Churchill and Foreign Secretary Eden asking them to consider "united action" in Indochina, and "to join the fight if necessary." On April 10–13, Dulles conferred with Eden in London, after which he went on to Paris to meet with Bidault before returning to Washington on April 15. Here a major "misunderstanding" took place.[2] Dulles went away from his meetings with Churchill and Eden convinced that they supported his views. (He later indicated that he had a "reluctant agreement" from Bidault, who, he said, preferred immediate U.S.

intervention to the "cumbersomeness of combined international forces.") But Dulles did not convince the British. They certainly did not openly support his proposals, as can be seen from a careful reading of their joint communiqué of April 13. But it may be argued, nonetheless, that secret arrangements had been made. Eden said on April 13, in a reply to a question in the House of Commons, that Britain's interest in these matters "will at least be greatly influenced by what happens at Geneva." What is clear is that England had already moved in the direction of the Geneva Conference; that Eden saw it as a device to get a partition of Viet Nam and a Locarno-type agreement by which the two sides— Communist and Free World—would guarantee the future of the Indochinese states. This, of course, was an anathema to Dulles.

On April 27, Prime Minister Churchill confirmed the Eden understanding. He told the House of Commons that no political or military commitment had been undertaken for Indochina, that Great Britain would not take any military action in advance of the results of the Geneva Conference. Between April and June, relations between Washington and London deteriorated. On June 23, in a speech to the House of Commons, Eden reaffirmed Britain's interest in "an international agreement of any settlement that may emerge at Geneva." He reported favorably on the improvement in Anglo-Chinese relations (a temporary illusion); he had words of praise for Chou En-lai and even for Molotov; he went on to praise Premier Mendès-France, who had replaced Laniel after the latter's resignation on June 12, and who on June 17 vowed to find a solution for the Geneva Conference in an acceptable cease-fire, or resign, by July 20. He scorned as "a present panacea" Dulles' proposal for a collective defense agreement with teeth. In Eden's view, this was not a "new" proposal. "It is quite wrong to suppose," Eden said, "that it suddenly sprang into the light of day a few weeks ago, fully armed, like Minerva from the head of Jupiter."

This public attack on Dulles, who, it must be said, was trying to find a way to save Indochina as an area of three free, non-Communist states, reaffirmed American suspicions of Eden's policies vis-à-vis Moscow and Peking. The attack came only two days before Churchill and Eden arrived in Washington to clear up the "misunderstanding." Churchill's great skill and warm relationship with President Eisenhower managed publicly to patch over the fracas. During his five days in Washington, June 24–29, he agreed to a fine-sounding "Potomac Charter." Gone, in words, was Eden's Locarno-type agreement. Churchill agreed "to press forward with plans for collective defense" while getting Washington to agree to a policy for an Indochina settlement, already foreshadowed at Geneva; partition, exchange of populations, and other devices that were to create more problems than the Geneva Conference was to consider and settle. The collective-defense agreement ended up as the Manila Pact of September 8, 1954—a pact that created the Southeast Asia Treaty Organization (SEATO) but lacked the capacities for action that had been at the heart of the Dulles plan.

Dulles was not deceived. On July 8, he announced that neither he nor Under Secretary Walter Bedell Smith would return to Geneva for the negotiations on Indochina—the Korean question had ended in a stalemate on July 15. Under pressure, he sent Smith—but it had become clear to all that the United States no longer believed that Geneva '54 would help the prospects of peace, security, and independence for Viet Nam, Laos, and Cambodia.

4. Two other factors are worth noting before we turn to the Geneva Conference itself, which opened on April 26, 1954, and began discussion of the Indochina question on May 8—the day Dien Bien Phu fell. The first is that on April 28, Paris and Viet Nam agreed to two treaties—they were signed on June 4 by Laniel and Buu Loc, Premier of the State of Viet Nam—which were to recognize "the total independence of Viet Nam and its full and complete sov-

ereignty"; and Viet Nam's willingness to retain an association with the French Union.[3] Premier Laniel had now fulfilled his program for "perfecting" or "completing" the independence of the three states, though the specifics for the transfer of power and the form of the association were left for the future. However, his agreement with Bao Dai's Viet Nam obviously could not commit North Viet Nam under Ho Chi Minh; in any event, it came years too late.

In failing to take advantage of United States willingness to try to save the Associated States from Communism and its threats, the Allies passed up a golden opportunity. No one knows the outcome of unfought battles. But if battles must be fought, then the twin springs of Dulles' drive—anti-Communism and anticolonialism—were worthy of the flag in April, 1954. Obviously he failed, but it is unfortunate that the cause he espoused was also set back for years. That France, after years of exhausting warfare, decided to go along with Eden's view rather than with Dulles' may be explained in terms of her desire to save something from her Indochinese empire in the French Union. The American policy was a further military risk and, if successful, would certainly welcome the independence of the former states of French Indochina in or out of any French association. In any event, after the departure of Laniel and Bidault and the arrival of the Mendès-France government, there came an end to Franco-United States negotiations for United States intervention.

The second factor was the role of India. However much weight India carried as a Commonwealth member, there is no doubt as to the influence of the late Prime Minister Nehru. On April 24, he denounced U.S. proposals for a Southeast Asian security pact. On April 28, he signed an agreement with Peking acknowledging the People's Republic of China's seizure of and full sovereignty over Tibet, and withdrawing Indian troops which for decades had acted as guard units in various Tibetan route towns; he also agreed to the so-called Five Principles of Peaceful Coexistence as the guide to

Sino-Indian policy. Clearly, India exerted its weight on the side of London against the United States. Krishna Menon, a major diplomatic thorn in the flesh of United States diplomacy, was the unofficial but ubiquitous representative of Nehru at Geneva. As one journalist noted, "there is no antechamber where one does not find oneself face to face with Mr. Krishna Menon."[4]

The Geneva Agreements

The Conference, which opened in Geneva on April 26, 1954, held its first of eight plenary sessions on the Indochina question on May 8. Most of its work was carried on in restricted meetings between various delegations. On May 29, in order to break the existing deadlock, Eden proposed that the military representatives of France and the Democratic Republic of Viet Nam (North Viet Nam) should meet to work out "armistice agreements." In the period that followed, Cambodia insisted successfully on negotiating for itself. On July 21, the results of these negotiations were incorporated into what were called "Agreements on the Cessation of Hostilities" in Cambodia, Laos, and Viet Nam. These three separate agreements were signed by the Vice Minister of National Defense of the D.R.V.N. The first agreement was also signed by the Commander in Chief of the Khmer (Cambodian) National Armed Forces, and the other two by the Commander in Chief of the Forces of the French Union in Indochina. These are the only signed agreements of Geneva '54. All other documents, including the various limiting Declarations and the Final Declaration, were merely "noted" by the participants of the Conference at its last plenary session on July 21, 1964.

Thus the Geneva Conference produced the following documents:[5] The Final Declaration (13 paragraphs); the three signed agreements relating to the cessation of hostilities; Cambodia (33 articles), Laos (41 articles), Viet Nam (47 articles and Annex); and seven separate, limiting Declarations of one or more unnumbered paragraphs: Cambodia (2), Laos (2), France (2), and the United States (1). Although the official British publication of these documents refers to two brief interventions by Tran Van Do, Foreign Minister of the State of Viet Nam, it does not reprint his re-affirmation of the official presentation of his country's position, delivered on May 12, 1954 (in which he rejected partition and called for international supervision of the cease-fire terms, future national elections, and recognition of the State of Viet Nam as sole sovereign in Viet Nam), nor his protest against and criticism of the "hasty conclusion" of the armistice signed by the French "alone," and their yielding to the Viet Minh territories still in the possession of Vietnamese troops, especially in the southeastern area of the Red River delta. His government reserved "complete freedom of action to guarantee the sacred right of the Vietnamese people to territorial unity, national independence and freedom."[6]

Since it is rather clumsy to refer to participants who "noted" and others who "signed" these documents, I shall in the following discussion refer to all countries present at Geneva as either participants or signatories. In international law there is of course a distinction between these terms, but for the purposes herein I shall ignore it unless strict reference to text is required.

The distinguished Chairman of the U.S. Senate Foreign Relations Committee is one of those who have urged that in seeking an effective and reasonable settlement of the current war in Viet Nam, "much [may] . . . be said for a return to the Geneva Accords in 1954, not just in their 'essentials' but in all their specifications."[7] Close study of these Agreements leads to an opposite conclusion: neither the "essentials" nor the "specifications" of Geneva '54 should be sought again. They were written in haste and ended in compromise with, and excessive concessions to, the Communist powers. They

add up to political folly. These Agreements helped Communist North Viet Nam to *initiate* further struggle against South
Viet Nam and prevented any objective peace-keeping machinery from performing its assigned function. They also fed
the Pathet Lao in Laos and helped to bring that country almost to ruin. (The Western solution proposed in the Geneva,
1962, Agreements for Laos—majority voting within the Control Commission, more careful definition of the controls,
freedom of movement for the Commission with provisions
for its movement—is better than that of 1954, but is still not
good enough. These provisions have been effectively negated
by the Pathet Lao military hold on the territory now legally
assigned to them—territory contiguous to China and to North
Viet Nam which they have illegally held since and because of
ambiguities in Geneva '54.)

Cambodia, the last country to be attacked by the Viet
Minh and the one least bothered by internal dissident movements, was the only beneficiary among the Indochinese states
of Geneva '54. The cease-fire in this instance worked: the
Viet Minh invaders withdrew; the local Viet Minh supporters,
one wing of the Khmer Issarak (Free Cambodian) movement,
led by a Vietnamese-Cambodian Communist, Sieu Heng, dis-
integrated; and Norodom Sihanouk first as King, then, after
his abdication, as Premier, succeeded in rallying his people to
his conceptions of Cambodian independence and reforms—
and he has continued to do so since 1954–55.

The cochairmen of the Geneva Conference were Anthony
Eden of Great Britain and V. M. Molotov of the Soviet
Union; their countries retained the obligation, as cochairmen,
to oversee the execution of the agreements. Participants were
France, Britain, and the United States for the West; the
Soviet Union, the People's Republic of China, and the Demo-
cratic Republic of Viet Nam, representing the Communist
bloc. Three associated states were represented—Cambodia,
Laos and the State of Viet Nam. There was some doubt at
the beginning whether the Communists would be willing to

participate if their demand that the national liberation movements (the Khmer Issarak and Pathet Lao) be represented at the conference was not met. The Western nations and the Royal Cambodian and Lao delegations refused to allow this because they did not recognize the existence of these "paper" governments. It was finally decided that the Pathet Lao would be referred to as "combat units" rather than as a political force.

The 1954 Agreements and Declarations contain some seven-score specific paragraphs and multiparagraph articles. It is quite probable that those who recommend these "essential" and "specific" Geneva Agreements have not fully studied them—or, in many cases, even read them. Obviously, they brought about a partition of Viet Nam at the 17th parallel; temporarily, they brought about a cease-fire, but they by no means ended the hostilities between the two Viet Nams and between the Viet Minh and Laos. Reference has already been made to the rejection of Geneva '54 made by the State of Viet Nam—soon to become a republic. The United States explicitly took "note" of the three signed "cessation of hostilities" agreements and of the first twelve paragraphs of the Final Declaration; it rejected the concluding paragraph, which called for consultations among "members of the Conference": the United States wanted no part of further consultations with Communist China and the D.R.V.N. It also issued its own declaration.

The United States declaration held that it would abide by the Geneva Declaration *provided* the signatories refrained in the future from the threat or use of force; it also indicated that "any renewal of the aggression in violation of the . . . Agreements" would be viewed "with grave concern and as seriously threatening international peace and security," and that it would "not join in any arrangement which would hinder" the peoples of Viet Nam in determining "their own future."

In this connection, it should be emphasized that though

neither the United States nor the Republic of Viet Nam was a signatory of the Geneva Agreements of 1954, this fact in itself did not wholly relieve either government from observing the provisions of these signed and unsigned Agreements and Declarations—*provided all other parties to them abided by them.* There is precedent in international law for observing treaties and agreements which cover a zone or subject of interests even if a government is not a signatory of the treaty. However, any breach of the articles of the agreement by any of the contracting parties automatically suspends or destroys the basis for compliance by other contracting or related parties; it certainly relieves nonsignatories from any actual or implied obligation to observe the provisions of the treaty or agreement.

It is clear that the United States representatives at Geneva had little confidence in the Conference's Declaration and Agreements, that they expected trouble, and that they therefore provided legitimate tests by which the United States could legally and honorably determine its course of action. Any objective examination of the post-Geneva conduct of North Viet Nam with respect to the key provisions of the signed Agreements—military matters, treatment of civilian populations in the zone of the South from which its cadres were to depart and in its own territory, and aiding and abetting internal subversion—yields data sufficient to prove that the Democratic Republic of Viet Nam violated the Agreements almost as soon as they were signed. Those who now say that the United States was (and is) guilty of "violation," when in the critical years 1954–56 it applied the tests written into the Agreements to determine the bona fides of the contracting parties, are either misinformed or dupes of the Communist propaganda line.

The various non-Communist state delegations at Geneva were to some extent the victims of the political pressure created by French Premier Mendès-France, who came to power in mid-June, 1954, on a policy which promised a solution to the Geneva Conference and the end of the Franco-Vietnamese war by July 21 or his resignation. Premier Mendès-France was openly in opposition to the United States –supported European Defense Community concept—as was the U.S.S.R. He thereby gained (in secret sessions) some co-operation from Molotov, but at the expense of compromises and concessions which the Western powers and the State of Viet Nam had not wanted to make. Since the Geneva Conference was called to end the hostilities in French Indochina, and since France was to be the co-signer of the "cessation of hostilities" agreements, along with the North Viet Nam, Democratic Republic of the Western powers reluctantly and unwisely acquiesced in France's position. Little thought was given—or, more accurately, none was publicly expressed—as to how France, which had agreed to the *independence* of what would now be four states (Cambodia, Laos, the D.R.V.N., and the State of Viet Nam), could guarantee compliance in the future with the terms of Geneva '54 by any of the independent states.

The British were perhaps the best prepared of the Western nations because they came into the conference with a plan to partition Viet Nam and, despite all of the arguments put up by everyone else, this was the plan that was finally accepted. There was a particular lack of communication and coordination among the Western powers. It appears that they had made no provision for concerted action, nor had they even prepared beforehand a plan for the settlement of the Indochina dispute. The initiative was given to the Communists.

The chief areas of disagreement at Geneva were mainly the following: the timing and supervision of a cease-fire; choice of areas for regrouping and withdrawal of military forces; foreign military assistance after the cease-fire; the question of general elections for the various states; the composition, voting procedure, authority, and controls of the international supervisory body; and the responsibilities of the Geneva powers as guarantors of a peace settlement. In their arguments the Communists, unlike the Western powers, invariably stuck together. The United States continually walked away from the conference table because it refused to recognize the Chinese and felt it was being blackmailed into recognition by sitting at the same table with them. The French were pressing for a settlement of any kind, so long as it was a quick one. Their bargaining power was further diminished by Mendès-France's thirty-day time table. He had to finish or else forfeit his office.

The assorted paragraphs and articles of the Geneva Agreements treat five major topics: the cease-fire; regroupment of forces and treatment of populations; post–cease-fire military assistance; elections; and international supervisory arrangements to guarantee the first four.

1. Cease-fire. The Western powers wanted to ensure agreement on a cease-fire before political questions were discussed. The Communists insisted on their being coupled; they won out, since the military situation had been steadily going against the French. The Communist delegations made a determined bid to include the Communist Khmer Issarak (Cambodian) and Pathet Lao forces as regular members of the Geneva Conference on the grounds that these were "national liberation forces." On this point, the opposition of the Royal Lao and Cambodian governments prevailed over the delegation from Hanoi. But the latter won a major concession, as we shall see, when this type of question came up under regroupment. Though the cease-fire agreements prohibit the "resumption of hostilities" (Articles 8, 10, 19, and 24)[8] and refer to "armed forces" and "regular troops," the Americans and the British did not succeed in persuading the French negotiators to insist that "irregular," i.e., guerrilla, forces be included in this prohibition.

Withdrawals of the regular armed forces, including equipment and supplies (Article 15), were to be completed within 300 days. They were to take place without hindrance, destruction, or sabotage of public property and without injury to the civilian population. As a matter of record, the withdrawal of the Viet Minh forces from the zone of the South was accompanied by considerable looting and destruction of public buildings and railroads, systematic destruction or theft of the files, documents, and especially land registries in the upper provinces close to the 17th parallel, and kidnaping or murder of local officials. But compared with the activity of the "irregulars" who were left behind, these were minor woes visited upon the government and people of South Viet Nam.

Immediately after the Geneva Agreements were signed, the leader of North Viet Nam, Ho Chi Minh, publicly vowed to bring about the reunification of his state with that of the State of Viet Nam. There is nothing reprehensible in such a view. Many Vietnamese, like many Germans and Koreans, are pledged to the eventual reunification of their country. What is at issue are the methods employed to achieve the goal. This is what Ho said on July 22, 1954:

We must devote all possible efforts during the peace to obtain the unification, independence and democratization of the entire nation. . . . We shall struggle infallibly . . . to obtain [these for] all Viet Nam, together with the peoples of the other sectors of the country. The struggle will be long and difficult; all the peoples and soldiers of the north and south must unite to conquer victory.

This is not a call for peaceful reunification of a country, nor a pre-election broadcast. Rather, it is yet another call for protracted warfare in the current Communist mode. And in 1955, the Viet Minh "irregular" cadres in the South organized what came to be called the "Army of Liberation" and, as we shall see, began their military, terror, and kidnaping operations against the Republic of Viet Nam. The country was at war with an enemy led, trained, inspired, and encouraged by Communists whose loyalty was to Hanoi and who were attempting to overthrow a legitimate government that had become an independent state the previous year.

The "irregulars," using arms and ammunition cached prior

to the withdrawal of the regular armed forces, were the cadres of the Viet Minh, i.e., the Communist North, left behind in the South to carry out guerrilla warfare as planned. They operated under various names: the "Patriotic Front," "United Front," or "Fatherland Front." Estimates vary, but between 5,000 and 10,000 of these "irregulars" were available in the South to conduct warfare. And though the "armed forces" of the contracting parties were not to commit acts and operations, nothing was said in the Agreements about infiltration, terrorism, assassination, and covert military operations—classic aspects of Communist tactics—which could be and were conducted by these irregulars.

2. Regroupment and treatment of the population. The aim of the Communists was to insist on large regroupment and assembly areas which could then be controlled by their forces. The Western powers apparently never agreed on what they wanted. The Cambodians won out on having *no* regroupment area in their state—only withdrawals. But the Communists won out elsewhere by demanding the north and northeastern provinces of Laos and then settling for those provinces contiguous to Communist China and North Viet Nam—a position reinforced by the Geneva '62 agreements! As the *Survey of International Affairs 1954* puts it: "The least satisfactory of the agreements . . . was probably that concerning Laos . . . it was not made . . . clear how the royal government was to resume control of this . . . area. . . . Thus the arrangement presented the possibility of hardening into partition or of being interpreted by the Pathet Lao as conferring on them political control of the area concerned."[9] And this is what happened.

The State of Viet Nam, with incidental but inadequate support from the United States, tried to secure regroupment areas of small "pockets," which would have had the effect of avoiding partition, since French and Vietnamese troops were on both sides of the 17th parallel. But Britain had long since opted for partition. France had gone along because it intended in fact to withdraw its soldiers from the North; and the Communists were pleased to acquire all of Viet Nam above the 17th parallel because they had been unable to eliminate the French Expeditionary Corps from Hanoi, Haiphong, and key areas in the southern Red River delta area.

Each party (Article 14c) undertook to refrain from "reprisals or discrimination against persons or organizations on account of their activities during the hostilities and to guarantee democratic liberties." The Communists used this to attack the Diem government when it sought to repress the (northern) Army of Liberation which began to operate (on its territory) in 1955. But it used terror, assassination, and suppression to wipe out dissident, anti-Communist leadership in the North. And inspections could not be or were not undertaken.

According to Article 14d, during the 300 days assigned to military regroupment and exchanges, civilians were to enjoy the option of choosing to remain or to depart from residence. This period was extended by agreement to a new cut-off date, July 25, 1955. By that time, approximately 861,000 persons left the North for the South, as against fewer than 5,000 choosing the North. To this latter figure must be added the approximately 100,000 Viet Minh troops and their dependents who went North as part of the military exchange. However, the obvious disparity in numbers led the North to impose restrictions and brutal punishments on those who *sought* to go South. Summary arrests, denial of permits, intimidation by "show trials" of those who served as leaders of the exodus, and executions served to inhibit the exercise of the option. Residual petitions affecting 95,000 persons in the North were presented to the International Control Commission. Nothing ever came of these. An unknown number were thus never allowed to leave the Democratic Republic of Viet Nam. The refugee problem was one of the most far-reaching issues at the time.[10] There is much supporting evi-

dence for the approximated 861,000 figure used above. It
climbed in subsequent years by illegal immigration—perhaps
another 100,000.

3. Military assistance (Articles 16–19). These articles ban-
ned "troop reinforcements," "additional military personnel,"
new war material, new bases, and foreign-controlled bases.
These terms either were not defined or were ill defined. Ro-
tation, replacement of war material, etc., were permitted
under inspection. But the inspection teams were not allowed
to function—particularly in the restricted military security
areas of North Viet Nam close to the Chinese border! And
though the American military advisers *replaced* the French
after 1955–56, the Viet Minh argued that they were illegal—
they protested while their own forces were augmented by
Sino-Soviet materials and advisers, and while they were aug-
menting the Viet Cong forces in South Viet Nam. The
French were permitted to maintain two bases and 5,000 troops
in Laos. Nothing was said in these Agreements about the size
of national armies, local production of arms, and other aspects
of war-potential which might make it possible for one state
to threaten the security of another.

4. Elections. This, one of the most debated questions in
the 1965 minority expression of opposition to United States
policy, hardly merits the attention it has received. Paragraph
7 of the Final Declaration reads:

The Conference declares that, so far as Viet Nam is concerned,
the settlement of political problems effected on the basis of respect
for the principles of independence, unity and territorial integrity,
shall permit the Vietnamese people to enjoy the fundamental freedoms, guaranteed by democratic institutions established as a result
of free general elections by secret ballot. In order to ensure that
sufficient progress in the restoration of peace has been made, and
that all the necessary conditions obtain for free expression of the
national will, general elections shall be held in July 1956, under the
supervision of an international commission composed of representatives of the Member States of the International Supervisory

Commission, referred to in the agreement on the cessation of hostilities. Consultations will be held on this subject between the competent representative authorities of the two zones from July 20, 1955, onwards.

Though the Western powers originally suggested that the elections be postponed until security was established, the Russians proposed that elections be held in one year; because of Mendès-France, they secured an agreement that election consultations be started in one year (July, 1955) and elections held not later than July, 1956. The French thereby agreed to a provision which they would have no future right or power to ensure.

The United States had in its own declaration addressed itself to the issue of Paragraph 7. It insisted that nations "divided against their will" have United States support "to seek to achieve unity through free elections, supervised by the United Nations to ensure that they are conducted fairly." This was a direct endorsement of the position taken by the State of Viet Nam in its May 12 proposals.[11] Lest there be any doubt, the United States declaration went on to say that "with respect to the statement made by the Representative of the State of Viet Nam, the United States reiterates its traditional position that peoples are entitled to determine their own future and that it will not join in an arrangement which would hinder this. Nothing in its declaration just made is intended to or does indicate any departure from this traditional position." Clearly, the United States was skeptical about the future of free elections in both parts of Viet Nam. And with equal clarity, it endorsed the position of the State of Viet Nam taken both in May and in the closing days of the conference. For the State of Viet Nam, under Premier Ngo Dinh Diem, had instructed the Vietnamese delegation to protest the Geneva Agreements, particularly the partition and the arrangements for the 1956 elections. It had reserved to itself complete freedom of action, with the exception that it would "not use force to resist the procedures for carrying the cease-fire into effect, in spite of the objections and reservations that the State of Viet Nam has expressed, especially in its final statement."

The State of Viet Nam had indicated that it would accept elections only if the country were not partitioned and if the United Nations would supervise such elections "so as to ensure their freedom and genuineness." Obviously such conditions never were met. And by 1956, the Viet Minh organs of repression within the Democratic Republic of Viet Nam had made it well-nigh impossible to hold free elections within that Communist country.

It may be said that neither side wanted or expected that "free elections" would follow Geneva '54 because by the very nature of the case free elections could not, would not be held.

5. The International Control and Supervision Commission (ICC). On the very first day of the Geneva Conference on Indochina, French Foreign Minister Georges Bidault made a speech in which he advocated an international commission to supervise the carrying out of any cease-fire agreements. This proposal was in line with the agreements reached in the earlier Korean conference. As later expanded, this idea included the supervision not only of the cease-fire (which initially was to be handled by joint commissions), but of political and military activities as well.

From the beginning, the conference participants agreed in principle to the need for international supervision. The Communists suggested a four-power commission which was to be made up of "neutral" nations, including India, Pakistan, Poland, and Czechoslovakia. Western countries found this unacceptable and countered with proposals for U.N. supervision or for a commission made up of five Asian nations. After much discussion, it was decided that the commission was to be made up of Poland, Canada, and India. It was also decided that the latter was to serve as chairman.

Similar commissions were already operating in Cambodia and Laos. The records of these three commissions fill volumes, volumes largely of frustration. The Cambodian ICC, typically, encountered least difficulty, because the Cambodian Government faced few if any of the political and insurrectionary problems encountered by its neighbors. Laos, under the Souvanna Phouma government of 1957 and with the endorsement of the Pathet Lao, the Viet Minh, and Peking, requested the ICC to retire. When the successor government of Premier Sananikone confirmed this, the same groups clamored for the restoration of the ICC. In Viet Nam, the ICC suffered from the division between Hanoi and Saigon and from the political character of its own membership. The ICC was charged with control and supervision of all the foregoing operations (points 1–4). It was to set up fixed and mobile inspection teams. If the inspection teams could not settle an incident, they could report to the Commission. The latter had the power to decide some issues by majority vote (Article 41), but "questions concerning violations, or threats of violations, which might lead to a resumption of hostilities . . . must be unanimous" (Article 42). The latter, of course, were the major issues. Further, any member of the ICC could insist that a question at issue came under Article 42, rather than Article 41. Unanimity meant that any recommendation that was not unanimous would not be made, and that any that were unanimous would depend upon the goodwill of the party or parties to which it was made.

The effect was stultification. This was the first application of Moscow's "troika" principle, later advanced for the United Nations itself. Poland could always veto an issue if it was not consonant with Communist policy—and did so. India, especially before the Chinese Communist invasion, refused to cast a majority vote even on many lesser questions for fear that this would "increase tensions." As a result, the ICC, unable to provide for its own mobility, frequently deprived of necessary help from both Viet Nam states, powerless to come to a decision on important matters, served little if any useful purpose. Even Canada, in the first critical months of the ICC, chose to interpret its role as an "impartial" one and sought to play out the game as if its impartiality would assist in an ultimate decision-making potential within the ICC. On those rare occasions when the ICC arrived at recommendations, it lacked sanctions to enforce them. If one of the states refused to accept a recommendation, the best the ICC could do was to refer the matter to the Geneva Conference cochairmen, the United Kingdom and the U.S.S.R. (Article 43). Obviously the Soviets had yet another forum for their built-in veto.

The Geneva Agreements were thus inept, ill defined, hopelessly ensnared in a mess of irresolution, with no policeman capable of handling any but the most unimportant complaints and minor violations. To go back to their "essentials" or their "specifications" is to go back to a political sieve helpful only in advancing the Communist cause of warfare at the lower end of the spectrum: infiltration, subversion, guerrilla activity—the so-called "wars of national liberation."

As another Johnson (Dr. Samuel) said, "Let there be an end on it, sir."

part three

*The Republic of Viet Nam—
The Diem Regime*

5. *The War Between the States Begins*

The purpose of the Geneva Conference of 1954 had been to end armed conflict in the Indochinese peninsula. The general intent of the Free World was to halt further Communist expansion through the creation of a favorable atmosphere for the peaceful growth and development of the newly independent Cambodia, Laos, and the State of Viet Nam. The direct goal was the establishment of politically stable and economically viable countries which would not become pawns in the East-West power struggle. Both the intent and the goal were to be thwarted.

The effectiveness of the bargaining position of the Western nations had been hampered by two serious obstacles. First, the Communists were winning militarily in this part of Southeast Asia; France, and England had been compelled to resort to diplomatic negotiations as a last-ditch effort to halt further Communist expansion. Second, the Western nations held widely divergent objectives concerning their future involvement in Southeast Asia. The United States placed its faith not in the Geneva Declarations and Agreements—to which it had declined full assent, though it had signified its interest in seeing that the accords were not violated—but in "united action" (by which military action was meant) and in the regional security system (foreshadowed in November, 1951, by Dean Rusk when he was Assistant Secretary of State for the Far East, and developed into SEATO in September, 1954). Though the Protocol of the Manila Pact threw a mantle of multilateral protection over the three newly independent states, it was, in the final analysis, U.S. bilateral commitments to South Viet Nam that helped to preserve that country's independence. After eight draining years of fighting in Indochina, the French had little interest or reserve effort for containing Communist expansion in this part of the world, and were, in fact, clearly resentful of the Americans as their apparent successors in Indochina. As one informed student writes, "The French were much more concerned with extricating themselves from Indochina than with establishing a meaningful peace and machinery adequate to perpetuate it." The British had been equally anxious for a settlement and were desirous of avoiding further military involvement beyond their active concern in Malaya, where they were then engaged in suppressing Communist insurgency.

The Communists, on the other hand, bargaining from a position of military strength, sought to consolidate their gains and keep both the U.N. and the United States out of Indochina. The Soviets and Chinese, clearly sharing the same international objectives in 1954, were putting forward a "moderate" or "soft" foreign-policy line, and apparently sought to enhance their image among the new neutral nations by cooperating in arriving at peace in Indochina. This was the period when Chou En-lai became the foremost proponent of the Five Principles of Peaceful Coexistence that he hawked so expertly with Prime Ministers Nehru of India and U Nu of Burma before going on to his political triumphs at Geneva and at the Bandung Conference of April, 1955. To further this "moderate" policy, the senior Communist leaders apparently exerted some pressure on the more intransigent Viet Minh to accept the Geneva settlement as an interim gain. The Communists were confident of future success in the three states after a brief period of consolidation. They now had a solid base, stretching from Moscow to Hanoi and as far south as the military demarcation zone at the 17th parallel, with territorial salients from Communist China and

Communist Viet Nam into Laos. In North Viet Nam, there was now a strong Communist regime which had also been building cadres for Communist activity in the other states of Indochina for many years.

The Advent of Ngo Dinh Diem

In 1954, South Viet Nam was certainly in confusion, and near chaos. The head of state, Bao Dai, spent his time in France, apparently having made a considerable profit out of selling the vice and gambling concessions in the Saigon-Cholon area to the Binh Xuyen, a gang whose leaders and troops had also served as security police for the French. When France and Viet Nam signed the two treaties for Independence and Association on June 4, 1954, Bao Dai once again offered the premiership to Ngo Dinh Diem, the incorruptible nationalist who for the previous twenty years had opposed both the French and the Communists. Diem accepted; he replaced Premier Prince Buu Loc, Bao Dai's cousin, on June 16, and formed an independent government in Saigon on July 7. It was his government that vigorously rejected the Geneva Declaration, though it accepted in principle (and reaffirmed in April, 1956) the cease-fire agreement that had been signed by the French and the Democratic Republic of Viet Nam. The clauses on the elections to be held in 1956, were contained in the unsigned Declaration that Viet Nam had rejected. Viet Nam was a sovereign state, and Diem's government had the legal and moral right to stipulate its terms and take the consequences of its position at Geneva.

This is not the place to present the man who as premier and then as a constitutional president held—tightly held—the reins of government from June, 1954, to November, 1963. That will come. His critics are many. And justifiable criticism is in order. But it is appropriate here to point out that few persons expected that Ngo Dinh Diem would manage to hold his country and government together during the trial of

strength which began in his first months in office. The French
had as little respect for Diem as he had for them; since 1933,
he had consistently rejected their colonial subterfuges. Initially, the American officials did not know him. Ambassador
Donald Heath, and his successor, General Lawton Collins,
in the early months after his appointment in November,
1954, were inclined to accept the French interpretation of
Vietnamese internal policies and conditions, including the
French disparagement of Diem and their maneuvers against
him. Diem was a Roman Catholic in a predominantly Bud-
dhist-Confucianist land, a man from Hué in the Center, with
few political allies or roots in Saigon or Cochinchina. He had
to establish his government's rule over the Binh Xuyen gang
and over the two powerful religious sects, the Cao Dai and
the Hoa Hao, who, though they were opposed to the Viet
Minh, had established satrapies in South Viet Nam in which
they ruled and maintained private armies of their own with
French subsidies. The leaders of these sects opposed Diem. He
was also opposed by General Nguyen Van Hinh, the Army
Chief of Staff, who had been appointed by Bao Dai, still chief
of state. (Bao Dai was removed and Diem became the president of the Republic of Viet Nam by referendum vote in
October, 1955.) Hinh attempted a coup in September, 1954; it
was unsuccessful, and he was recalled to France by Bao Dai
and became a regular officer in the French Air Force.

After the collapse and withdrawal of the French colonial
regime, civil administration in South Viet Nam was largely
nonexistent. Diem had to reconcile and rebuild a government
and administration that rested on the former French government of Cochinchina (which had been a colony) and of
part of Annam (which had been a protectorate). France
still held the controls of the central bank and customs—Diem's
government acquired these only on January 1, 1955; other
fiscal and defense matters were not finally and fully turned
over to Viet Nam's control until 1956; the last of the French
military forces departed in July. In short, Diem faced the task

of creating a government in a newly sovereign state the borders of which had just been redrawn and the parts of which had previously been under a variety of domestic and external jurisdictions. Only divided Pakistan faced a similar problem of administration at its birth as a sovereign state—but Pakistan did not have to win over dissident religious sects with private armies, nor acquire control over divided military and police forces, nor face incipient Communist insurgency.

Robert Shaplen, one of the few capable and experienced reporters on Viet Nam, has described—in his study *The Last Revolution*[1]—Diem's takeover, his victory over the sects and the Binh Xuyen, and his consolidation of governmental authority during the crucial months between July, 1954, and October, 1956, when the new constitution was promulgated. There are, of course, other detailed accounts of these two years, but Shaplen's book ably re-creates the drama of the days during which Diem, "except for his family and a few Vietnamese friends and his American supporters, literally stood alone. For a time Diem's actual authority scarcely extended beyond Saigon itself, where he had only a single battalion of loyal troops upon which he could completely depend."

Diem's problems were complicated by two other factors deriving from the partition of the country at the 17th parallel: the unbalanced economy and the Communist insurrection. The first of these, eased by United States economic support, was less significant than the second, and was on its way to a reasonable resolution after the first years. It arose from the fact that the two parts of Viet Nam had been economically interdependent: the mineral resources (coal, iron, and bauxite) and the main industries (cement, textiles, glass, railroad repair shops) were in North Viet Nam, which was deficient in rice and other food products; the South had virtually no industry but was the granary for the whole country and, under normal conditions, was an important rubber-producing and exporting area. The North, relative to its resources, was overpopulated; the South, less densely populated in relation to its supplies, had to care for nearly 1 million refugees from the North between July, 1954, and July, 1955. The United States stepped in, from the fall of 1954 on, with massive aid that averaged $250 million annually over the next few years, in aid for refugees, in economic support, and in military support and financing (excluding classified military aid). The speed with which American assistance and influence increased once the United States had decided to support Diem disturbed many Frenchmen. As one wrote: "The progress of the Americans has been so fast that it threatens to wipe out within a few years the vestiges of almost a century of French presence."[2]

From the low point of 1954, the Diem regime managed, with the support of the indomitable and independent peasantry, to restart an economy that was near collapse after fourteen years of warfare. Rice production in South Viet Nam in the two crop years 1956–57 and 1957–58 was 3.3 million tons, about what Cochinchina had produced in 1942. The country was able to feed itself and to have a small surplus for export. Rubber production went up from 54,000 tons in 1954 to 70,000 tons in 1958. Rubber and rice accounted for over 80 per cent, by value, of all exports. Production of other crops— maize, copra, sugar cane, tobacco, and livestock—also rose. Roads, canals, railroads, and port facilities were restored and improved. There was, however, no comparable improvement in building up an industrial base for the country. Though the production figures in themselves are not startling, and though South Viet Nam's large budgetary deficits—incurred chiefly for defense and for the acquisition of manufactured goods from abroad—had to be made up by United States aid funds, it could be said not only that Diem had survived these early years, but that his government, in domestic affairs, at least, was making progress.

The situation was ably summed up at the June 1, 1956, conference in Washington, D.C., of the American Friends of

Viet Nam (which had been organized the year before), in a speech delivered by a United States Senator:

It is an ironic and tragic fact that this Conference is being held at a time when the news about Viet Nam has virtually disappeared from the front pages of the American press, and the American people have all but forgotten the small nation for which we are in large measure responsible. The decline in public attention is due, I believe, to three factors: First, it is due in part to the amazing success of President Diem in meeting firmly and with determination the major political and economic crises which had heretofore continually plagued Viet Nam. Secondly, it is due in part to the traditional role of American journalism, including readers as well as writers, to be more interested in crises than in accomplishments, to give more space to the threat of wars than the need for works, and to write larger headlines on the sensational omissions of the past than the creative missions of the future. Third and finally, our neglect of Viet Nam is the result of one of the most serious weaknesses that has hampered the long-range effectiveness of American foreign policy over the past several years—and that is the overemphasis upon our role as "volunteer fire department" for the world. Whenever and wherever fire breaks out—in Indochina, in the Middle East, in Guatemala, in Cyprus, in the Formosan Straits—our firemen rush in, wheeling up all their heavy equipment, and resorting to every known method of containing and extinguishing the blaze. The crowd gathers—the usually successful efforts of our able volunteers are heartily applauded—and then the firemen rush off to the next conflagration, leaving the grateful but still stunned inhabitants to clean up the rubble, pick up the pieces and rebuild their homes with whatever resources are available.

The role, to be sure, is a necessary one; but it is not the only role to be played, and the others cannot be ignored. A volunteer fire department halts, but rarely prevents, fires. It repels but rarely rebuilds; it meets the problems of the present but not of the future. Let us briefly consider exactly what is "America's Stake in Viet Nam":

First, Viet Nam represents the cornerstone of the Free World in Southeast Asia, the keystone to the arch, the finger in the dike.

Burma, Thailand, India, Japan, the Philippines, and obviously Laos and Cambodia are among those whose security would be threatened if the red tide of Communism overflowed into Viet Nam. The fundamental tenets of this nation's foreign policy, in short, depend in considerable measure upon a strong and free Vietnamese nation.

Secondly, Viet Nam represents a proving ground of democracy in Asia. However we may choose to ignore it or deprecate it, the rising prestige and influence of Communist China in Asia are unchallengeable facts. Viet Nam represents the alternative to Communist dictatorship. If this democratic experiment fails, if some one million refugees have fled the totalitarianism of the North only to find neither freedom nor security in the South, then weakness, not strength, will characterize the meaning of democracy in the minds of still more Asians. The United States is directly responsible for this experiment—it is playing an important role in the laboratory where it is being conducted. We cannot afford to permit that experiment to fail.

Third, and in somewhat similar fashion, Viet Nam represents a test of American responsibility and determination in Asia. If we are not the parents of little Viet Nam, then surely we are the godparents. We presided at its birth, we gave assistance to its life, we have helped to shape its future. As French influence in the political, economic and military spheres has declined in Viet Nam, American influence has steadily grown. This is our offspring—we cannot abandon it, we cannot ignore its needs. And if it falls victim to any of the perils that threaten its existence—Communism, political anarchy, poverty and the rest—then the United States, with some justification, will be held responsible; and our prestige in Asia will sink to a new low.

Fourth and finally, America's stake in Viet Nam, in her strength and in her security, is a very selfish one—for it can be measured, in the last analysis, in terms of American lives and American dollars. It is now well known that we were at one time on the brink of war in Indochina—a war which could well have been more costly, more exhausting and less conclusive than any war we have ever known. The threat of such war is not now altogether removed from the horizon. Military weakness, political instability or economic failure in the new state of Viet Nam could change almost overnight the apparent security which has increasingly characterized that area under the leadership of President Diem.

And before we look to the future, let us stop to review what the Diem government has already accomplished by way of increasing that security. Most striking of all, perhaps, has been the rehabilitation of more than three-fourths of a million refugees from the North. For these courageous people dedicated to the free way of life, approximately 45,000 houses have been constructed, 2,500 wells dug, 100 schools established and dozens of medical centers and maternity homes provided.

Equally impressive has been the increased solidarity and stability of the Government, the elimination of rebellious sects and the taking of the first vital steps toward true democracy. Where once colonialism and Communism struggled for supremacy, a free and independent republic has been proclaimed, recognized by over forty countries of the Free World. Where once a playboy emperor ruled from a distant shore, a constituent assembly has been elected.

Social and economic reforms have likewise been remarkable. The living conditions of the peasants have been vastly improved, the wastelands have been cultivated, and a wider ownership of the land is gradually being encouraged. Farm cooperatives and farmer loans have modernized an outmoded agricultural economy; and a tremendous dam in the center of the country has made possible the irrigation of a vast area previously uncultivated. Legislation for better labor relations, health protection, working conditions and wages has been completed under the leadership of President Diem.

Finally, the Vietnamese army—now fighting for its own homeland and not its colonial masters—has increased tremendously in both quality and effectiveness.

But the responsibility of the United States for Viet Nam does not conclude, obviously, with a review of what has been accomplished thus far with our help. Much more needs to be done; much more, in fact, than we have been doing up to now. Military alliances in Southeast Asia are necessary but not enough. Atomic superiority and the development of new ultimate weapons are not enough. Informational and propaganda activities, warning of the evils of Communism and the blessings of the American way of

life, are not enough in a country where concepts of free enter-
prise and capitalism are meaningless, where poverty and hunger
are not enemies across the seventeenth parallel but enemies within
their midst. As Viet Nam's Ambassador Tran Van Chuong has
recently said: "People cannot be expected to fight for the Free
World unless they have their own freedom to defend, their freedom from foreign domination as well as freedom from misery,
oppression, corruption."

I shall not attempt to set forth the details of the type of aid program this nation should offer the Vietnamese—for it is not the
details of that program that are as important as the spirit with
which it is offered and the objectives it seeks to accomplish. We
should not attempt to buy the friendship of the Vietnamese. Nor
can we win their hearts by making them dependent upon our
handouts. What we must offer them is a revolution—a political,
economic and social revolution far superior to anything the Communists can offer—far more peaceful, far more democratic and far
more locally controlled. Such a revolution will require much from
the United States and much from Viet Nam. We must supply
capital to replace that drained by the centuries of colonial exploitation; technicians to train those handicapped by deliberate policies of illiteracy; guidance to assist a nation taking those first
feeble steps toward the complexities of a republican form of government. We must assist the inspiring growth of Vietnamese democracy and economy, including the complete integration of
those refugees who gave up their homes and their belongings to
seek freedom. We must provide military assistance to rebuild the
new Vietnamese Army, which every day faces the growing peril
of Viet Minh armies across the border.

And finally, in the councils of the world, we must never permit
any diplomatic action adverse to this, one of the youngest members of the family of nations—and I include in that injunction a
plea that the United States never give its approval to the early na-
tionwide elections called for by the Geneva Agreement of 1954.
Neither the United States nor Free Viet Nam was a party to that
agreement—and neither the United States nor Free Viet Nam is
ever going to be a party to an election obviously stacked and sub-
verted in advance, urged upon us by those who have already

broken their own pledges under the agreement they now seek to enforce.

This is the revolution we can, we should, we must offer to the people of Viet Nam—not as charity, not as a business proposition, not as a political maneuver, nor simply to enlist them as soldiers against Communism or as chattels of American foreign policy—but a revolution of their own making, for their own welfare, and for the security of freedom everywhere.

The Senator was John F. Kennedy, speaking, as he said, as a "proud member" of the American Friends of Viet Nam.

"The Red Tide of Communism Overflowed into Viet Nam"

It was this "red tide," as Senator Kennedy called it, that was the second factor stemming from partition that threatened the freedom and stability of South Viet Nam.

It has variously been said that the Communist insurgency in South Viet Nam followed, and was the result of, the refusal of Diem's regime to agree to the July, 1956, elections that had been stipulated in the Final Declaration at Geneva; or, that it broke out in 1958 or 1959 because the Communist regime of North Viet Nam, in economic and political difficulty at home and resentful of the economic and political successes of the Diem regime, sought to deflate its southern rival, bolster its popularity at home, and acquire the southern rice granary. It is true that these explanations are correct insofar as they explain the *continuation* and *increasing tempo* of Communist insurrectionary activity, but they do not relate to the time or the reason for the *initiation* of this policy.

The plan for the Communist insurgency in the South is related to over-all Communist policy in Viet Nam, and this antedates by far the Geneva Conference of 1954. It was put into operation in the independent State of Viet Nam with the speech of Ho Chi Minh on July 22, 1954, in which he called for a protracted struggle by "all the peoples and soldiers of the North and South [united] to conquer victory."

During and immediately after World War II, the Communists in Indochina had operated under various "front" names. The first of these was Viet Minh (League for Independence). This was the name by which the Communists of the North became popularly known, and though this name was subsequently changed a number of times, this is the name that has been generally retained in this book to refer to the Communists who established the Democratic Republic of Viet Nam in 1945 and to the Communists within the Democratic Republic after the partition of 1954. In Saigon, the Communists are referred to as Viet Cong, from Cong San, or Communist; accordingly, Viet Cong are the Vietnamese Communists operating within the South, and the term is so used in this book. For various "political" reasons, the Viet Minh changed its name, first to Lien Viet (Vietnamese Alliance), then to To Quoc (Fatherland Front), and finally to Thong Nhat Quoc Gia (National Reunification Front).[3] The name of Ho Chi Minh's own Communist Party (the major constituent within the Viet Minh) was officially changed in March, 1951, to Dang Lao Dong, or Lao Dong (Labor Party), officially translated as the Workers Party.

When the Lao Dong, or Workers Party, was reorganized in March, 1951, it published its manifesto, a standard Leninist anti-imperialist call for struggle against colonialism and for the liberation of the "whole Viet Nam nation" under the leadership of the Party and "the leader of the people, President Ho Chi Minh."[4] Except for one paragraph, the manifesto refers exclusively to its tasks in Viet Nam. In this one paragraph it "recommends that the people of Viet Nam closely unite with and help the peoples of Cambodia and Laos in their struggle for independence, and [that the Lao Dong], jointly with them, liberate the whole of Indochina." The Lao Dong issued a secret directive in November, 1951, to supplement its public manifesto. This is reported and analyzed by Professor P. J. Honey, one of the foremost students of North Viet Nam. He quotes from it:

Sections of the Communist Party now exist in Cambodia and Laos [as well as in Viet Nam as a whole] and are developing; Cambodia and Laos already possess unified Liberation Fronts. At the center of the organizations are groups of faithful Communists who constitute delegations of the Indochinese Communist Party, from which they receive their orders. The Vietnamese Party retains a permanent right of supervision over the activities of the fraternal Cambodian and Laotian Parties. Later when conditions permit, the three revolutionary parties of Viet Nam, Cambodia and Laos will unite to form a single party.

This secret directive, Honey indicates,

strongly implies, though it does not affirm in so many words, that the intention of the North Vietnamese Communist leaders is to unify the territories of the former French Indochina—Laos, Cambodia and Viet Nam—under the rule of a single Communist Party. In the past the Vietnamese Communist leaders have been remarkably successful in concealing their Communism and thereby receiving support, aid, or acceptance from quarters which would not have accorded any of these to a purely Communist regime. They have done this by working from within a "front" movement. The practice was employed by them when they established the Viet Minh, the Lien Viet and the Fatherland Front, and is today still being used in South Viet Nam where the insurrection is under the control of the National Front for the Liberation of South Viet Nam (NFLSV).[5]

The formation of the National Liberation Front was publicly announced on December 20, 1960. It was another name in the parade of Communist "fronts"—the Viet Minh, the Lien Viet, and the To Quoc—that had been fighting against the French in all parts of Viet Nam before 1954. In 1954, the "front" name was To Quoc (Fatherland Front), a synonym for the "Army of Liberation," which, by the terms of the signed Agreement, should have withdrawn to the northern zone, the D.R.V.N.

Difficulties with North Viet Nam arose soon after the close of the Geneva Conference. The cease-fire agreement signed by the French and the Viet Minh came into effect progressively: for the North (Tonkin), on July 27, 1954; for the Center (Annam), on August 1; and for the South (Cochinchina), on August 11. The exchange of prisoners was completed in September. The regroupment of forces on both sides of the demarcation line was carried out within the three hundred days stipulated. The French evacuation of Hanoi and Haiphong was completed by May 18, 1955, and the transfers of civilian population ended in July. Earlier, in February, the North had asked the South to join it in establishing "normal relations." Consultations on the elections were to begin, according to the Final Declaration of Geneva, in July. Neither the consultations, nor, of course, the elections, were ever held. On July 16, and again on August 9, Ngo Dinh Diem stated his government's policy—that it was "not bound" by the Final Declaration since it had not signed it. He again announced that, although his government favored "free elections," he was "skeptical concerning the possibility of fulfilling the conditions of free elections in the North [where the] regime does not permit each Vietnamese citizen to enjoy democratic freedoms and the basic fundamental rights of man." He charged also that the Viet Minh were "violating their obligations [under the cease-fire agreement, which his government had not signed but had accepted] by preventing our countrymen of the North from going South [and] by recently attacking with the communist Pathet Lao, the friendly state of Laos."[6]

North Viet Nam protested the elections issue to the cochairmen of Geneva. Talks between the British and Russians were held in 1956. Foreign Minister Gromyko urged proper implementation but little else. On the whole, it appeared that none of the principal participants really expected that the elections would be held; the absence of elections, however, served the cause of Communist propaganda.

A more disturbing problem was that created by the Viet Minh "irregulars" who had been left behind in the South after the withdrawal of regular troops and the exchange of prisoners. Somewhere between 5,000 and 10,000 Viet Minh fighters had been picked to remain in the South at carefully selected points, especially in the mountain area along the Laotian and Cambodian borders, in the coastal area immediately south of the 17th parallel, and in the Mekong delta area. This Communist network, made up of southerners trained by the Viet Minh as well as northerners who were infiltrated into the South with the refugees, began to trouble the South Vietnamese authorities by 1955. By then they had infiltrated the apparatus of government, the police and the armed forces; in the rural areas, the insurgents were making a base for guerrilla operations.

In July, 1955, Diem's government, alarmed by the deterioration of security in the northern provinces of Quang Nam and Quang Tri close to the demarcation line, set up a "Campaign for Denunciation of Communist Subversion." The campaign was made national in scope in May, 1956, and could, according to Secretary of the Ministry for Information Tran Chanh Thanh, "mobilize all military, administrative, and technical services" to help it. Between July, 1955, and May, 1956, the campaign claimed to have taken more than 15,000 Viet Minh agents and uncovered more than 700 caches of arms and ammunition. Although it is probable that not all these agents were Viet Minh, an appreciable number certainly were. The campaign also captured seventy-five tons of "documents" which contained instructions "to create troubles, first in the economic then in the political field"; to engage in "clandestine activities . . . so as to conceal the strength of the [Lao Dong] Party," and to organize the "Fatherland Front" as a successor to the Viet Minh and the Lien Viet. Some of these decisions were made, according to a spokesman for Diem's government, at the "Eighth Congress of the Viet Minh Communist Party,

held in August, 1955." There is nothing in the character of
these South Vietnamese reports which cannot be substantiated
by reference to Hanoi sources.

At Ben Tre, insurgents set fire to villages and refugee camps,
seized ballot boxes, and killed voters in order to obstruct the
elections held by the South in October, 1955, and in March,
1956. A pattern of Communist terror began to emerge that
"cost the Republic [South Viet Nam] the lives of several hundred troops and civil administrators since 1954."[7] In mid-
1956, this writer toured the Mekong delta area, visiting installations of the Philippine-manned Operation Brotherhood
(a nongovernmental medical and social work aid effort), and
the Cai San resettlement villages for refugees from the North
who had "voted with their feet" against the Communists. In
both areas our jeeps and canal boats were subjected to fire
from Communist terrorists and required military protection.

Confirmation of the nature and extent of Communist insurgency in South Viet Nam comes also from the Communist
North itself. Unlike the South, the North made full use of the
International Control Commission created at Geneva to publi-
cize its complaints.[8] With mounting frequency, between 1955
and 1957, Hanoi's High Command of the Peoples Army of
Viet Nam charged that the South was violating Article 14c of
the cease-fire agreement by arresting "former" resistance
fighters, by creating "concentration camps," and by arresting
members of the "Movement for Defense of Peace"—a creation
of the Fatherland Front.

These complaints are significant more for what they reveal
about the accuser than about the accused. As Bernard B. Fall
pointed out,[9] most of the complaints received by the ICC from
the Viet Minh regarding alleged reprisals against "former resistance members" were sufficiently precise in detail to show
that they were based on information given to the North Vietnamese by Viet Minh agents who had remained in the South
in 1954, or had subsequently infiltrated. Moreover, on com-
paring the location of alleged reprisals with the location of re-

cent rebel activities as reported by South Viet Nam, Fall found a striking correlation: their geographic distribution was almost identical. On the basis of this evidence he concluded that coordination between the Democratic Republic of North Viet Nam and rebels in the South almost certainly existed.

Thus, eye-witness accounts and other substantial data reveal that Diem's government in 1955–56 faced a determined Communist enemy whose policies and operations had already begun to attack South Viet Nam by political and military means. That Diem and others were aware of this is true; that Diem and his American supporters failed to deal adequately with this genuine threat to security is also true. Their fault was not in the lack of recognition of the problem (though in 1965–66, opponents of the Republic of Viet Nam have tried to suppress, distort, or excuse this early Communist effort to subvert, infiltrate, and otherwise destroy the young republic). Their fault lay in not prescribing and executing adequate counters to the threat.

6. *The Search for Security, Stability, and Improvement in the Conditions of Living, 1955–63*

Today's detractors of Ngo Dinh Diem and his regime tend to see him in the pure and simple terms of a no-good dictator who, with the support of the United States, "violated" the Geneva Declaration and Agreements of 1954, and thereby, in effect, invited the Viet Minh to pursue reunification by the only remaining alternative, by force. This distortion and irresponsible presentation of the events is matched to some extent by the views of those who continue to portray the Diem regime in terms of the "miracle" of 1954–56. To them Diem remains a national hero brought down by fate—fate being a combination of his avowed enemies, his former friends, and, as an after-thought, "his own flawed nature."

Ngo Dinh Diem, whatever his faults, was an outstanding Vietnamese nationalist and patriot; his record as such reaches back at least to the early 1930's. He was anti-French because France was the colonial master; since the compliment was amply returned by most French spokesmen, he remained deeply suspicious of the French even after his country gained full independence in 1954. He knew that the French had been involved in an attempt to prevent his appointment as premier in the first place, and in several subsequent attempts to overthrow his government before the French finally left Viet Nam. He was rigidly anti-Communist, in part because his religious and philosophical outlook rejected Communism, in part because the Viet Minh and the Viet Cong plotted and fought for his overthrow from the very beginning, in part because at least two members of his family, a brother and a nephew, had been murdered by the Communists and he himself had been imprisoned by them. Like the hero of a classical tragedy, it may well be that Diem's flawed nature—his stubbornness, inflexibility, and excessive self-confidence—was the key to his eventual failure and to the final denouement, his ignominious assassination following the coup of November, 1963.

Senator John F. Kennedy's penetrating analysis quoted in the preceding chapter serves as an excellent benchmark from which to examine the years of Diem's rule. Kennedy, like President Eisenhower, regarded Viet Nam as "the cornerstone of the Free World in Southeast Asia, the keystone to the arch, the finger in the dike." He believed it represented "a proving ground of democracy in Asia [which] we cannot afford to permit to fail." Viet Nam was a "test of American responsibility and determination in Asia," a test which could among other things "be measured in terms of American lives and American dollars." What we must do, Kennedy said, is to offer the Vietnamese "a revolution—a political, economic, and social revolution far superior to anything the Communists can offer—far more peaceful, far more democratic and far more locally controlled. Such a revolution will require much from the United States and much from Viet Nam." Such a revolution is not "charity" and not a "business proposition," it is to enhance "the security of freedom everywhere."

The views of the young, liberal Democratic Senator were identical at that time with the officially expressed policy of the Republican Administration. Speaking at the same conference at which Senator Kennedy spoke, Assistant Secretary of State for Far Eastern Affairs Walter S. Robertson told of his second visit to Viet Nam, in the company of Secretary of State John Foster Dulles. They had been impressed, he said,

at the progress toward stability, security and strength. The United States is proud to be on the side of the effort of the Vietnamese people under President Diem to establish freedom, peace, and the good life. Our policies . . . may be simply stated as follows:

To support a friendly non-Communist government in Viet Nam and to help it diminish and eventually eradicate Communist subversion and influence.

To help the Government of Viet Nam establish the forces necessary for internal security.

To encourage support for Free Viet Nam by the non-Communist world.

To aid in the rehabilitation and reconstruction of a country and people ravaged by eight ruinous years of civil and international war.

Our efforts are directed first of all toward helping to sustain the internal security forces consisting of a regular army of about 150,000 men, a mobile civil guard of some 45,000 and local defense units which are being formed to give protection against subversion on the village level. We are providing budgetary support and equipment for these forces and have a mission assisting the training of the army. We are also helping to organize, train, and equip the Vietnamese police force. The refugees who have fled to South Viet Nam to escape the Viet Minh are being resettled on productive lands with the assistance of funds made available by our aid program. In various ways our aid program also provides assistance to the Vietnamese Government, designed to strengthen the economy and provide a better future for the common people of the country. The Vietnamese are increasingly giving attention to the basic development of the Vietnamese economy and to projects that may contribute directly to that goal. We give our aid and counsel to this program only as freely invited.

Robertson concluded his address with a caution:

I do not wish to minimize the magnitude of the task that still remains and of the problems that still confront this staunch and valiant member of the free world fighting for its independence on the threshold of the Communist heartland of Asia.[1]

There were other appraisals, less official, that confirmed what the Senator and the Assistant Secretary of State had said about Viet Nam at that time. Some of these are worth noting, in view of their authors' present attitudes to the problems of Viet Nam. Professor Hans J. Morgenthau, since 1965 an outspoken opponent of the Administration's Viet Nam policies, had this to say at the same conference in June, 1956:

If you consider . . . the defeatist policy of the French [before the Geneva Conference of 1954], working toward an accommodation with the Communists in anticipation of their complete victory, then you realize what kind of miracle has been wrought in recent years in South Viet Nam. Actually, the provision for free elections [in the Geneva Declaration] which would solve ultimately the problem of Viet Nam, was a device to hide the incompatibility of the Communist and Western positions, neither of which can admit domination of all of Viet Nam by the other side. It was a device to disguise the fact that the line of military demarcation was bound to a line of political division as well. There will be—and here I shall leave the role of analyst and become a prophet without running any great risk—no elections in Viet Nam in the foreseeable future.[2]

Robert Guillain, a prominent French journalist, had written in *Le Monde* in 1957:

We have underestimated the chances of the South. It is good, for a journalist and for others as well, to have the opportunity to acknowledge this. We did not believe in Monsieur Diem, but in two years of effort he has dispelled this pessimism. We may not like the political style of the regime or find in the personality of its leader certain traits which displease us, but is it still our business? In spite of all our reservations, a reality emerges here which we can no longer ignore: the Republic of Viet Nam has taken substance as a State. We must fully take into account its existence and its importance.[3]

Bernard B. Fall, a persistent critic of United States and South Vietnamese policies subsequent to the Geneva Conference of 1954, pointed out in an article in *Pacific Affairs*[4] (which began with the above quotation from Guillain) that Guillain had been one of those who, in 1954, had expected the demise of South Viet Nam to take place even before the July,

1956, date set for elections by the Geneva Declaration. "With very few exceptions," wrote Fall, "no French observer of the Vietnamese scene deviated from Guillain's judgment until after the 1956 deadline passed without incident." The period from October, 1955, to October, 1956, had been "the high point in the regime's popularity and countrywide security," in the view of "Vietnamese in general," Fall continued, a conclusion he neither affirmed nor denied for himself.

Clearly, then, the leading admirers and the leading detractors were agreed on the success of Diem's first years in office, a "miracle" that enjoyed "popularity."

Survival with Progress

When Diem and his cabinet took office in July, 1954, the premier's position was, to say the least, insecure. He was opposed by a powerful group of mandarins (chief civil servants). "It was in their interest to have a premier who would continue the policy of collaboration with the French." In their view a weak executive power meant that they "could continue their monopoly of top administrative posts."[5] Ngo Dinh Diem, who was, of course, passionately opposed to collaboration with the French, was able to rally sufficient anti-French sentiment to prevail over this powerful sector of the bureaucracy.

Diem was also opposed by the two sects, the Cao Dai and the Hoa Hao, and by the Binh Xuyen gang group which, under the French and under Bao Dai, had enjoyed a monopoly of vice revenues in Cholon, the twin city of Saigon. Diem initially solved the problem of the sects in September, 1954, by adding four representatives from each group to his cabinet. At the turn of the year, with the assistance of Colonel Edward G. Lansdale, then (as in 1965–66) on the staff of the American Embassy in Saigon, Diem won over an important Cao Dai general, Trinh Minh The, who supported the Premier with his 2,500 troops through the later fighting with the Binh Xuyen. Also in September, 1954, Diem successfully crushed the coup attempted by his Army Chief of Staff, General Nguyen Van Hinh.

At one stage in this bizarre configuration of opposition plot and counterplot, the sects and the Binh Xuyen formed an anti-Communist, anti-Diem "United Front" with the Cao Dai "pope," Pham Cong Tac, as president, the Binh Xuyen's General Bay Vien as commander, and with Generals Tran Van Soai and Ba Cut representing the Hoa Hao. This United Front sent an ultimatum to Premier Diem on March 5, 1955, demanding that he reorganize his cabinet and give them a greater share in it. At the same time, they requested Emperor Bao Dai (then in France) to remove Diem as premier. Diem rejected their ultimatum and on March 27 the eight sect members of his cabinet resigned. The Binh Xuyen, which had been deprived of considerable revenues when the government had closed down its gambling and vice operations in Cholon, was determined to press the fight. In the closing days of March, clashes broke out between the Binh Xuyen and loyal government troops. Paul Ely, the French general, was able to arrange a truce; for various reasons, not all wholly honorable, the French still had some powers of persuasion over the Binh Xuyen, though General Ely was entirely free from any of the tar on the brush. He was, in fact, regarded by competent authorities as devoted in his support for the Viet Nam Government.[6]

The truce was broken by the end of April. Heavy fighting, with many casualties and much damage, resulted. In the midst of this Bao Dai summoned Diem to France for "consultations" and indicated that he would appoint Inspector-General Nguyen Van Vy as military commander. Diem regarded General Vy as a pro-French, pro-Bao Dai figure and ignored both the summons from Bao Dai and the appointment of Vy. The events of the next few weeks, during which Diem emerged victorious from his battle with the Binh Xuyen, are not easy to disentangle. At one stage, apparently, General Vy helped the government against the Binh Xuyen. At another stage, April 30–May 1, Vy attempted a coup to remove Diem. He lacked

the support of other high-ranking officers, his coup failed, and
Vy went into exile in France. Backed by the loyal military,
Diem now proceeded in two ways. His civilian supporters were
encouraged to organize a People's Revolutionary Committee
which called for the removal of Bao Dai and the withdrawal
of all remaining French armed forces. His military supporters,
with the aid of the Cao Dai group under General The, were
able to defeat the Binh Xuyen in the Saigon-Cholon area during the first half of May, during which they pursued, and
finally liquidated, the remnants of this gang in the countryside. General The lost his life in the action. (A number of
Binh Xuyen leaders, it is charged, were given French assistance to escape to France.) The loyal military, now called the
National Army, then went after the dissident Hoa Hao troops
in the southwest. In April, 1956, the Army captured their
leader, General Ba Cut, and destroyed most of his force. (Ba
Cut was guillotined in July.) The fight against the sects and
the Binh Xuyen was now, to all intents, over.

The difficulties encountered by Diem during the winter of
1954 and the early months of 1955 were not lost on official
American observers. The United States Ambassador to Viet
Nam, General Lawton Collins, had apparently lost confidence
in Diem's ability to weather the storm and was prepared to see
changes in the government of Viet Nam; according to Robert
Shaplen, Collins conveyed this view to the President and to
the State Department. It seemed at the time that the preserva-
tion of Viet Nam's security and stability would require a government stronger and more representative than any Diem
could head. While the situation was being analyzed in the
United States, no clear decisions could be arrived at. It was at
this juncture, when others were taking the most pessimistic
views, that Diem exhibited the characteristic traits of his personality to the best advantage: with stubbornness, unwavering
adherence to his planned course, and full confidence in his
personal outlook, he took the offensive against the Binh Xuyen

and won. This success immediately earned him support from many quarters, within Viet Nam and without, that had previously been denied him.

Earlier, in 1954, a French mission had vainly sought American backing for the removal of Diem. On September 29, 1954, a joint French-American communiqué was issued detailing the future relations and attitudes of the two countries to the now independent states of France's former Indochinese empire. The United States announced that American aid for these states, which had earlier, in part, been channeled through France, would go to them directly after January 1. In the case of Viet Nam, this was an oblique, but public, rejection of the French attempt to unseat Diem. In October, President Eisenhower wrote to Premier Diem (addressed by his then official title, President of the Council of Ministers):

I have been following with great interest the course of developments in Viet Nam, particularly since the conclusion of the conference at Geneva. The implications of the agreement concerning Viet Nam have caused grave concern regarding the future of a country temporarily divided by an artificial military grouping, weakened by a long and exhausting war and faced with enemies without and by their subversive collaborators within.

Your recent requests for aid to assist in the formidable project of the movement of several hundred thousand loyal Vietnamese citizens away from areas which are passing under a de facto rule and political ideology which they abhor, are being fulfilled. I am glad that the United States is able to assist in this humanitarian effort.

We have been exploring ways and means to permit our aid to Viet Nam to be more effective and to make a greater contribution to the welfare and stability of the Government of Viet Nam. I am, accordingly, instructing the American Ambassador to Viet Nam to examine with you in your capacity as Chief of Government, how an intelligent program of American aid given directly to your Government can serve to assist Viet Nam in its present hour of trial, provided that your Government is prepared to give assurances as to the standards of performance it would be able to maintain in the event such aid were supplied.

The purpose of this offer is to assist the Government of Viet Nam in developing and maintaining a strong, viable state, capable of resisting attempted subversion or aggression through military means. The Government of the United States expects that this aid will be met by performance on the part of the Government of Viet Nam in undertaking needed reforms. It hopes that such aid, combined with your own continuing efforts, will contribute effectively toward an independent Viet Nam endowed with a strong government. Such a government would, I hope, be so responsive to the nationalist aspirations of its people, so enlightened in purpose and effective in performance that it will be respected both at home and abroad and discourage any who might wish to impose a foreign ideology on your free people.[7]

The United States offer of help was followed by the sending of a new Training Relations Instruction Mission to help train the Vietnamese army. The mission was headed by General John ("Iron Mike") O'Daniel; Colonel Lansdale was a member of his staff. O'Daniel had earlier headed the United States Military Assistance and Advisory Mission to the French forces in Indochina in the years preceding the Geneva Conference.*

President Eisenhower's letter made reference to the refugees from the North. Almost 1 million of these reached South Viet Nam after the Geneva Conference. The process was largely financed by the American aid program. Transportation for at least three-quarters of a million refugees was provided by the U.S. Pacific Fleet (310,848 persons, plus cargo, between August 8, 1954, and May 18, 1955), French ships and aircraft, and China Air Transport, a private airline. Scores of thousands came south by their own means, many of them on foot. The refugees left behind their homes, their land, their livestock, and all but a few personal possessions. Many who had lived

---

* O'Daniel, on his retirement, became chairman of the American Friends of Viet Nam; he resigned in 1963.

away from protected evacuation points were forcibly prevented by the Viet Minh from leaving; others who tried to
leave were killed or imprisoned. About 80 per cent were Roman Catholics; the rest were mostly Buddhists, with a few
Protestants. Some preparation had been made in South Viet
Nam for about 250,000 refugees. When almost four times that
number materialized—equivalent to one out of twelve or thirteen of South Viet Nam's population—the problems of resettlement and care were, of course, enormous. Resettlement centers
were rapidly created in twenty-five of the forty-odd provinces of the country, as a prelude to relocation and ultimate
absorption. One such relocation settlement, at Cai San, deep
in the Mekong delta area, was started in November, 1955, for
about 40,000 persons. When I visited it in July, 1956, it was
already producing a crop of rice on what had once been
abandoned lands. Cai San was, for several years, a showplace
of what could be achieved by determined peasants with some
security, aid, and a land reform program. It is a tribute to
Diem and his government that they were able to cope effectively with the refugee problem at a time when they were
beset by so many other problems. In a speech in the town of
Honai on October 11, 1956, Diem referred to the task that the
refugees posed as "immense" and the achievements as "gigan-
tic." It was no overstatement.

The victory over the Binh Xuyen and the sects, and the renewed decision of the United States to support Diem as premier, added momentum to the next course of events. Working
within a remarkable, self-imposed timetable, Diem set about
building the institutional arrangements that he believed his government and his country needed. His proposals for government
reform—deposition of Bao Dai, the ending of government-
by-decree, the establishment of some form of representative
government—found a responsive note in the country. Civil
servants below the top mandarin level met and endorsed the
reform resolutions of Diem's People's Revolutionary Committee and formed local committees. In all likelihood, the local

committees were the result of direct inducement by the central authority; but the popular response to their calls for support was undoubtedly largely spontaneous. In the last week of April, 1955, in the midst of the crisis provoked by the United Front of the sects and the Binh Xuyen, Ngo Dinh Diem announced his plans for elections for a Constituent Assembly with universal suffrage for men and women over eighteen, when the voters would be able to decide the future of their country. In a speech on May 8, the day after his victory over the Binh Xuyen, Diem said: "The Vietnamese population has expressed in various demonstrations what it disapproved of and what it wished for. It will determine its destiny by democratic means, principally by elections, which must be prepared for at once."

During the summer of 1955, Diem repeated this theme on a number of occasions; he coupled it with a call for a free, independent, and modernized economic policy in a speech, on September 17, at the reopening of the big Dong Cam dam. The electoral rolls were meanwhile being prepared. On October 6, he announced a referendum, to be held on October 23, to determine Viet Nam's form of government. A cable from Bao Dai, on October 18, in which the former emperor sought once more to dismiss Diem from office, was ignored. On the eve of the referendum, Ngo Dinh Diem broadcast to his people.

Tomorrow, October 23, for the first time in our history, men and women of Viet Nam, you will exercise one of the fundamental rights of all democratic countries: the right to vote. In compliance with the unanimous wish that you have clearly expressed, you are called upon to exercise your sovereignty by deciding whether or not you agree to withdraw legally the title of Chief of State from a man whose overthrow you have demanded.

Twenty-two years ago, when I was in office, I insisted on the installation of an elected Assembly. Since men and circumstances opposed it, I handed in my resignation. Thus, the event of a democratic regime is not due solely to circumstances. It corresponds with an ideal for which I have never ceased to struggle. The first act that you will perform as citizens of a free nation will open the way to other consultations on the political life of the country, especially to the holding of the coming general elections throughout Free Viet Nam.

In all circumstances, I will continue to serve the country as in the past, with all my might. If, by approving the policy I have adopted since my return to Viet Nam, you will entrust me with a new charge tomorrow, you will have voted for the building of a free and democratic Viet Nam in which all of us will have equal rights in the handling of public affairs, social progress, and collective prosperity. It depends only on you whether or not I will be put in a position to proclaim the Republic.

The vote next day was ninety to one for the deposition of the former emperor. It is generally conceded that this near unanimity was carefully "engineered"; it is also generally conceded that this maneuver was largely superfluous, for the issue was certain of gaining the votes of a majority of the people. Ellen J. Hammer, no great admirer of Ngo Dinh Diem, summed up the situation in a moderate understatement:

If there were those who criticized the fairness of certain aspects of the government-sponsored referendum in which Bao Dai was voted out of office by an overwhelming majority, there was no one in 1955 who could produce any evidence that the onetime emperor had a popular following in Viet Nam. Bao Dai, ever since he had been brought back by the French as chief of State in 1949, had demonstrated a persistent inability to act in the national interest or indeed to act at all.[8]

Ngo Dinh Diem, by contrast, had won notable public support during his fifteen months in power. On October 26, 1955, he proclaimed the Republic of Viet Nam. His proclamation speech was highlighted by a stirring promise for democracy:

Democracy is not a group of texts and laws, to be read and applied. It is essentially a state of mind, a way of living with the utmost respect toward every human being, ourselves as well as our neighbors. It requires constant self-education, careful practice, flexible and patient attention, in order to achieve a harmonious balance between the desirable diverse conceptions of men and the inevitable complexity of reality. Democracy demands from each of us, then, infinitely more efforts, understanding and goodwill than any other form of government.

Confident in the unity which you proved during the difficult times we endured, confident in the moral strength of our people whose spirit has been enriched by elements from the oldest and most highly developed civilizations, I know that together we will be able to throw off all forms of oppression and to build the ideal political and economic state to which our people aspire with such fervor.

It is in this spirit that the Constitution of our country will be written and the members of our National Assembly elected.

On that day, Diem became the first President of the Republic. He could properly be described as an accepted leader who had steered his country through a most extraordinary experience and who had gained approval both at home and abroad. Now the pace of his timetable was accelerated. In November, Diem appointed a commission to prepare the draft for a democratic constitution. In January, 1956, he announced March 4 as the date for national elections, to be preceded by two weeks of campaigning. A Constituent Assembly was to be elected, consisting of 123 members apportioned on a constituency basis with at least one delegate for each province. Some 400 candidates ran for election; these included candidates of parties that supported the government, non-Communist opposition candidates and independents. The Viet Minh's Fatherland Front called for a boycott of the elections and, in a number of places, Viet Minh supporters burned down the schools in which the voting was to be held. On the whole, however, there was little violence and disorder on election Sunday; 80 per cent of the registered voters cast their ballots.

The composition of the Constituent Assembly was as follows:[9]

Designation	Deputies
Movement for National Revolution (Phong Trao Cach Mang Quoc Gia)	61
Citizens Assembly (Tap Doan Cong Dan)	25
Revolutionary Labor Party* (Can Lao Nhan Vi)	15
Movement to Win and Preserve Freedom (Phong Trao Tranh Thu Tu Do)	8
Dai Viet [Greater Viet Nam] Progressive Party (Dai Viet Cap·Tien)	1
Independents	11
TOTAL	121†

Thirty-three candidates who had stood as independents became affiliated with a party when they joined the Assembly. Most of the eleven deputies who remained as independents, and the lone Dai Viet deputy, formed the "opposition"; the other deputies may all be regarded as supporters of Diem. The Assembly convened on March 15 and promptly protested the work of the earlier constitution-drafting commission; this was therefore set aside. On April 17, Diem outlined to the Assembly the democratic principles on which he thought the constitution should be based. A committee of the Assembly thereupon went to work to draft a new constitution; it finished its task during the summer.[10] The Constituent Assembly adopted the Constitution in October. It was promulgated on October 26, 1956, the first anniversary of the proclamation of the Republic; on that day, Diem took the oath of office as President under the new Constitution.

The National Constituent Assembly, its work completed, now became the National Assembly, and reconvened as such on November 9.

* The full name was Can Lao Nhan Vi Cach Mang Dang (Revolutionary Labor Personalism Party); *nhan vi* (personalism) represented the "philosophy" of Ngo Dinh Diem and his brother Ngo Dinh Nhu, head of the party. Madame Ngo Dinh Nhu was elected as an independent candidate.

† Two deputies were refused their seats for violations of the Electoral Law. They were subsequently replaced in by-elections.

The South Vietnamese Constitution followed, in part, the outlines of the U.S. Constitution. It vested executive power in a president who was both head of state and head of government; it provided for an independent judiciary and a unicameral legislature (the National Assembly). All elections were to be by universal suffrage. The president and vice president were to be elected for five-year terms and were eligible for two additional terms. The Assembly was to be elected for three-year terms, and was to convene twice a year. The government of the Republic of Viet Nam was not a federal one. The Constitution (which had ten chapters and ninety-eight articles) incorporated certain French and Vietnamese provisions that enhanced the power of the president and of the national government. Though it stipulated the powers of the judiciary, it was silent on how the judiciary should be instituted. It enumerated both "rights" and duties" of the citizen. Article 25 recognized the family "as the foundation of society" and a charge on the responsibility of the State. The Constitution (Chapter VII, Articles 82–84) also created a National Economic Council, not composed of members of the Assembly, which had the function of "suggesting ideas and rendering its opinion on economic matters and proposals." The powers of the president, as provided in Chapters III and X, Article 98, were large. A majority of three-quarters of the Assembly was required to override a presidential veto. The president could issue executive orders between sessions of the Assembly (Article 41), including limited though substantial budgetary orders (Article 43). In addition to the usual emergency powers granted to a president, Article 98, the concluding one, gave to him, during the Assembly's first legislative term, the right to decree a temporary suspension of the rights of freedom of circulation and residence, of speech and the press, of assembly and association, and of formation of labor unions and strikes, in order to meet "the legitimate demands of public security and order and of national defense."

A sober appraisal of the work of the Assembly and the

progress in administration in the Republic of Viet Nam was published in *Current Notes on International Affairs,* a monthly publication of the Australian Department of External Affairs, in August, 1959:

During its first term the National Assembly tended to concentrate on the technical and administrative aspects of legislation while the formulation of policy was left largely to the executive. The Assembly was encouraged to adopt a constructive and responsible approach towards its duties and to acquaint itself as closely as possible with the efficacy of laws it had passed and the requirements of the electorate. At the same time, high priority was given to the training of the administration as an honest and efficient body. A National School of Administration was established and Ministers and senior civil servants were urged to attend to the training of their staffs. By these means the President hoped to avoid political instability and disorder during the early days of the Republic and to lay the foundation of a future which will embrace both Western political concepts and Vietnamese national traditions.

In his first years in office, President Diem clearly had restored a large measure of internal security to his disturbed country and had taken a number of significant steps to create the institutions necessary for political stability. Though the new constitution fell short of Western conceptions of democracy, it is certainly true that it extended democratic measures beyond anything that had previously obtained in the country, and perhaps beyond what was then warranted by the security conditions of the country. At the very least, Diem's efforts constituted a "promissory note" for the next period ahead— for tackling the problems of refugee relief and rehabilitation, of economic restoration and growth, and of the next elections, only three years away. One could easily argue, especially with hindsight, that Diem introduced his "promissory note" too soon. This view was held by one of his later critics who, in 1963, wrote that it was "unfortunate that full-scale elections and democratic trappings should have been introduced into Viet Nam during a period of great transition when its rulers' lack of confidence, the ideological tensions within the society, and the importance of the issues at stake have all militated against the growth of fragile democratic institutions."[11]

A negative aspect of Diem's early years as president was the extraordinary, and frequently clandestine, actions by his family and intimate circle to control or inhibit any nationalist opinion, even when strongly anti-Communist, that differed from the family's outlook. The Can Lao party of Ngo Dinh Nhu was from its origins a secret-cell, cadre party designed to have its members work in and through the mass parties, particularly the Movement for National Revolution. Most probably, it was Ngo Dinh Nhu who organized the incredible ninety-to-one vote in the referendum that deposed Bao Dai. He was a little less zealous in the elections for the Constituent Assembly. Diem's personality was not of the type that would have helped him become a popular leader in the Western, democratic image. Though a voluble, thoughtful, and highly expressive individual in private conversation, he was not effective as a public figure. He was a bachelor in his fifties, a recluse by temperament, and not at ease among the people. In the twenty-one years he had spent in the political wilderness, from 1933 to 1954, he had acquired a skeptical—if not suspicious—outlook with respect to those Vietnamese who had not experienced his own type of political and spiritual exile from his country. He was ruled by his deep devotion to the concept of family loyalty; he was under the always questionable influence of his brother Ngo Dinh Nhu, whom he named his official advisor. Nhu and his wife—the beautiful but vicious Tran Le Xuan, who acted as if she were a Vietnamese queen of old—lived in Independence Palace, the President's residence and former seat of France's governors-general, where Mme. Nhu was official hostess for bachelor Diem. The family's less pleasant activities were facilitated by the limitations on civil liberties that were written into Article 98 of the Constitution.

The herculean efforts of Ngo Dinh Diem during his first two years in office—from July, 1954, to the convening of the

legally constituted National Assembly in November, 1956—
revealed an unexpected capacity to triumph over conflicts and
obstacles. His goal was the independence and the security of
the Republic of Viet Nam. His desire, clearly and effectively
expressed, was to achieve security, stability, and improvement
in the conditions of living, by and through democratic principles. Once, when questioned on the wisdom of making haste
slowly in applying such principles, he said: "If you want to
emerge rapidly from this humiliating condition [colonial
status] and not in a few centuries, you are led to adopt some
sort of forced march. The democratic problem consists precisely in our ability to determine the limits of this forced
march, which is in itself indispensable, even *without* the added
pressure of Communist neighbors."

And so Diem proceeded on his "forced march," convinced
that he had what he called a "sound vision and true cause."[12]

7. *The United States and the Diem Regime*

Whether it was the "miracle" that some observers called it or not, the fact is that President Diem's government managed not only to survive the rough years 1954–56 but even to make some progress. There was an understandable disposition by 1956 to get on with the many formidable tasks ahead, and to leave for the future the implementation of full democracy. The "flawed nature" of, and the inconsistency in, Diem's rule —the democracy he preached and which was defined in the Constitution, but which was abridged and curtailed in practice by the use of clandestine political and overt police controls, initiated and applied by his brothers—was temporarily overlooked or accepted as a passing feature. The National Army was reorganized as a defense force, cut back to 150,000 men, retrained, supplied, and positioned to guard the demarcation line against a Korean-type invasion from the North. The Communist terrorists, left behind as cadres by the Viet Minh after its incomplete withdrawal in 1954, now active in the border areas near Laos and Cambodia and also in the lower reaches of the Mekong delta, were being hunted down and their political and terror campaigns had to be counteracted. A century of French occupation and administration had to be transformed into a Vietnamese administration. Nationalist dissident groups had to be neutralized and, where possible, won over. International relations were established with countries of the Free World and with neutral nations.

Most important of all, the basic agricultural economy of South Viet Nam had to be restored and reinvigorated. After years of warfare, the farmhands, the tenant-farmers, the small holders, and the uprooted peasantry—who among them made up the majority of the population—had to be given the opportunity once again to live productively and securely. Like all peasants everywhere, they wanted land they could own or acquire and pass on to their children, without the crushing, cyclic burden of debt imposed on them by rapacious landlords and usurious money-lenders. They required livestock, for much of what they had once owned had been consumed or destroyed during the war years. Drainage canals and irrigation systems, and waterways and transport facilities that would enable their produce to reach the markets, had to be rebuilt. The peasants were entitled to a new life without harassment, their only tribute in government taxes in cash or kind, without the added burden of "taxes" imposed by the Communist rebels.

To Aid the Republic of Viet Nam: A Commitment of Three Presidents

The offer made by President Eisenhower "to assist the Government of Viet Nam in developing and maintaining a strong, viable state, capable of resisting attempted subversion or aggression through military means"[1] was soon implemented. This commitment by the United States to the government and people of Viet Nam is a continuing commitment, first stated by President Eisenhower and reiterated by Presidents Kennedy and Johnson. President Eisenhower, in the following letter sent to President Ngo Dinh Diem on October 26, 1960, expressed it in these words:

My countrymen and I are proud to convey our good wishes to you and to the citizens of Viet Nam on the fifth anniversary of the birth of the Republic of Viet Nam.

We have watched the courage and daring with which you and the Vietnamese people attained independence in a situation so perilous that many thought it hopeless. We have admired the rapidity with which chaos yielded to order and progress replaced despair.

During the years of your independence it has been refreshing for us to observe how clearly the Government and the citizens of Viet Nam have faced the fact that the greatest danger to their independence was Communism. You and your countrymen have used your strength well in accepting the double challenge of building your country and resisting Communist imperialism. In five short years since the founding of the Republic, the Vietnamese people have developed their country in almost every sector. I was particularly impressed by one example. I am informed that last year over 1,200,000 Vietnamese children were able to go to elementary school; three times as many as were enrolled five years earlier. This is certainly a heartening development for Viet Nam's future. At the same time Viet Nam's ability to defend itself from the Communists has grown immeasurably since its successful struggle to become an independent Republic.

Viet Nam's very success as well as its potential wealth and its strategic location have led the Communists of Hanoi, goaded by the bitterness of their failure to enslave all Viet Nam, to use increasing violence in their attempts to destroy your country's freedom.

This grave threat, added to the strains and fatigues of the long struggle to achieve and strengthen independence, must be a burden that would cause moments of tension and concern in almost any human heart. Yet from long observation I sense how deeply the Vietnamese value their country's independence and strength and I know how well you used your boldness when you led your countrymen in winning it. I also know that your determination has been a vital factor in guarding that independence while steadily advancing the economic development of your country. I am confident that these same qualities of determination and boldness will meet the renewed threat as well as the needs and desires of your countrymen for further progress on all fronts.

Although the main responsibility for guarding that independence will always, as it has in the past, belong to the Vietnamese people and their government, I want to assure you that for so long as our strength can be useful, the United States will continue to assist Viet Nam in the difficult yet hopeful struggle ahead.[2]

President Kennedy enlarged upon this commitment, as the

Communist insurgency mounted. On December 14, 1961, he wrote to President Diem:

I have received your recent letter in which you described so cogently the dangerous condition caused by North Viet Nam's efforts to take over your country. The situation in your embattled country is well known to me and to the American people. We have been deeply disturbed by the assault on your country. Our indignation has mounted as the deliberate savagery of the Communist program of assassination, kidnaping and wanton violence became clear.

Your letter underlines what our own information has convincingly shown—that the campaign of force and terror now being waged against your people and your Government is supported and directed from the outside by the authorities at Hanoi. They have thus violated the provisions of the Geneva Accords designed to ensure peace in Viet Nam and to which they bound themselves in 1954.

At that time, the United States, although not a party to the Accords, declared that it "would view any renewal of the aggression in violation of the agreements with grave concern and as seriously threatening international peace and security." We continue to maintain that view.

In accordance with that declaration, and in response to your request, we are prepared to help the Republic of Viet Nam to protect its people and to preserve its independence. We shall promptly increase our assistance to your defense effort as well as help relieve the destruction of the floods which you describe. I have already given the orders to get these programs underway.

The United States, like the Republic of Viet Nam, remains devoted to the cause of peace and our primary purpose is to help your people maintain their independence. If the Communist authorities in North Viet Nam will stop their campaign to destroy the Republic of Viet Nam, the measures we are taking to assist your defense efforts will no longer be necessary. We shall seek to persuade the Communists to give up their attempts of force and subversion. In any case, we are confident that the Vietnamese people will preserve their independence and gain the peace and prosperity for which they have sought so hard and so long.[3]

President Johnson restated the United States commitment on numerous occasions. On July 28, 1965, at a press conference in the White House, he said:

Moreover, we are in Viet Nam to fulfill one of the most solemn pledges of the American Nation. Three Presidents—President Eisenhower, President Kennedy, and your present President—over eleven years, have committed themselves and have promised to help defend this small and valiant nation.

Strengthened by that promise, the people of South Viet Nam have fought for many long years. Thousands of them have died. Thousands more have been crippled and scarred by war. We cannot now dishonor our word or abandon our commitment or leave those who believed us and who trusted us to the terror and repression and murder that would follow.

This, then, my fellow Americans, is why we are in Viet Nam.[4]

On an earlier occasion, President Johnson had summed this up by saying, "Our commitment is to help these people help themselves."

Aid to Viet Nam

It is not easy to convey the difficulties of building a secure and viable state in the partitioned country that became the Republic of Viet Nam. As one careful observer stated, the task was "to build a nation, where, indeed, only a temporary building permit existed at the moment." To carry the analogy further, the "architects"—official Vietnamese and American—were essentially in conflict over such broad issues as industrialization, land reform, the kind of military and police establishment necessary; the "contractors" frequently worked at cross-purposes because their "blueprints" were not identical; and the working staffs were members of a variety of "craft unions" whose jurisdictions were not always clear. Language problems —communication between the indigene and the advisor—also contributed to the discordance. And inflation, black-marketeering, and other forms of human frailty were ever-present dangers.

It is an incontrovertible fact that much got done despite these not uncommon aspects of the aid relationship—much more than might seem from a record of the errors of omission and commission. One can certainly say that the genuine improvement in the lives of the South Vietnamese was one of the factors that helped to sustain their resistance to Communist dictatorship. Although dissatisfaction with the Diem government certainly grew, it was coupled with recognition that there had been numerous and genuine gains. Had this not been so, the Communists would most probably have been able to convert their military-guerrilla success into a genuine political hold and would have been able to consolidate their gains into a contiguous territorial command, such as Ho Chi Minh and General Giap had achieved when fighting against the French after 1950. The Communists—Fatherland Front, National Liberation Front, or Viet Cong—hold some important enclaves in South Viet Nam, but they have never been able to link these up to form a large continuous and viable base area that they can control by day as well as by night.

The United States aid program during the Diem regime, from 1955 to 1963, contributed in no small measure to the failure of the Communist attempt. Total United States aid to the regime in these years exceeded $2 billion. During all the changes of government in Viet Nam, and during successive administrations in the United States, the aid program held to five basic objectives:

To finance the import of essentials, such as oil, steel, medicines, and machinery, needed for the economy; and, through various anti-inflationary measures, to support the budgets for the Vietnamese military and counterinsurgency efforts.

To supply the skills, the training, and the goods required at the village level to raise farm output, to provide health services and education, and generally to improve the lot of the people.

To utilize United States surplus farm products to make up for local shortages in food and fibers.

To help Viet Nam make all levels of government more effective and more responsive to the needs and aspirations of the people.

To support the war effort.

For most of these years, the United States alone carried this burden. More recently, substantial contributions in the form of loans, grants, and commercial credits have been provided by more than thirty nations, including Australia, Britain, Canada, France, West Germany, Japan, Korea, New Zealand, the Philippines, Nationalist China (Taiwan), and Thailand. The main burden, however, continues to be borne by the United States. This is as it should be: it was the United States that assumed the bilateral commitment to defend this country against Communist aggression and that sponsored the multi-lateral commitment through SEATO.

The early phase of the aid program was essentially a crash program. About 70 per cent of the annual allocations was for defense and police purposes; the remainder was allotted to economic and technical assistance, including aid for refugees and rural resettlement. This is how economic aid was apportioned in fiscal year 1956–57:[5]

Economic and Technical Assistance with Estimated Expenditure, Fiscal Year 1956–57
(in thousands of dollars)

Agriculture and Natural Resources	
Small water-control systems	1,374
Administration of agrarian reform	607
Land development (rural resettlement)	10,034
General livestock development	1,169
Development of marine fisheries	430
Agricultural extension and information	351
National Agricultural College and general training	687
Research in diversified crops	337
Agricultural credit and cooperatives	190
Agricultural economics and statistics	111
Total	15,290
Industry and Mining	
Nong Son coal-exploration survey	56
Telecommunication development	719
Electric-power development	843
Paper-industry survey	25

Sugar-industry survey	36
Industrial Development Center	10,000
General industrial survey	804
Rural water-supply development	417
Saigon-Cholon water-system survey	122
Handicraft development	99
Total	**13,121**

Transportation

Highways and bridges	20,694
Viet Nam railway system	4,413
Saigon port loan	229
Waterways of Viet Nam	298
Improvement and expansion of aeronautical ground facilities	3,006
Total	**28,640**

Labor

Labor school	200
Labor ministry organization	40
Total	**240**

Health and Sanitation

Malaria eradication program	1,231
Medical and allied education	3,554
Health services development	1,410
Total	**6,195**

Education

Technical vocational education	883
Elementary education	1,002
Secondary education	480
Teacher training and higher education	1,450
Adult literacy training	350
Textbook development and special services	204
Total	**4,369**

Public Administration

Civil police administration	5,787
Training civil tax expert	8
Fellowship on taxation and public finances	150
National Institute of Statistics	214
National Institute of Administration and MSU (Michigan State University) administrative support	2,037
Travel costs for Vietnamese scholarship students to and from Viet Nam	100
Total	**8,296**

General and Miscellaneous

Development of government information facilities	779
National radio network	882
General program administration	5,072
Total	**6,740**
GRAND TOTAL	82,891

One particular and unusual characteristic of the United States aid program at that time (which is not reflected in the above table) was the way in which the heavy military and security portion of the Vietnamese budget was financed and made possible. Since the new government could raise in annual revenues only about $200 million, and since its approved budget for expenditures was more than twice that sum, the United States aid program made use of a variety of fiscal devices, including conversion of dollars at official rates into piasters, to help the government balance its budget. The Vietnamese authorities also engaged to sell on the local market certain equipment and supplies provided by United States aid, and to use the local-currency proceeds to finance government expenditures. This was called the "commercial import" program.

The character of this program was popular with neither the United States Congress nor the Vietnamese and American civilian aid personnel, who would have preferred to see American aid used for development projects. Their preference is understandable; their lack of comprehension of the security requirements in a situation such as was present in Viet Nam after 1954, and of the United States financial capacity for larger aid grants, is perhaps less understandable. The situation was correctly summed up by R. G. Casey, then Australia's Minister for External Affairs: "This 'crash' operation, and the urgent imposition of new systems of exchange and import control, would have tested the capacity of any administration. Under such conditions, the Vietnamese government and the United States aid administration made a remarkable achievement in limiting economic and commercial dislocation and in attaining the vital, immediate objective of supporting the Vietnamese budget and covering current expenses, in particular those involved in security and the maintenance of the refugees."[6]

Over the years, the words that were used to denote the objectives of the program changed. But the objectives, as also the major outlines of the program and the fiscal devices used to implement it, remained fairly constant. For fiscal years 1954–66, the dollar value of American economic assistance to Viet Nam approximated $3 billion; the aid activities continued to include agriculture, health, education, public works, public safety, public administration, labor, industrial development, provincial operations (resettlement and refugees, etc.), development loans, communications, food-for-peace—not very different from what they had been in 1956–57.

A fuller picture of developments in South Viet Nam and of the projects that were completed there with United States aid during the first half of the Diem regime can be obtained from the *Annual Reports* published by the United States Operations Mission (USOM) in Saigon. The director of the USOM program at that time was Leland Barrows, a reliable reporter not given to puffery. He presented a summary of the program and its results at the fourth conference of the American Friends of Viet Nam, held in 1959; the report of the conference was published under the somewhat extravagant title *Aid to Viet Nam—An American Success Story*. This is what Barrows said in 1959:

In the first place, Viet Nam is a free nation today, stronger militarily, politically, and administratively than most people thought possible four years ago.

In the second place, Viet Nam has made the transition from colonial status and an inflated wartime economy to political independence and a normal level of economic activity without a fall in the standard of living and without loss of political or economic stability.

In the third place, agricultural production has been restored and refugees equal to 7 per cent of the population have been received and resettled.

Parenthetically, I would like to say that Viet Nam has been slow to return to the world rice export market, but that, I think, is because of increased domestic consumption, attributable in part to the refugees, because actual production, I believe, has already reached and surpassed the pre-war level.

Fourth, much of the physical destruction caused by the civil war and the years of occupation has been repaired.

Fifth, a program of industrial development has been launched.

Finally, the nation has been enabled to maintain the military strength required by the constant threat of Communist aggression.

In fact, so much has been accomplished in the past four years that one can easily forget that Viet Nam remains a divided country, not enjoying the blessings of peace, but protected only by an armistice. The threat of subversion and violence within and of infiltration from without and the danger of actual invasion are always present. This, I think, is why the Government of Viet Nam is sometimes obliged to put considerations of security ahead of economic objectives and why defense continues to absorb such a large proportion of the total national budget and of American aid.[7]

Certainly, the most important aspect of the aid program related to the peasant and the land. The countryside in South Viet Nam contains 85 per cent of the population; the heart of the problem facing the government was to bring stability and progress to the countryside and safeguard it against Communist terror and insurrection. "Land to the Landless" has always been one of the most potent and most hypocritical of all Leninist appeals, and it was being put to good propaganda use by the Communists operating in South Viet Nam. If Diem could have instituted and sustained a genuine land reform program he would have been able to solidify support for his government even without holding national elections; elections were of interest to the Saigon intellectuals but not to the peasantry.

The southern part of South Viet Nam, like the delta areas of Cambodia, Thailand, and Burma, is part of the rice bowl of mainland Southeast Asia. It is usually cultivated in small units of five to twenty acres, through the use of a short metal-tipped plow drawn by buffaloes. Plowing, planting, transplanting,

growth, and harvest all take place within the limits of the season of moonsoon rains, from mid-May to October. The yields
are low in comparison to yields in Spain, Italy, Japan, and the
United States. Generally there is only one crop a year, although with the proper guidance and assistance the farmer
could grow a second crop. The French, as the British in colonial Burma and elsewhere, helped to develop rice-growing in
the delta areas, but for the most part they were engaged in the
rice-export trade and concentrated modern methods and machinery in developing rubber plantations.

In 1955, early in his administration, Ngo Dinh Diem was
fortunate to secure by direct contract the services of Wolf
Ladejinsky as land reform expert and technical consultant.
Ladejinsky had previously served in a similar capacity in
occupied Japan, under General Douglas MacArthur, and in
Taiwan. He served Diem until 1962. There has been criticism—both justified and unjustified—of the land reform program in Viet Nam as it was conceived, and as it was actually
carried out. Ladejinsky has never answered the critics of his
work in Viet Nam directly, although he has done so indirectly in a number of articles he has published on the general
subject.[8]

As Ladejinsky indicated in his early (and unpublished)
reports to President Diem, "when we talk of farmers in South
Viet Nam we refer to tenants. In all of South Viet Nam the
majority of the farmers do not own the land they cultivate."
The landlords, money-lenders, and suppliers of agricultural
credits were French, Chinese, and a small Vietnamese upper
class; the French landowners were eventually bought out by
the French Government and by Diem's government. The
Vietnamese landlords, both before and after Viet Nam's independence, were no better than their predecessors. They occupied the superior economic positions; frequently, they or
their sons became the national and provincial officials who
were to administer whatever reforms were adopted by the
Diem government. The term "land reform" was used in

Viet Nam to cover the resettlement of refugees and others on abandoned or newly reclaimed or cleared lands as well as the distribution of land to the landless. The program began slowly under Diem. His original conception was based on the "notion that a reform must make all parties equally happy . . . he tended to overlook the fact that under Vietnamese conditions this would have meant no reform." Half the cultivated land was owned by approximately 2.5 per cent of the landowners, who owned more than 100 acres each; these landlords were obviously not going to be "equally happy" with any reform which curtailed their holdings and their power over the peasantry.

But Diem did move—in two stages. First came Ordinances 2 and 7, in January and February, 1955. The ordinances were to be executed by what later, in 1957, became the Commissariat-General for Land Development, headed by Bui Van Luong, who had earlier acted as the able director of the refugee program. Land reform got underway in late 1955, with the Cai San resettlement scheme as one of its first successes. It subsequently acquired momentum, but also opposition. Between 1957 and 1959, about ninety rural resettlement centers were created on 120,000 acres, to take care of about 125,000 relocated persons, of whom about 5 per cent were classed as non-Viet *montagnards*. By 1963, some 200,000 persons had been relocated in the centers. Opposition came from the United States Operations Mission, which disagreed with Diem's policy of locating most of these centers in the uplands of central Viet Nam and in the border provinces near Cambodia and Laos. Diem's purpose was to create with these new settlers a "living wall" against the Communists; however, in the absence of adequate security provisions, these centers were certain to be exposed both to the Viet Cong and to the highland non-Viet tribes, who regarded the Viet lowlanders as intruders on what were their tribal lands.[9] These resettled peasants were given lease-holds and were offered rent-reduction and other advantages so that, it was hoped, their communities would become self-supporting after a period of government assistance.

The second and perhaps more decisive stage came with Ordinance 57, in October, 1956. This provided for the distribution of all rice lands in excess of 250 acres that were held by landlords. Of this remainder landlords could in principle cultivate at least 30 per cent and lease or sell the balance. All holdings in excess of the permitted maximum were to be acquired by governmental purchase and sold to former tenants, farm workers, war veterans, or refugees, under a plan by which these new owners would repay the government in six annual installments; the new owners could neither lease nor mortgage such land for ten years after acquisition. The former owners were to receive compensation for their land in cash and in interest-bearing twelve-year government bonds which they could use as tender to pay off agricultural debts or to invest in government-sponsored economic development. (The latter device had been used in Taiwan with some success.) About 1.5 million acres of land formerly held by landlords were thus acquired during the next few years. Surveying, acquisition, and the preparation of new titles proved to be a time-consuming affair that slowed down the program. By December, 1960, the formalities had been completed for about 930,000 acres, and three-fourths of this was already under cultivation by the 120,000 new tenant-owners.

Criticism of the program came because the pace of redistribution was slow; the annual installments to be paid by the new owners to the government were too high and not spread over a long period; and an excessive price had to be paid to the former owners. Particularly unhappy were the peasants who had squatted on the lands of absentee landlords during the war years, 1940–54, when the owners were not in a position, because of the security situation, to collect rents; now, as the peasants obtained title to land which they had long been cultivating free of rent, land they already regarded as their own, they were being forced for the first time to make substantial annual payments.

The Communists utilized these resentments over the land distribution program in their propaganda campaign against the government of South Viet Nam. The impact of their propaganda was blunted, however, by the trouble into which North Viet Nam's own land reform program had run. In the Quynh Luu area of the province of Nghe An, villagers who had protested the harsh treatment by the Communists were put down in a bloody massacre. News of the peasant uprising appeared in two Communist publications in the North, *Nhan Dan* and *Hoc Tap*, and soon became known in the South. Radio Hanoi itself broadcast in November, 1956, the "self-criticism" of Truong Chinh, Secretary-General of the Communist Party in the Democratic Republic of Viet Nam; he admitted that he had been "unjust" and that he had arrested and accused many for opposing "the program of land reform." The extent of the peasant uprisings, the mass arrests, and the executions in the North during the land reform and rent reduction campaigns in 1954–56—which deserves to be better known—is documented by Hoang Van Chi in *From Colonialism to Communism—A Case History of North Vietnam*.[10] At the Tenth Congress of the Central Committee of North Viet Nam's Communist Party, General Vo Nguyen Giap "read a long list of errors." The errors included "indiscriminately" attacking the landowning families; executing "too many honest people"; "seeing enemies everywhere"; and resorting to "terror, which became far too widespread" (whether "terror" which was not "too widespread" would have been permissible, he did not say). He added:

The Party had failed to respect the principles of freedom of faith and worship . . . [and] attacked tribal chiefs too strongly. . . . Instead of recognizing education to be the first essential, we resorted . . . exclusively to . . . disciplinary punishments, expulsion from the Party, executions. . . . Worse still, torture came to be regarded as a normal practice during party reorganization.[11]

The rebellion in Nghe An province temporarily halted North Viet Nam's land and rent reform program.

Land reform also created certain problems in the South, but against that it solved many problems for several hundred thousand peasant families. It was a valid and important component of the general improvement within South Viet Nam. Other improvements were the reopening of through-railway traffic between Saigon and Hué; the growth in elementary-school enrollment from 400,000 to 1.5 million; the renewal of export earnings from the production of rice, rubber, seafood, coffee, tea, beer, and handicrafts; and increased production of textiles, sugar, coal, and hard fibers, and the accompanying saving in foreign-currency expenditures; the development of medium-sized industrial plants to produce textiles, glass, cement, refined sugar, paper, furniture, and other consumer items; better health facilities with malaria prevention, health, and maternity stations; and the preparation of the (unfortunately stillborn) Five-Year Plan for economic development. *Current Notes on International Affairs* summed up its review of the economy of South Viet Nam by saying that the "Government of Viet Nam has very substantial achievements to its credit since the end of the war in Indochina . . . it has . . . to face the problem of putting the economy on a sound basis and reducing its dependence on foreign aid."[12]

Senator Mike Mansfield, then chairman of the Senate Subcommittee on State Department Affairs, wrote in an official report, *United States Aid Program in Viet Nam*,[13] dated February 26, 1960, that South Viet Nam "has made a great deal of progress as an independent nation under its able President, Ngo Dinh Diem, and the aid program has been a significant factor in that progress." What Mansfield felt was needed was more planning and a reshaping of the program "eventually to bring about a termination of the need for it." A current of impatience ran through this report, impatience at the less than effective use of aid funds, impatience at South Viet Nam's continuing dependency on United States aid, impatience at what was considered to be the low level of productivity and exports.

In August, 1959, the Republic of Viet Nam held its second national elections for the National Assembly. Again the parties supporting the government won "overwhelming victories," with even fewer "opposition" candidates elected than in 1956. Even with scrupulously fair elections, Diem's supporters would most probably have soundly defeated the opposition candidates in that year. "It would seem that the Ngo Dinh Diem government has been unnecessarily cautious and has at times acted for narrow advantage in dealing with the problem of political freedom," reported Robert G. Scigliano,[14] who was in South Viet Nam in 1958–59 as an administration adviser. Scigliano considered the non-Communist nationalist opposition to Diem to be weak and fragmented, revolving around a few leaders and "having little or no real organization and but few direct followers." The opposition, Scigliano wrote, was agreed on the fact that the regime was "a family dictatorship run by a man who is incapable of sharing power and will go to almost any length to preserve it. It [the opposition] doubts the regime's integrity and ability though it often excludes the President himself from the first of these judgments and disbelieves in its [the regime's] good motives."

Scigliano, a critic of the Diem regime, found that the opposition, for the most part, did not differ from the government on social and economic programs, but that there was no agreement within its ranks on "how much democracy Viet Nam can afford to have beyond the need for 'basic freedoms' " The problem of coupling democracy with prudence was one that troubled many, a problem that had no easy solution. No one seemed able to find the Aristotelean mean between basic freedoms and the requirements of internal security.

In his concern over the rising vehemence of the Communist campaign of terror, insurgency, and assassination, Diem tended to overlook such issues as the freedom of the press, the honesty of the elections, the role of the National Assembly, and the rights of the legitimate (though puny) non-Communist political opposition. This was another manifestation of the "flaw" in his character that, in 1960, lead to the aborted coup whose aim was reform.[15]

The Attempted Coup of November, 1960

The 1960 "coup" turned out not to be one. The issue, despite the frequent use of the word "democracy" by both Diem and his non-Communist critics, was not democracy in any Western sense of the term. That Diem was responsible, prematurely and sincerely, I believe, for introducing the idea of democracy in his talks and constitutional endeavors is true. That he, personally, was influenced by French, Anglo-Saxon, and Roman Catholic concepts of individualism, democracy, and morality is also true. But Ngo Dinh Diem, like his non-Communist critics, remained deeply imbedded in the aristocratic and authoritarian tradition of his family and his Confucian-influenced Vietnamese culture. That his regime was an authoritarian one, despite the trappings of a constitution and elected National Assembly—he also stood in 1961 for re-election as president against two opposition slates—is also true. In this respect, he personally was responsible for holding out more—of democracy—than he was ever prepared to see carried out.

The demand for some degree of sharing in matters of government continued to mount. In April, 1960, eighteen prominent citizens, including former Cabinet ministers, issued a manifesto which they described as an "objective balance of the situation." They called for a liberalized regime that would "promote democracy, guarantee minimum civil rights, recognize the opposition so as to permit citizens to express themselves without fear, thus removing grievances and resentments, opposition to which now constitutes for the people their sole reason for existence."[16] Discontent continued. On November 11, a coup was attempted by a group of paratroopers. Led by two colonels, they surrounded the Presidential Palace. They demanded, not the end of Diem, but the liberalization of his regime and the curtailment of his family's influence in the affairs of the Republic. Diem, their prisoner, engaged the leaders in thirty-six hours of talks. At the end of that time, the loyal armed forces and the police—the mass of the people, in Saigon as in the countryside, was apparently uninvolved—suppressed the coup. A week later, Diem announced a new reform program; despite this, the eighteen signers of the April manifesto were arrested.

The reforms were made public in February, 1961. They promised a measure of electoral activity for self-governing village councils; a reorganization of the President's executive agencies so as to assign a number of them to appropriate ministries; and a regroupment of various ministries under Coordinating Secretaries of State for Economic Development, for Security, and for Social and Cultural Affairs, with the aim of promoting efficiency and rooting out opportunities for corruption. In addition, the regime fostered the creation of an "opposition" to contest the forthcoming presidential election; a Committee on National Union was formed to encourage legitimate political discussion and pre-election activity. The elections, held on April 9, 1961, according to the date stipulated in the Constitution, offered the electorate a limited choice of slates and were preceded in Saigon by a genuine election campaign. There was less "unanimity" than in the referendum of 1955 that deposed Bao Dai and elected Diem to his first term: Diem received 88 per cent of the votes cast throughout the country and 64 per cent of those cast in Saigon.

Saigon, at this time, was a hotbed of intrigue and rumor. The elites in Saigon were increasingly affected by the regime's authoritarianism. Almost everyone had a friend who had been arrested at one time or another; everyone was aware of the suppression of newspapers (not all of them venal) and of other avenues of expression. Unquestionably, there were many bona fide nationalists who had fought long and honorably against the French and the Communists, who were not supporters of the sects or of the Binh Xuyen, and who were nevertheless denied the right to voice their opposition to Diem's regime.

But one can neither assert nor deny the existence of similar attitudes in the countryside, even though there were isolated reports of resentment when local village elections were suspended. There, the majority of the people lived and had their being seeking—and one knows this more by inference and experience than by scientific evidence—the security and stability of a livelihood and the pleasures of ceremony and occasional holidays. As far as one can tell, they were not directly affected by the regime's authoritarianism. They were affected, however, by the regime's effort to improve their lot through the various aid programs, including land resettlement and redistribution, and by the promise of security—a condition they had not fully enjoyed for a generation.

For the villager lived his life in his village, seldom moving from its orbit. And in the village, the villager could and did participate in the concerns of his family, associated families, and village group life.

Political affairs in Saigon and the pursuit of more genuine democracy were therefore of little concern to the vast majority of Vietnamese. However, as Diem's close friend and land reform expert Wolf Ladejinsky pointed out, "this is not to say that the country would not profit from a climate of political tolerance, with an active loyal opposition. In Viet

Nam, however, as in a good many other ex-colonial countries; opposition does not foster compromise; more often than not it stands for hatred bordering on the pathological. The problem the President faces is whether in the midst of a life-and-death struggle against the Communist conspiracy he dares to risk the full exercise of Western democratic practices. The fear that the enemy would try to pervert them for the ultimate destruction of the new state is much too real."[17]

"To risk the full exercise of Western democratic practices," is the first of two operative clauses in this capsule analysis. There were some, especially in the journalistic and academic worlds in the West, but also in Viet Nam, who would have advocated running this "risk"; these persons never accepted Diem nor appreciated the fullness of the problem in Viet Nam. I know of no *responsible* American official or true friend of Viet Nam, however, who proposed this "risk." In the unsettled and explosive state in which Viet Nam has been since 1954, it would be impossible to define and to carry out the full exercise of democratic practices. Full for whom? Under what conditions? In the light of what existing Vietnamese traditions and institutions? Democracy, if it is to succeed, requires certain minimum conditions. There must be unifying forces in the society, not only divisive ones. Over and above the shared experience of being *against* something—colonial power, Communist or other dictatorship—there must be some *positive* shared experience that is valued by most and considered worth preserving. There must be some common symbols for respect and allegiance; responsibilities as well as rights. It is not that all these were absent in South Viet Nam. It is that their potentials had not yet had the time to be articulated cohesively in the society.

"A life-and-death struggle against the Communist conspiracy" is the second operative clause in the quotation. Had there been no such struggle, it would be easy to dismiss Diem today as a stubborn bungler or, worse, as one who persisted in flouting all advice but that of his family. The fact is that there was such a struggle, the character of which is only recently becoming understood. Diem's self-deluding propaganda in 1956–57 had the effect of lulling some Vietnamese and some Americans into believing that his regime, by its truly bold actions against the sects and the Binh Xuyen in 1955 and by his rejection of Ho Chi Minh's overtures in 1955–56, had won the day against the Communists as well. In 1956, for example, he boasted that he had restored peace and control even in the Camau peninsula—where the Communists are still entrenched to this day. Diem failed to have—certainly he failed to voice—a clear perception of the Communist danger until well into 1957. But when he did, in 1958 and 1959, others —Americans and Vietnamese—thought he was crying wolf; they suggested as the cure-all more democracy, or more non-military aid, or some social or economic program that could not get to the root of the problem, which was the Communist attack on the security of the countryside.

What should have been done to counter the Communist danger is a complicated question. Various approaches were attempted. The United States helped to build up a Vietnamese army to defend the Republic of Viet Nam against direct invasion, in Korean fashion, from the North. The Protocol of the Southeast Asia Treaty Organization was designed to throw the mantle of protection over Viet Nam, as well as Laos and Cambodia. Since the bulk of American aid to the country was to be devoted to defense against Communism, General John W. ("Iron Mike") O'Daniel was led to prophesy: "The [Vietnamese] Army will be, above all, according to American ideas on the subject, a police force capable of spotting Communist guerrillas and Communist efforts at infiltration."[18] Even in 1961, the United States White Paper still ignored the extent of Communist aggression in the earlier years, though it pointed out the increased tempo of Communist guerrilla activities in 1959 and, especially, in 1960, *after* the formation of the National Liberation Front was publicly announced by Hanoi. Diem had also attempted an approach to counter Communist insurgency with the creation of the *agrovilles*, the forerunners of the later strategic hamlets and their successors. But the security of the countryside against the Communist conspiracy and attack, which had been the primary aim, was the one thing that was not achieved.

The failure of Diem was twofold. He never really understood the nature of the enemy's strategy and tactics. His awareness of general principles, his own and those of the Communists, crowded out an effective concern for countervailing practice. In this failure to cope with the Communist danger his American allies share responsibility, though they at long last responded with more appropriate measures. Diem's second failure flowed from his lack of understanding of the nature of Communist protracted warfare. He chose, in the final analysis, to be loyal to one Vietnamese institution, the family, rather than to acknowledge his errors and redirect his energies into announced paths of reform which he had seen but not fully comprehended. His own family's misbegotten and misguided advice prevailed. He might have fallen in any case, but perhaps less ignominiously.

8. *The Protracted Conflict, or Long War, Short Campaign*

In the years 1959–60, the Republic of Viet Nam was not quite the success that its friends advertised. Its leaders had not yet found the practical political means for democratic accommodation. Nevertheless, the Republic of Viet Nam had made considerable progress, both in absolute terms and in comparison with its aggressive neighbor to the north. It is conceivable that had it been given time and freedom from attack and militant subversion South Viet Nam would have been able to solve its domestic political problems. But the country and its leaders did not have the time, and they were never free from the threat of Communist aggression and from Communist campaigns designed to destroy the government and take over the country.

Defense against direct invasion from the Communist North was accomplished. Preparation for this was relatively an easy task. When Lieutenant General Samuel ("Hanging Sam") Williams arrived in South Viet Nam at the end of 1955 to relieve General O'Daniel as head of the United States Military Assistance Advisory Group (MAAG), he set about building, training, and providing for an army of 150,000 men, organized for conventional warfare in regiments, divisions, and corps. This military force was mechanized, motorized, and road-conscious; it did not, during the crucial years 1956–59, have the mission assigned to it earlier: direct responsibility for local security, for what O'Daniel had called "spotting Communist guerrillas and Communist efforts at infiltration." These functions were now turned over to the Civil Guard and to the village-based Self-Defense Corps, both of which were put under the jurisdiction of civilian departments of the Vietnamese Government. Since the MAAG did not have responsibility for these units, they were poorly trained, inadequately equipped, and—in the case of the Civil Guard—inadequately paid. They were never equal to the task of countering the Viet Cong.

The decision to change the function and mission of the newly formed Army of the Republic of Viet Nam—a near fatal decision—was made by the Vietnamese Government, but it had the full support of United States officials in Viet Nam and in Washington. It removed from the army the role of providing local security action and the concomitant civic action, such as helping the villages to build access roads, clearing land, providing basic health facilities and medical assistance, and digging wells. The decision was reversed in 1960, after having been hotly argued by military and civilian analysts; it was described in subsequent American military studies as "an error in emphasis and orientation of the nature of MAAG's effort, during the 1956–59 period." The error, as much American as Vietnamese, provided an abundant opportunity for North Viet Nam's aggressors in South Viet Nam to "swim like fish" in the South Vietnamese "sea."

Communist Strategy After 1956

Ho Chi Minh had begun his campaign to take over South Viet Nam, as indicated above, even while the Geneva Conference was still in session. Viet Minh cadres had been picked to remain in the South at carefully selected points; they were later reinforced through the infiltration into the country of Viet Minh soldiers who had gone North during the exchange of forces in 1954–55. The Communists' politico-military network in South Viet Nam remained relatively undetected at first as it started up its separated but planned attacks in the rural areas and infiltrated into the government and into other institutions in the cities.

North Viet Nam's position was not too strong in 1956. It had just lost the battle over the Geneva elections. It had failed to solve its recurring problem of rice deficiency, and this failure had led to a well-publicized peasant uprising against the regime. The regime had become economically dependent on the Soviet Union and on Communist China, receiving from them, in goods and credits, about the same amount in aid—approximately $250 million per year (aside from classified military aid)—that was supplied by the United States to the South. Despite its weaknesses, North Viet Nam was determined to engage in protracted warfare, in the "long war and short campaigns" of Maoist terminology. Saigon's decision to divest its army of local security and police functions played right into Hanoi's hands.

In 1956–57, the Communist network in South Viet Nam stepped up its activity. A campaign of terror, extortion, assassination, and guerrilla action was used to undermine village security. Targets of such activities always include local village officials, civil guards, the members of the Self-Defense Corps, teachers, and, especially, officials sent out from the capital as local administrators of one kind or another. Sometimes these officials were "put on trial" by the Communists, then "sentenced" to death; after execution the bodies were left exposed with a notice pinned on them to indicate that the sentence had been carried out by the "Liberation Forces." The pattern of selective terror grew. By mid-1959, Viet Cong violence of this type accounted for between fifteen and twenty assassinations of provincial-government officials per month; how many less prominent villagers were similarly treated is not known, but many particularly brutal cases of beheading and disembowelment were reported. In May, 1961, President Kennedy indicated that 4,000 low-ranking officials had been killed during the preceding twelve months; the figures mounted in subsequent years. Estimates vary, but as many as 14,000 provincial and local officials, police, teachers, and other personnel are said to have been assassinated by the Viet Cong during Diem's regime.

The strategy of terror paid dividends. When the Viet Cong killed an unpopular government official—and there were scoundrels among the officials—the local population would approve and support the Viet Cong. When the Viet Cong killed a popular one it served as a caution for the local population lest they suffer too. Accommodation with the Viet Cong in the relatively unprotected villages became a way of insuring one's life. In villages remote from regular defense forces, with only intermittent protection, at best, from the police and local security personnel, survival depended on forced cooperation with the superior and resident Viet Cong power.

It should not be inferred, however, that the Viet Cong used terror as the sole weapon to hold the villagers; terror is effective in intimidating the terrorized, but otherwise insufficient to gain positive acceptance. To terror, therefore, the Communists added propaganda about the evils of the central government, never an object of love for the villagers. Their biggest trump was the promise of land, free from fear of returning landlord or other claimant. This use of a combination of terror, propaganda, and land can be seen in a translation of a captured report dated October 14, 1961, made by a delegate to an inter-district meeting of the National Liberation Front.[1] The report describes the experiences of "turning XB village in Kien Phong province into a combattant [Communist-supporting] village." The author of the report explains that in 1959 the "Party members" were instructed to reestablish in this area a Party base that had been destroyed. The first step was to tackle the land question—"the right of owning land or reduction of land rent." The second step was to blacken the reputation of the village leaders, charging that they would favor the landlords. Simultaneously, the Party members wooed "the sympathy of the families" of these same leaders. "It was," writes the unknown author, "a good method." The Party then grew bolder; it "developed and used this slogan: 'Kill the Land Robbers' "—with the clear implication in the report that the slogan was indeed acted on against those who obstructed the Party. The author adds: "Farmers are now free to farm, without paying either land rent or agricultural tax." This "victory" led to the growth and influence of the Party, which, we learn, "also attends to the other needs of the people, such as public health, sanitation, education, maternity facilities . . . [and] marketing their produce at high prices." Once the Party is established in the village, it enrolls the villagers as guerrilla fighters and explains that the "Viet Cong flag means that the people have land to till." In the "self-criticism" section of the report, the author admits that "the Party only led the people to the point where they passively opposed our enemies and were content if the latter did not terrorize the village."

In 1959, the Central Committee of the Lao Dong (Communist) Party of North Viet Nam stepped up its offensive, calling for national unification by "all appropriate means." Despite what has been said to the contrary in recent years, the Northern Communists made no secret at that time of their intention to take over the Republic of Viet Nam. In September of that year, the Viet Cong's 2nd Liberation Battalion routed two companies of South Viet Nam's 23rd Division. In the following January, the same battalion, reinforced to about 500 men, attacked and badly mauled the 32nd Regiment of the South's 21st Infantry Division. In both attacks, the Viet Cong captured weapons and ammunition. Reporting on the second attack, Radio Hanoi on February 5 indicated: "Our attack has inflicted serious losses on the enemy. On our part, thanks to the skill of our commander and the good will of our soldiers, we completely destroyed the enemy."[2]

The political pace was also quickened. The Third Congress of the Lao Dong Party, meeting in September, 1960, resolved "to carry out the socialist revolution in North Viet Nam" and "to liberate South Viet Nam from the ruling yoke of U.S. imperialists, in order to achieve national unity and complete independence and freedom throughout the country." Techniques were to include the rallying of "national and democratic forces" in a "broad national united front directed against the U.S.–Diem clique" in a "protracted struggle."[3] In an address to the congress, Ho Chi Minh spoke of the need to "step up the socialist revolution in the North and the national democratic people's revolution in the South." Here he was restating the familiar Leninist-Maoist strategy of the two-stage revolution: first "national-democratic," then "socialist." Speaking at the same congress, Le Duan, First Secretary of the Party's Central Committee, stressed that the Party must "constantly intensify our solidarity and the organization and education of the people of the South—especially the workers, peasants, and the intellectuals—and must uphold the revolutionary fighting spirit of all strata of patriotic compatriots."

Truong Chinh, a member of the Party's Politburo who had been ousted from office in 1956 because his harsh policies had been held responsible for the peasant uprising, but who was now back in favor, stated in the Party's journal, *Hoc Tap* (April, 1961), that the Third Congress had set forth two strategic objectives: to carry out the socialist revolution within North Viet Nam and to liberate South Viet Nam from the "U.S. imperialists" and their "henchmen" in order to achieve national unity. To attain the second objective, Truong Chinh declared, North Viet Nam is "providing good support to the South Vietnamese revolution, and is serving as a strong basis for the struggle for national reunification."

The broad front that had been foreshadowed at the Party congress was proclaimed on December 20, 1960, by the Communists operating within South Viet Nam, under the name "National Front for the Liberation of South Viet Nam" (NFLSV, or NLF). The Front's manifesto was broadcast by Radio Hanoi in two different versions; the first version, broadcast on January 29, was toned down to conceal its Communist origin and character; the later version, broadcast on February 11, bore a remarkable similarity to the speech made by Le Duan before the Party congress in Hanoi, even using some of the same terminology to describe the Front's aims. A ten-point program was outlined in the manifesto. It declared that the immediate task of the Front was to over-throw the Saigon government—through armed revolution, it was implied. Once South Viet Nam's government had been overthrown, the Front would form a "broad national demo-cratic coalition administration" to "negotiate" with North Viet Nam on "reunification." These and other goals of the Front, such as the adoption of a foreign policy of "peace and neutrality" and the redistribution of land in the South, were identical with the actions long advocated for South Viet Nam in Hanoi's propaganda broadcasts. In the manifesto, however, the goals were phrased in such a manner that the politically inexperienced masses in the South would under-stand them to mean little more than the replacement of the current Saigon government by a more "representative, hu-mane" administration.

The National Liberation Front is a creation of the Lao Dong Party. The over-all direction of the Front is the re-sponsibility of the Lao Dong's Central Committee, within which there exists a "Committee for Supervision of the South." For administrative purposes, the Lao Dong Party has divided South Viet Nam into zones—the highlands and the coastal regions, and the south and southwestern provinces including the Mekong delta. Each zone has an executive com-mittee operating under the Committee for Supervision of the South in Hanoi. The activities of the executive committees include propaganda, training, subversion, and military bases.

Militarily, the Viet Cong operation is directed by the High Command of the People's Army of Viet Nam under close Party supervision. The High Command is responsible for the selection of major targets, for operational plans, for the assignment of the Viet Cong's regular units, for tactical intelligence, and for supplies. The military organization parallels, and is dominated by, the political organization. For example, General Nguyen Don, who is in charge of military affairs in the South-Central zone, is responsible to Tran Luong, Secretary-General of the zone and a member of the Lao Dong Central Committee; the same is true of the other zone, where General Huc Xuyen is responsible to Secretary General Muoi Cuc.

The Central Research Agency, an arm of the Lao Dong and the People's Army of Viet Nam, is an intelligence organization that maintains its headquarters in Hanoi. Its directing committee includes Premier Pham Van Dong and Defense Minister Vo Nguyen Giap. Its principal function is to further the war effort. It maintains special centers throughout Indochina for administration in "liberated" areas, for cadres, communications, infiltration, and espionage. At Vinh, there is a center responsible for intelligence operations in Laos and Cambodia, and at Vinh Linh, one responsible for sending agents and supplies south by sea.

The organizational structure of the National Liberation Front has been analysed by Wesley R. Fishel. Committees were formed

at the regional, provincial, district, and village levels . . . in a structure that paralleled exactly that of the Viet Cong in the South, which in turn was patterned after the Lao Dong Party in the North. A few top leaders were named, all of them with lengthy Party-connected backgrounds. The Chairman, Nguyen Huu Tho, is a lawyer who was involved in pro-Communist political agitation as early as 1947. The first Secretary-General of the Front, Nguyen Van Hieu, was a known pro-Communist journalist who had spent most of his career as head of the "Overt and Covert Propaganda" section of the Communists in the South. Huynh Tan Phat, the present Secretary General, has been involved in Party activities since the mid-1930's. In an attempt to conceal the extent of Communist domination, the NFLSV formed an additional piece of machinery December 19, 1961. The new organization, given the name of the People's Revolutionary Party (Dang Nhan Dan Cach Mang), was to play the role of a separate South Vietnamese Communist Party, thus to lend currency to the fiction that the Communists in the South are independent of those in the North, while simultaneously suggesting that the NFLSV is in truth a union of diverse revolutionary forces, of which the Communists are only one.

Two other "political parties," the Radical Socialist Party and the Democratic Party, were also established and announced to be constituent bodies of the NFLSV. It is interesting that the only two political parties (aside from the Lao Dong Party) permitted to exist in North Vietnam bear almost identical names. In the DRVN they supply a façade of democracy to the political process in the country, and are intended to attract support from the intellectuals and bourgeoisie. One may presume that their function in the South is intended to be of the same character.[4]

This Front comprises a variety of organized units from each significant segment of Vietnamese society—soldiers, peasants, youths, workers, women, intellectuals. In May, 1961, its clandestine radio announced the Front's readiness to carry out the decisions of the Third Congress of the Lao Dong Party "concerning the revolution" in South Viet Nam. The broadcast added that the "exigencies of the revolution" demanded that "cadres and members of the Front as well as those who love their fatherland and the revolution in South Viet Nam must strictly execute the basic and immediate mission determined by the [North Vietnamese Communist] Party." As the Hanoi resolution had indicated, this "is a protracted, hard, and complex process of struggle, combining many forms of struggle of great activity and flexibility." The Viet Cong, the armed Communist forces operating in the Republic of Viet Nam, were the chief instrument of this revolution.

The End of Diem

From 1960 onward, the Communists intensified the struggle both at the guerrilla level and at a level approaching conventional warfare. The Civil Guard and the village Self-Defense Corps proved unequal to the well-prepared attacks staged by the Viet Cong. The South Vietnamese army, which at that time was not prepared to deal with this type of war-fare, had to be retrained, reorganized, and made ready once again—physically and psychologically—for a task that had been shelved four years earlier. As reported by the government, the number of South Vietnamese killed during this transition phase rose from 138 in 1959 to more than 4,000 in 1961. Weapons lost by the Army of the Republic of Viet Nam were reported as being sufficient to equip "twenty or more" Viet Cong battalions. Estimates of the size of the Viet Cong's battalions then ranged from 150 to 300 men, and there was uncertainy about their location.

In 1961, shortly before the April presidential election, the Army of the Republic of South Viet Nam dealt four consecutive defeats to an over-confident Viet Cong. This was just before the monsoon rains slowed down all military activities, and it served to give the Saigon government a chance to take stock and to seek further American assistance. In May, President Kennedy sent Vice President Lyndon B. Johnson to Saigon. It was a reflection of heightened United States concern for the defense of the Republic of Viet Nam. A joint communiqué was issued by Vice President Johnson and President Diem at the close of the visit, on May 13, 1961:

Both Governments recognize that under the circumstances of guerrilla warfare now existing in free Viet Nam, it is necessary to give high priority to the restoration of a sense of security to the people of free Viet Nam. This priority, however, in no way diminishes the necessity, in policies and programs of both Governments, to pursue vigorously appropriate measures in other fields to achieve a prosperous and happy society.

The following measures, agreed in principle and subject to prompt finalization and implementation, represent an increase and acceleration of United States assistance to the Republic of Viet

Nam. These may be followed by more far-reaching measures if the situation, in the opinion of both Governments, warrants.

First, it was agreed by the two Governments to extend and build upon existing programs of military and economic aid and to infuse into their joint actions a high sense of urgency and dedication.

Second, it was agreed, that regular armed forces of the Republic of Viet Nam should be increased, and that the United States would extend its military assistance programs to include support for an additional number of regular Vietnamese armed forces.

Third, it was agreed that the United States would provide military assistance program support for the entire Vietnamese civil guard forces.

Fourth, it was agreed that the two Governments should collaborate in the use of military specialists to assist and work with Vietnamese armed forces in health, welfare and public works activities in the villages of free Viet Nam.

Fifth, it was agreed that the assistance of other free governments to the Government of the Republic of Viet Nam in its trouble against Communist guerrilla forces would be welcome.

Sixth, it was agreed that, to achieve the best possible use of available resources, the Vietnamese and the United States, in prosecution of their joint effort against Communist attacks in Viet Nam, a group of highly qualified economic and fiscal experts would meet in Viet Nam to work out a financial plan on which joint efforts should be based.

Seventh, it was agreed that the United States and the Republic of Viet Nam would discuss new economic and social measures to be undertaken in rural areas, to accompany the anti-guerrilla effort, in order that the people of Viet Nam should benefit promptly from the restoration of law and order in their villages and provinces.

Eighth, it was agreed that, in addition to measures to deal with the immediate Viet Nam guerrilla problem, the two Governments would work together toward a longer range economic development program, including further progress in the fields of agriculture, health, education, fisheries, highways, public administration, and industrial development.

These longer range plans and programs would be developed in detail after further consideration and discussions.

Their goal would be a Viet Nam capable of a self-sustained economic growth.

The Vice President's visit was followed up in October, when the President sent General Maxwell D. Taylor to investigate the military situation in South Viet Nam. The reports presented to President Kennedy by these two missions were, in part, responsible for the reshaping of American policy. In October, President Kennedy ordered a massive increase in military and nonmilitary aid. The President's letter of December 14 (see page 143), a reply to a letter of December 7 from President Ngo Dinh Diem, reaffirmed the agreements worked out between Johnson and Diem.

The Geneva Agreements of 1954 had limited foreign military training missions in South Viet Nam to a total of 327 officers and men. Though not a signatory of these agreements, the United States adhered to the limitation until 1961. Then, after the Lao Dong, the National Liberation Front, and the Viet Cong revealed their plans, the United States doubled the size of its training mission, to approximately 700 officers and men. As the war grew in character and intensity, United States commitment to the Republic and the people of Viet Nam also grew. In 1964, the 700 became 16,000; there were 23,000 at the beginning of 1965, and between 200,000 and 250,000 at the beginning of 1966, direct combat personnel among them. Before February, 1965, the task of the MAAG was to train, supply, and advise the Vietnamese Army, but not to engage in direct combat; it was an unprecedented mission and its duties changed with the ever-changing situation. At that time, nonclassified aid by the United States to Viet Nam, aside from the cost of its own military efforts in the country, was estimated at close to $2 million per day.

In March, 1962, President Kennedy issued an order to all U.S. military and civilian departments in any way involved with the war in Viet Nam to study and to train for the requirements of what became called counterinsurgency. This was the first full and official recognition by the United States Government that it had to prepare more thoroughly for what the Communists had been calling for decades "wars of national liberation"—warfare at the lower end of the spectrum, including guerrilla warfare—warfare not responsive to the arsenal of strategic weapons that had been in America's possession since the end of World War II. Much had been written before then about the Communist wars of national liberation; about the enemy's strategy and tactics of the long war and the short campaign, about American experience of guerrilla warfare since pre-Revolutionary days (for example, Rogers' Rangers in the French and Indian Wars); about utilizing our Asian experiences in World War II (for example with the Chindits, the Marauders, the Kachin Rangers); about learning the lessons of how the Filipinos, under President Magsaysay, defeated the Communist guerrillas; about how the British and the Malays defeated the Communist guerrillas; about how the Burmese withstood and wore down the Communist guerrillas. Nevertheless, the United States had not officially *organized* the men and material to fight such wars where they would be most likely to occur, and had not even initiated a proper study. In Viet Nam, there was a better understanding of the problem. In the words of John Mecklin: "Among guerrilla warfare experts there was no disagreement about the merits of existing principles of strategy and tactics in Viet Nam, if only they could be applied: to patrol and fight at night just as fearlessly and aggressively as the Viet Cong, to bring honest government to the hamlets, to dismiss corrupt officials and inept military commanders, to press home attacks, in short to get out in the muck of the paddies and jungles and destroy the Viet Cong where they lived."[5] Such a policy would have given security to the villagers, and, had it been sustained over a long enough period, it would have made it

possible to effect improvements and ultimately win the full
support of the villagers.

The combination of circumstances and efforts should have
been enough, at that time, to bring an improvement in the
military situation in South Viet Nam. President Diem, re-
elected to a second term, had promised reforms. President
Kennedy had made further commitments to the Vietnamese
and had proceeded to implement them under the new military
and diplomatic team headed by General Paul D. Harkins and
Ambassador Frederick E. Nolting, Jr. In the wider sphere of
political strategy, the United States participated in the Geneva
Conference of 1962 and was a signatory of an agreement that
promised an uncertain future for Laos;[6] it had also taken
steps to assist Thailand beyond the commitments stemming
from the Manila Pact and SEATO, which should have helped
the over-all position in South Viet Nam.

But the fighting and the cause in Viet Nam did not go as
expected. The initiative remained with the Viet Cong. Reports of the fighting spoke for the most part of Viet Cong
—initiated "incidents" and "attacks" and of Vietnamese
"counterattacks" and "defensive operations." Raids, ambushes,
assassinations, kidnaping, extortion, bombings in Saigon, hit-
and-run guerrilla actions, and small-scale skirmishes followed
one upon the other with little, if any, apparent strategic purpose. We heard of far-off places where these occurred and
tried to locate them on unfamiliar maps. We read about the
Communist ability to supply men and matériel through Laos
and Cambodia by way of the so-called Ho Chi Minh Trail; also
across the northwestern corner of the 17th parallel, and even
by sea. There were reports of large areas of Viet Nam occupied in strength, by the Viet Cong, and of other areas of
the countryside where the Viet Cong did not have control by
day but were in control at night. Other reports spoke of the
"strategic hamlets" sponsored by Diem that were supposed to offer protection to the villagers and were said, in
November, 1962, to number between 4,000 and 6,000—

scarcely a year after the program was begun—with a total of 12,000–14,000 planned. There were reports of distrust and animosity between the various ethnic and religious groups within South Viet Nam. Estimates of the time required to put down the Communist insurgency varied between an optimistic three years and a pessimistic fifteen; how these estimates were reached was not made clear. These intermittent flashes of information were typical of a fluid battleground. Disconnected items were reported more or less accurately; the putting together of the separate pieces took place more or less out of sight and sound of the general public. Retrospectively, it has become clear that the decisions taken by President Kennedy and his advisers were essentially of a defensive nature: they prevented the military collapse of the Republic of Viet Nam and denied to the Viet Cong the takeover that they confidently expected.

United States power was there to serve the cause of a free and independent Republic of Viet Nam. It was, so to speak, on loan to the Vietnamese; it was untrammeled by the specter of the reimposition of French colonialism. The difficulties that arose from the use of that power were real. Mistakes were made. The presence of American military advice and matériel was no automatic guarantee of victory in battle. American officers, too, had to learn from experience as well as from military doctrine what combination of men and weapons would be successful under the conditions obtaining in Viet Nam.[7]

For the military problems there were solutions. For the problem posed by Diem and his family there was none—but not for want of trying; the internal political issues between the Diem family on the one side and the large group of equally patriotic, non-Communist Vietnamese on the other proved to be insoluble. Diem preached democracy, but did not practice it—though, apparently, when preaching it he thought he was truly practicing it too. To the peasants, that meant little; they wanted security, stability, and improvement in their living conditions—in that order—without giving much thought to democratic ideals. But Diem was never able to convince the peasants that he was fighting on their side to attain their aims and, as a result, he could not enlist their full support in fighting against Viet Nam's Communist enemies. What Viet Nam needed was support for the concept "unite and fight." Diem was not the man to encourage this. He alienated his near peers, the educated and semi-educated civilian and military "elites." By suspicion, mistrust, and disdain; by the bribery, corruption, and sycophancy that were instruments of his policy; by power ploys engineered by his brother Ngo Dinh Nhu on the classic formula "divide and rule," he lost their support.

President Kennedy and Ambassador Henry Cabot Lodge tried to save Diem, essentially by trying to disengage him from his supreme political adviser, his evil (and at the end, perhaps crazed) brother Ngo Dinh Nhu, and the sinister Madame Nhu. The President and the Ambassador tried persuasion; they tried pressure by suspending a portion of the nonmilitary aid program, the commercial import projects on which the Diem government depended for budgetary support. They sent personal emissaries and messages.

In the end, Diem remained loyal to his family. There have been many and varied accounts of Diem's ultimate fall; blame has been variously apportioned. The search for the full story will go on, but it is doubtful whether it will ever be fully ascertained.[8] The final incidents that led to the coup were a train of abuses, no single one of which was necessarily more important than any other, even though the dramatic Buddhist crisis (the riots in Hué in May, 1963; the self-immolation of Buddhist monks; and, finally, the resignation of Viet Nam's Foreign Minister and the Ambassador to Washington —Madame Nhu's father—in August) is frequently cited as the final straw; it was one straw, a dramatic one. The elections for the National Assembly on September 27, in which Ngo Dinh Nhu and his wife were returned unopposed, did not propitiate the growing opposition. Finally, on November 1, the leading generals in the army staged a coup. The Presidential Palace was taken the following morning; Ngo Dinh Diem and Ngo Dinh Nhu escaped, were captured, and put to death. A similar fate later befell a third brother, Ngo Dinh Can, the "War Lord of the Center."

The United States Commitment Stands

Lyndon B. Johnson, succeeding to the Presidency after the assassination of President Kennedy in November, 1963—just three weeks after the overthrow of Diem—was faced immediately by the turmoil in Viet Nam. The instabilities of its governments, the musical chairs played by rival generals, the intermittent emergence of respected but conflicting civilian leaders, gave rise to cynical scoffing coupled with shock and dismay. President Johnson had to decide afresh the ways in which America's treaty ally, the Republic of Viet Nam, could best be helped.

Until February, 1965, President Johnson continued the general lines of the policies that he had helped to formulate in the joint communiqué with Diem in Saigon on May 13, 1961, as they were further amplified during 1962–63. In line with this policy, the United States continued to supply, train, and advise the Army of the Republic of Viet Nam on an increasing scale. At the beginning of 1964, the Vietnamese Army numbered over 200,000 men, with an equal number in the Civil Guard and Self-Defense Forces. At that time the Viet Cong was estimated to have some 30,000 highly trained hard-core troops operating in platoon, company, battalion, and even regiment-sized units. The Viet Cong was supported by an estimated 80,000–100,000 men in local guerrilla and paramilitary units. Thus, in 1964, the Vietnamese Army outnumbered the Viet Cong by nearly four to one. Earlier military experience in Malaya and elsewhere in Southeast Asia had suggested that the desirable ratio for defeating similar insurrections should be ten or even fifteen to one; such ratios, though frequently quoted, are misleading. The helicopter, for example, which was not available for wide use in earlier counterinsurgency wars, has been invaluable as a weapon in South Viet Nam, where its mobility and versatility have made a substantial difference in the ratio of forces required to counter guerrilla action. By February, 1966, it was estimated that the number of Vietnamese soldiers, in military and paramilitary units, and of Americans, Koreans, Australians, and New Zealanders fighting alongside them, totaled about 900,000 men; the Viet Cong forces, together with soldiers of the North Vietnamese Army fighting in South Viet Nam, totaled about 230,000. The ratio of four to one has thus remained unchanged.

The first noticeable change in the Administration's Viet Nam policy came in the summer of 1964. On August 2 and 4, North Vietnamese motor patrol boats attacked the warships U.S.S. *Maddox* and U.S.S. *C. Turner Joy* in international waters in the Gulf of Tonkin. President Johnson ordered an immediate reply, and on August 4 United States aircraft struck against bases from which North Viet Nam's torpedo boats had been operating.

On August 7, 1964, the United States Congress passed the following joint resolution:

Whereas naval units of the Communist regime in Viet Nam, in violation of the principles of the Charter of the United Nations and of international law, have deliberately and repeatedly attacked United States naval vessels lawfully present in international waters, and have thereby created a serious threat to international peace; and

Whereas these attacks are part of a deliberate and systematic campaign of aggression that the Communist regime in North Viet Nam has been waging against its neighbors and the nations joined with them in the collective defense of their freedom; and

Whereas the United States is assisting the peoples of Southeast Asia to protect their freedom and has no territorial, military or political ambitions in that area, but desires only that these peoples should be left in peace to work out their own destinies in their own way: Now, therefore, be it

Resolved by the Senate and House of Representatives of the United States of America in Congress assembled, That the Congress approves and supports the determination of the President, as Commander in Chief, to take all necessary measures to repel any armed attack against the forces of the United States and to prevent further aggression.

Sec. 2. The United States regards as vital to its national interest and to world peace the maintenance of international peace and security in Southeast Asia. Consonant with the Constitution of the United States and the Charter of the United Nations and in accordance with its obligations under the Southeast Asia Collective Defense Treaty, the United States is, therefore, prepared, as the President determines, to take all necessary steps, including the use of armed force, to assist any member or protocol state of the Southeast Asia Collective Defense Treaty requesting assistance in defense of its freedom.

Sec. 3. This resolution shall expire when the President shall determine that the peace and security of the area is reasonably assured by international conditions created by action of the United Nations or otherwise, except that it may be terminated earlier by concurrent resolution of the Congress.*

The Resolution, supportive of the SEATO Treaty and the various commitments of preceding presidents, was regarded by President Johnson as constituting prior Congressional approval for all subsequent action, but no further military measures were carried out against North Viet Nam during 1964.

In the fall of 1964, repeating a theme I had expounded several years earlier, I wrote that it was long past time to heed the advice of Clausewitz and proceed to the "swift transition to the attack [as] the most brilliant point of the defensive."

This calls for a major decision, beyond the defensive action in the Gulf of Tonkin, to reject the notion that the war must be fought

* The vote in the Senate was 98–2; in the House, 416–0. In 1966, an attempt to "terminate" this resolution was defeated by a motion to table, 95–5.

solely on R.V.N. soil. The way to defend Saigon is by threatening, penetrating, undermining and attacking North Viet Nam. If this "swift transition" is confined to a limited objective—namely, the defense of South Viet Nam—the risk of escalation is small. Interdiction of Communist resupply of men and material, not the conquest of North Viet Nam, is the goal. The accomplishment of this strategic mission—sealing off the borders against infiltration and invasion by offensive and defensive tactics—would eventually lighten the Vietnamese burden in countering Communist insurgency, for the Viet Cong would henceforth be deprived of external land and sea resupply of trained manpower and material. It would advance the timetable for victory.[9]

The basic change in the President's policy came in February, 1965. The Viet Cong, with fairly sophisticated weapons of Russian and Chinese manufacture that were supplied to them by Hanoi, had launched a series of attacks against the American forces in Pleiku in the central highlands and at Nha Trang on the coast. President Johnson, charging "provocations ordered and directed by the Hanoi regime," thereupon ordered an air strike at major staging and transportation centers around Dong Hoi, in the southern part of North Viet Nam. At long last, after years of political provocation and military aggression directed from Hanoi, the Vietnamese-United States alliance responded against the enemy *on his own soil*. The battle was now joined, on the conventional warfare level as well as on the guerrilla level practised by the Viet Cong.

Despite the outcry against the U.S. bombings of targets in North Viet Nam (of which I shall say more below), one would be hard pressed to find in recent history another example of self-restraint exercised by a big power over so long a period. North Viet Nam had deliberately made war on the South, though it had bound itself to refrain from war. The United States had become an ally of the South at a time when no further war between the two states had been expected. Eventually, after this unprovoked war had begun, the United

States recognized its obligation to its ally and slowly, and with many misgivings, assumed a responsible role in this alliance, a role which was defined, until as late as February, 1965, as one of assistance and advice only. It was only then that the decision was taken to punish the aggressor in the way aggressors should be punished: on their own territory. Even so, the United States has taken only limited action, pausing twice in its bombing attacks to explore the possibility of negotiating an honorable peace. Throughout most of 1965 and 1966, the United States made it clear that it was prepared for "unconditional discussions" among the governments involved, so as to achieve this peace. All such efforts have thus far failed.

The American commitment to the Republic of Viet Nam, in the several stages of its development under Presidents Eisenhower, Kennedy, and Johnson stands. No American who studies the full record can escape the commitment expressed in President Eisenhower's letter of October, 1954, and in the Manila (SEATO) Pact; no one can escape the facts of the further commitments by Presidents and Congress. At some date in the future, it is conceivable, such obligations may be withdrawn. For the present, and until they are repudiated, they cannot be denied. It is to the honor of our country that we have fulfilled a solemnly undertaken obligation. Obligations of this sort are responsive to change but, thus far, there is no reason to alter the commitment.

part four

What Is at Stake in Viet Nam?

9. *To Guarantee the Independence of the Republic of Viet Nam*

The Strike Against the North

On February 7, 1965, at President Johnson's order, forty-nine United States carrier-based fighter-planes bombed and strafed north of the 17th parallel, in what were at that time called "retaliatory and limited responses against Communist military installations." Intelligence had shown these installations to have been in active use by the North Vietnamese for the training and infiltration of Viet Cong personnel into South Viet Nam.

In a letter to the U.N. Security Council on that day, the Permanent Representative of the United States of America, Adlai Stevenson, spoke of the large numbers of armed and trained soldiers, and of military equipment, that had been sent into South Viet Nam from North Viet Nam: "Infiltration in such numbers can hardly be labelled 'indirect aggression,' though that form of aggression is illegal too. What we are witnessing in Viet Nam today is a sustained attack across a frontier set by international agreement." Mr. Stevenson said that the pattern of North Vietnamese aggression included:

. . . the infiltration of armed personnel to make war against the legitimate government of South Viet Nam, the arming of terrorist gangs in South Viet Nam, the assassination of local officials as an instrument of policy, the continued fighting in Laos in violation of the Geneva Agreements, and deliberate, systematic and flagrant violations of international agreements by the regime in Hanoi which signed them and which by all tenets of decency, law and civilized practice is bound by their provisions. The Republic of Viet Nam, and at its request the Government of the United States and other governments, are resisting this systematic and continuing aggression. Since reinforcement of the Viet Cong by infiltrators from North Viet Nam is essential to this continuing aggression, counter measures to arrest such reinforcement from the outside are a justified measure of self-defense.

On March 8, U.N. Secretary-General U Thant called for a preliminary conference to consider a settlement, naming the United States, U.S.S.R., England, France, Communist China, and the two Viet Nams as conferees. On the same day, Pham Van Dong, Premier of the Democratic Republic of [North] Viet Nam, issued a statement calling for the "correct implementation of the fundamental provisions" of the Geneva Agreements. His demands were, in brief:

The "basic national rights" of the Vietnamese people—independence, sovereignty, unity and territorial integrity—should be recognized. The United States Government should withdraw its troops and all war material from Viet Nam, dismantle its "bases" there, abolish its "military alliance" with South Viet Nam and stop its attacks on North Viet Nam.

Pending the peaceful reunification of Viet Nam, the military provisions of the 1954 Geneva Agreements must be respected. There must be no foreign military alliances, arms, or troops in either North or South Viet Nam.

The affairs of South Viet Nam must be settled by the South Vietnamese people themselves "in accordance with the program of the South Viet Nam National Front for Liberation without any foreign intervention."

The realization of the peaceful reunification of Viet Nam must be settled by the people of the two zones without any foreign interference.

The United States requested a clarification of Hanoi's terms but, to this date (July, 1966), such clarification has not been received. It is reported that, at that time, U Thant believed that the United States had not responded to his offer of assistance. What may have seemed unclear in March, 1965, was made perfectly clear in the next month, when North Viet Nam roundly rejected any U.N. initiative. The following week a group of seventeen nonaligned countries (Afghanistan, Algeria, Ceylon, Cyprus, Ethiopia, Ghana, Guinea, India, Iraq, Kenya, Nepal, Syria, Tunisia, Uganda, United Arab Republic, Yugoslavia, and Zambia) issued a moderate statement urging the parties concerned to start negotiations without any preconditions.

On April 7, President Johnson, referring to the appeal of the seventeen nations, made a major foreign policy address at Johns Hopkins University. In it, he defined the United States' purpose:

The world as it is in Asia is not a serene or peaceful place. The first reality is that North Viet Nam has attacked the independent nation of South Viet Nam. Its object is total conquest.

Of course, some of the people of South Viet Nam are participating in attack on their own government. But trained men and supplies, orders and arms, flow in a constant stream from North to South.

This support is the heartbeat of the war. . . . The confused nature of this conflict cannot mask the fact that it is the new face of an old enemy. It is an attack by one country upon another. And the object of that attack is a friend to which we are pledged.

Over this war, and all Asia, is another reality: the deepening shadow of Communist China. The rulers in Hanoi are urged on by Peking. This is a regime which has destroyed freedom in Tibet, attacked India, and been condemned by the United Nations for aggression in Korea. It is a nation which is helping the forces of violence in almost every continent. The contest in Viet Nam is part of a wider pattern of aggressive purpose. . . .

There are those who say that all our effort there will be futile, that China's power is such it is bound to dominate all Southeast Asia. But there is no end to that argument until all the nations of Asia are swallowed up.

There are those who wonder why we have a responsibility there. We have it for the same reason we have a responsibility for the defense of freedom in Europe. World War II was fought in both Europe and Asia, and when it ended we found ourselves with continued responsibility for the defense of freedom.

Our objective is the independence of South Viet Nam, and its freedom from attack. We want nothing for ourselves, only that the people of South Viet Nam be allowed to guide their own country in their own way.

We will do everything necessary to reach that objective. . . . We will not be defeated. We will not grow tired. We will not withdraw, either openly or under the cloak of a meaningless agreement. . . .

Once this is clear, then it should also be clear that the only path for reasonable men is the path of peaceful settlement.

Such peace demands an independent South Viet Nam securely guaranteed and able to shape its own relationships to all others, free from outside interference, tied to no alliance, a military base for no other country.

These are the essentials of any final settlement.

We will never be second in the search for such a peaceful settlement in Viet Nam.

There may be many ways to this kind of peace: in discussion or negotiation with the governments concerned; in large groups or in small ones; in the reaffirmation of old agreements or their strengthening with new ones.

We have stated this position over and over again fifty times and more, to friend and foe alike. And we remain ready, with this purpose, for unconditional discussions. . . .

No President could have been more explicit or more generous. The day after this address, U Thant said that President Johnson's announcement of U.S. readiness to enter into "unconditional discussions" was "both constructive and statesmanlike," and that it was likely to be very helpful.

On April 13, the Communist authorities in Hanoi publicly rebuffed the appeal of the seventeen nonaligned countries as "inappropriate," and branded as such "any approach tending to secure a United Nations intervention in the Viet Nam situation." Two days earlier, North Viet Nam had denounced

President Johnson's offer for "unconditional discussions." All other attempts by numerous Western and nonaligned parties, and by Pope Paul VI, aimed at bringing Hanoi to the conference table have thus far similarly failed. President Johnson tried on two other occasions to bring about an atmosphere for negotiations by suspending air attacks on North Viet Nam for five days in May, 1965, and for a thirty-seven day period in December, 1965, and January, 1966.

Various statements continued to be made by both sides on the conditions under which negotiations might be held, especially in January, 1966, during the pause in United States air strikes. The two positions at that time were summarized in *The New York Times* of January 17. The North Vietnamese had in no way departed from the Four Points of March, 1965. The United States had amplified its position and was offering a fourteen-point proposal:

1. The United States accepts the 1954 and 1962 Geneva accords as a "good enough basis for negotiation."

2. It would welcome a conference on Southeast Asia or any part of Asia.

3. It is ready for unconditional *negotiations*.

4. It is also ready, if Hanoi so prefers, for *informal* unconditional *discussions*.

5. A cease-fire could be the first order of business at a peace conference, or could be arranged preliminary to such a conference.

6. The United States is willing to discuss the North Vietnamese Four-Point Program.

7. It seeks no military bases in Southeast Asia.

8. It does not seek a continuing American military presence in South Viet Nam.

9. It will support the holding of free elections.

10. The question of the reunification of the two Viet Nams can be determined by the free decision of their peoples.

11. The countries of Southeast Asia may choose to be nonaligned or neutral; the United States seeks no new allies.

12. The United States is prepared to contribute $1 billion to a regional development program in which North Viet Nam could take part.

13. The Viet Cong would have no difficulty in having its views represented at a conference, after hostilities have ceased.

14. The bombing will be stopped if it is stated what would happen as a result of that.

Amplifications Nos. 6 and 14 offered no difficulties. The softening represented in the acceptance (Point No. 1) of the Geneva Agreements of 1954 and 1962 as a "good enough basis for negotiation" may create more problems than it solves. The reference to the Viet Cong (No. 13) ran into a wall of opposition from our Vietnamese allies—as it should. To offer the Viet Cong a position in the negotiations would be like the boy who murdered his parents and then asked the judge for clemency on the ground that he was an orphan. In any event, it became clear throughout the world that the United States *had* a policy and was determined to carry it out. No one could accuse the Johnson Administration of neglecting the Vietnamese issue!

There is little doubt that President Johnson's policy—both in its military and nonmilitary aspects—helped to save South Viet Nam from the internal dissensions that followed the successful coup against Diem and protected it against the vigorous thrusts of the Viet Cong, who were being bolstered by North Vietnamese Communist troops infiltrated for what the Communists had expected to be the final *coup de grâce*. Since June, 1965, a new regime of military figures, headed by Major General Nguyen Van Thieu as head of state and Air Marshal Nguyen Cao Ky as Premier, has held office in Saigon. Slowly but effectively, they managed—to the summer of 1966—to restore military discipline and civilian order to South Vietnamese life. The internal conflicts among various ambitious sectors of the South Vietnamese elites—military, religious, and civilian—seem to have abated. This was a reflection of the rise in morale that stemmed, in part, from the American determination to punish North Viet Nam for its aggression, and from the commitment of massive American forces—together with Australian, Korean, New Zealand, and other troops—to engage the Viet Cong in direct combat alongside the soldiers of South Viet Nam. But this was a respite from the round of controversy succeeding the coup in November, 1963. Where it will end at this writing is not clear. Once again national, free elections are to be held. Once again, the United States and its non-Vietnamese allies are fully engaged against the Communist enemy. But the Vietnamese have not yet resolved their internal arrangements—a task they have been working at since the first justified expression of dissatisfaction against Diem.

Just one year after President Johnson's long-overdue decision to carry the battle into North Viet Nam, in February, 1966, the United States and South Viet Nam met at Honolulu. At Honolulu there emerged a renewed and encouraging dedication to the execution of the requirements for the defeat of this Communist war of national liberation. These requirements were foreshadowed in President Eisenhower's decision of 1954, in Senator Kennedy's keen analysis of 1956, and in President Kennedy's order of 1962 to study counterinsurgency. Unfortunately, though each administration has added further elements of support—political, economic, or military— for the Republic of Viet Nam, the right combination had not been found that would enable the Vietnamese to liquidate the Communist insurrection. What helped to turn the tide were the decisions taken in February, 1965, which were implemented in Saigon during the months preceding the Honolulu Conference by the most experienced United States team yet fielded there—Ambassador Henry Cabot Lodge; his special counterinsurgency assistant, Major General Edward T. Lansdale (Ret.); and General William C. Westmoreland, commander of the United States forces in Viet Nam, each supported by loyal, hard-working American assistants, experi-

enced in economic aid, public information, and political and
military matters.*

Before we turn to the Honolulu meeting and its implications, we must first look at the curious phenomenon of an
aberrant American behavioral pattern—encouraged from
"friends" and enemies abroad—which erupted in the days and
months following President Johnson's decision in February,
1965, to bomb selective military targets in the aggressor's
North Vietnamese territory.

Reaction at Home

If President Johnson had with the vote of the Congress formally declared war on the D.R.V.N., much of what occurred
most probably would not have occurred. But he did not "declare" war. His reasons for not doing so were both directly
and obliquely indicated. In the first place, all the official acts of
the various Chief Executives and the Congresses had, in his
expressed view, already validated the actions—including the
attacks against the North—he had taken. Second, though he
had ordered air strikes against North Viet Nam, the targets
were zoned and limited to those military, transport, and communication facilities the incapacitation of which would slow
down or interdict the supply of military personnel and mate-

---

* In addition to the Presidential and Congressional documents cited
in the text in support of the American commitment to Viet Nam, the
following treaties and other agreements should be better known and
understood. The first of these dates from the Truman Administration,
an Economic and Technical Cooperation Agreement signed in Saigon in
September, 1951. In 1955, this Agreement was re-negotiated directly
with the State of Viet Nam. See *Treaties and Other International Agreements Series* (*TIAS* 2346 and 3640). The Protocol of the Southeast Asia
Collective Defense Treaty (*TIAS* 3170) specifically extended to "the free
territory under the jurisdiction of the State of Viet Nam" the economic
and social benefits enumerated in Article III of the Treaty, and the "common defense" provisions enumerated in the three paragraphs of Article IV.
Defense agreements of various types were negotiated in 1955 (*TIAS*
3563), and reiterated in a Joint Communiqué of President Eisenhower and
Premier Diem on May 11, 1957. A Treaty of Amity and Economic Relations (*TIAS* 4890) was signed in 1961.

rial from the North to the Viet Cong rebels in the South. Third, President Johnson was, as he said, desirous of avoiding escalating the war. And by this he meant at least two things. First, as he repeated frequently, he did not want to destroy North Viet Nam or its government. He aimed at negotiating with it for a future of possible peace. He had no designs on the Communist North except to have its leaders negotiate and for the end of the supplying and fighting in the South. The United States, in other words, was attacking the military potential with which aggression was directed against the South; it was not attacking the people of North Viet Nam. Second, although he did not explicitly say so, he wanted to avoid the *direct* involvement in the war of the U.S.S.R. or Communist China (or both). Though these Communist countries were aiding Hanoi as a country in the so-called socialist camp— Hanoi could not have successfully survived its domestic difficulties without Sino-Soviet aid since 1954—their military aid, consisting of skilled military officers, technicians, and material, had not yet exceeded these elements. A United States declaration of war and the use of United States power against North Viet Nam *as a state* ran the risk of inviting war with either the U.S.S.R. or Communist China, or both. Hence the declared objective of the President was interdiction, not destruction, of Hanoi. The risk was real; but it could be argued that a declaration of war, with the creation of a combined Allied war command, to a large extent would have settled the issue at home and would more rapidly end the actual war.

The undeclared war in Viet Nam commanded increasing and more critical attention in the United States, because of the costs in American casualties and funds, growing doubts as to the stability of successive South Vietnamese governments, and the risks of upward escalation since the first "retaliatory" strikes in the Gulf of Tonkin in August, 1964, and the "limited" strikes beginning in February, 1965. The Kennedy Administration had issued a two-part White Paper, *A Threat to the Peace, North Viet Nam's Effort to Conquer South*

Viet Nam, in December, 1961; the Johnson Adminstration followed a similar pattern with an updated, edited version of the same, *Aggression from the North, The Record of North Viet-Nam's Campaign to Conquer South Viet Nam*, in February, 1965. The intensity of the reaction to the second White Paper, in contrast to the tepid reception accorded the first, was immediately evident. Comment ranged from moderate approval—a better job could have been done with the data since 1961 instead of "lifting" so many paragraphs from the earlier White Paper—to widely expressed sharp antagonism.

United States Senatorial voices calling for "withdrawal" and its simulacrum, "negotiations," were supported by resolutions from the World Council of Churches (which also condemned the "artificial isolation" of Communist China from the United Nations), and by the U.N. Secretary General, who underlined his intervention with the blunt suggestion that the United States forces withdraw "from that part of the world." Sections of the academic and other intellectual communities became vociferous. Those who attended the "teach-in" in Washington, D.C., May 15, 1965, seemed preponderantly in favor of withdrawal and negotiation. Those aligning themselves with this position frequently argued that the Geneva Accords of 1954 or of 1962, or the U.N. Charter, or some combination of these, supported their views. Some alleged that the United States had violated one or more provisions of these instruments. Curiously and significantly, few of these voices were heard when these international agreements were breached by members of the Communist camp.

Those who oppose current United States policy in Viet Nam, i.e., the attacks on Communist North Viet Nam, base their argument on assertions such as these:

1. The conflict in South Viet Nam (the Republic of Viet Nam) is a civil war between contending forces.

2. The Saigon government is at best unrepresentative of the people of the R.V.N., at worst a despotic dictatorship.

In either case, it merits neither American official support nor sympathy; nor is it necessarily to be preferred to the opposition, the Viet Cong.

3. As a general principle, the United States should not intervene in affairs of this sort. The people of the country should determine their future. But if the United States remains involved in the affairs of South Viet Nam, it should certainly be willing to discuss or negotiate with both sides of this civil war, the leaders of Saigon and the leaders of the Viet Cong.

4. Therefore, the United States is in grave error, or is immoral, or is aggressive in attacking North Viet Nam, a country whose policies and actions have nothing to do with South Viet Nam. Worse, we are attacking and invading a country which has unredressed grievances because of South Viet Nam's unwillingness to abide by the decisions of the Geneva Accords of 1954.

Examination of these assertions demonstrates that they are either wholly or partially false, i.e., unfactual or untrue; that therefore they do not logically or historically support the conclusion summarized in item 4 above. Let us look at these assertions more closely.

The issue of "civil war": In a literal sense, the war in South Viet Nam is a "war between citizens." That is, a number of citizens of the R.V.N. are in conflict with citizens in and of the government of that country since it became a recognized government by international agreement in 1954. But there is nothing in international law or custom that prevents other governments from supporting governments in power when civil strife breaks out. And if the government in power has entered into agreements with external governments, the latter are presumably bound by the terms of such agreements, especially in the case of conflict.

The United States and the Republic of Viet Nam have, as indicated above, signed a variety of agreements since the latter was internationally recognized as a sovereign state in 1954. Thus, by law and custom, it is proper that the United States assist the successor governments of the newly established state until the mutually accepted agreements are no longer in force. We need not approve a government when we sustain an agreement with it. Many Americans, for example, were and are opposed to the Soviet Government before and since we exchanged instruments of recognition with it in the first Franklin D. Roosevelt Administration. Similarly, many Americans are opposed to Franco's government in Spain. But in neither case are we legally or morally relieved of our mutual obligations until such time as we denounce or abrogate the instruments which define such obligations. There is here, therefore, no contravention of international law or custom in American assistance to the successor governments of South Viet Nam. But this is only the beginning of the brief.

As has already been pointed out (in Chapter 4), neither the United States nor the State (Republic) of Viet Nam bound itself to the Geneva Declaration; in any event, both the Declaration and the signed Agreements were breached by the D.R.V.N., thereby relieving the United States and the R.V.N. from any voluntarily assumed obligations under Geneva's terms.

But most of all, the war in Viet Nam is not wholly a civil war, and there is serious question as to whether it was ever a civil war.

The issue of representative government. The government of the Republic of Viet Nam came into being under legitimate monarchical institutions. By referendum it became a republic. Four times since then its citizens have participated in national elections—once for the President and three times for members of the National Assembly. Whatever criticisms there may be of these elections, they are accorded in international law the sign of legitimacy. Since the coups of 1963, there have been military governments in power. These have been recognized by the United States and by other states. How representative of the people have these governments been? It is difficult to say precisely. But they are the existing governments. And the most recent one promises in time to restore the electoral process. The opportunity for change within the system, in contrast to the lack of such opportunity in a Communist system, establishes the basis for dealing with it in a friendly fashion.

The issue of intervention: Geneva 1954 provided for regroupment and exchange of partisans and supporters in the "zones" north and south of the 17th parallel. At least 860,000 northerners voluntarily came south. Some 100,000 Viet Minh cadres, inclusive of their dependents in the South, were repatriated to the North. French troops in the North were evacuated. But other Viet Minh cadres, the so-called irregulars not covered in Geneva 1954, were left in the South. Viet Minh cadres were Communist trained. They had led the fight against French imperialism throughout the states of Indochina and had also fought those anti-French nationalists who refused to join the Communist cadres.

It was these illegal, nonrepatriated Viet Minh cadres with caches of arms and munitions who in the South became the Fatherland Front, the Communist "Army of Liberation," the Viet Cong. As P. J. Honey has pointed out:

When Ho Chi Minh agreed to participate in the Geneva conference of 1954, Le Duan, First Secretary of North Viet Nam's Communist Party, was commanding the resistance movement in South Viet Nam and was not consulted. After his return to North Viet Nam he criticized Ho's decision as incorrect, arguing that public opinion in France at the time would not have permitted any French government to continue the war, so Ho might have successfully demanded control of the whole of Viet Nam by pursuing a more intransigent policy. The acceptance of negotiations, insisted Le Duan, led to the division of Viet Nam and the need for a further war. That such a war would indeed be necessary became clear when Ngo Dinh Diem restored peace to the South and a considerable measure of economic progress. Le Duan himself was appointed to go secretly to the South and establish the Viet Cong insurgent movement there, and he greatly enhanced his own reputation by taking credit for the Viet Cong's past successes.[1]

Le Duan is, according to Honey, one of the most powerful of the North Viet Nam Communist leaders, and has been supported in his intransigence by Peking, and has staked his party position on the war in the South.

This record of continuous armed intervention by the North in the South was and is either ignored by critics, or excused by them on two grounds. The first justifies the armed intervention as an act warranted by, or a consequence of, Diem's refusal to hold elections—a decision between the French and the Viet Minh which he explicitly rejected, as he had every right to do. Such reasoning for the Communist North's intervention can be found in the views expounded by Professors George McT. Kahin and John W. Lewis.[2]

The second view is more complicated—and more dangerous. In the words of Professor Hans Morgenthau, we should "disengage" in Viet Nam so as to ensure our "cooperation with the Soviet Union [against Communist China] in support of a Titoist [Ho Chi Minh] all-Vietnamese Government. . . . Our interests in Southeast Asia are identical with those of the Soviet Union: to prevent the expansion of the *military* power of China." He accepts China's political and cultural dominance over mainland Asia "as a fact of life." The only alternative: China has to be "conquered."[3]

These arguments against United States support for a treaty ally are designed to reward the aggressor or to offer a sacrifice on the altar of an illusory "balance of power" thesis. Not one shred of evidence exists that the Soviet Union wants an alliance—even if it were desirable—against Communist China. Nor has any convincing argument been made that Ho Chi Minh would or could become a Tito—since, unlike Yugoslavia's geographical position vis-à-vis the U.S.S.R., North Viet Nam borders on Communist China. And further, what merit does a Communist Ho-Tito have which is superior even to the military dictatorship of South Viet Nam? Especially since the latter wants to, and probably can, find the way to transform itself into a representative civilian regime?

Hanoi may have thought that with the gradual withdrawal of the French, who under the terms of Geneva 1954 retained certain military training and supply prerogatives in South Viet Nam, the latter would easily fall prey to the Communist "Army of Liberation," especially as the new government in the South was sorely tried by private armies of the then dissident sects, the Cao Dai and Hoa Hao, and by the Binh Xuyen.

The government in South Viet Nam did not fall then. Quite the contrary, it made significant security and economic gains. So, in 1958 Hanoi began to step up its campaign against Saigon. Its government radio broadcast instructions to the Viet Minh armed forces and political cadres in the South. The text of this monitored broadcast was supplied on September 16, 1958, to the International Control Commission created at Geneva in 1954. The ICC had been and remained stultified in its operations because (a) Hanoi would not permit it to make free inspections, and (b) its Indian chairman refused to act unless he had the unanimous approval of the two other members, Poland and Canada, and Poland never voted for an action which might turn to the disadvantage of the Communist North.

In October, Hanoi launched a special appeal to the *montagnards* of South Viet Nam to "fight against the South government," promising that "the government and the people of North are prepared to help. . . . Our beloved Ho is standing behind you." In 1959, Ho was quoted in the Belgian Communist *Red Flag*, July 10, 1959, as saying that the Communist North must complete the "anti-imperialist revolution in the South in order to unify the country."

Such statements, accompanied by acts of infiltration, attempted subversion, and warfare—the warfare of the so-called wars of national liberation—have continued in South Viet Nam since its independence in 1954. Even the ICC, in June, 1962—at a time when India momentarily was stung into action because of the invasion of its territory by the Communists from China—issued a Special Report of the majority of the ICC which declared that armed and unarmed personnel, arms, munitions, and other supplies have been sent from the zone in the North (the Hanoi government) to the zone in the South with the object of supporting, organizing, and carrying out hostile activities, including armed attacks, directed against the armed forces and administration of the zone in the South (the Saigon government).

The ICC added that these acts were violations of the Geneva Accords. To which, on December 11, 1962, the D.R.V.N. replied that the issue of subversive activities (in which, it did not deny, it was engaged) is a question which has no relevance to the Geneva Agreements, hence it would continue as it pleased.

This is war—undeclared in a formal sense—but war by invasion. And at long last, a President of the United States has so named it. The only response to this war is either capitulation or defense against invasion as well as suppression of its civil war aspects. And not until February 7, 1965, did the United States came to the assistance of its ally and friend, the government of South Viet Nam, with the *means* and with the *tactics* historically employed when possible to stop an invasion, that is *to stop invasion at its source in North Viet Nam.* This is what the Vietnamese, the Americans, and other allies are presently doing after some ten years of suffering from such attacks.

Finally, I submit that the principle of nonintervention requires additional scrutiny and more precise definition. In one sense, all countries intervene in the affairs of the countries with which they have diplomatic relations—they try to influence responses and behavior. This, together with less polite forms of intervention, such as intelligence gathering and espionage, is generally acceptable. Intervention as a consequence of treaty or other agreements, especially when invited by a contracting party, is always also acceptable. Intervention even in the absence of a treaty when called for by a friendly or otherwise recognized government is permissible. Unilateral intervention, that is, without agreement or invitation, becomes justly suspect. Self-defense and protection of lives and property are standard although not necessarily sufficient reasons to warrant intervening acts. The verdict of history must pass on intervention in such cases.

But there is another variety of intervention which may well set a new pattern in international relations. The Russian invasion of Hungary and the North Vietnamese invasion of South Viet Nam were designed to install governments of the aggressors' choice in countries with internationally recognized governments. In the instance of the Russians, physical measures were not used by others outside Hungary to stop them because, it was agreed, the Russians were merely forcibly changing their *own* guard, Kadar for Nagy. In the case of South Viet Nam, physical measures at long last are being used to stop the North Vietnamese because the latter wish to change the guard *and* the system which legally, morally, and otherwise creates the guard and which offers, potentially, an opportunity to choose guards. It is to safeguard that system —based in the long run on freedom to change—that intervention *even* in the absence of a treaty or an invitation may become justifiable—i.e., in a world in which the Sino-Soviet bloc seeks to impose its goals on others. However, in the case of South Viet Nam, we do not need to debate this type of intervention. *The United States is there by treaty and agreement and by invitation. It should legally, morally, and in every other sense do what is required to stop the invasion and help the Vietnamese stamp out the insurrection.* Happily, an increasing number of states and peoples the world over agree on this. As Thanat Khoman, Thailand's extremely able Minister of Foreign Affairs, said in London on May 3, 1965:

The chances for an enduring peace will become greater if we can see to it that aggressions against free nations either in overt or covert form, will not be profitable . . . what the Thai people desire most is not to have their names inscribed on a war memorial, but live their lives as free men and to be able to shape their own destiny.

The same can be said of the people of Viet Nam, and therein lies the reason for our stand in Viet Nam since February 7, 1965. The stand and its implications provide the chance for victory in that sad country. Victory means precisely what Thanat Khoman's words say and imply. It does not mean giving to those within the country who would take up arms against that country the status of negotiators. To negotiate with the Viet Cong is equivalent to a prosecuting attorney counseling with the guilty criminal as if the two were on the same legal footing.

The campaign against the Administration's position in 1965 acquired an inflammatory though always minority aspect. The pacifist movement, a traditional part of American culture since our Revolutionary War, joined with sections of the civil rights movement, with the so-called "New Left" and the orthodox Communists, to organize more than fifty teach-ins that drew large crowds of students from Berkeley to Washington, D.C. Viet Cong films smuggled into this country were shown. Draft cards were publicly burned and martyrs to the cause sacrificed themselves. In the meantime, as revealed in public opinion surveys, the majority of the American people, although legitimately disturbed by the fact of war, nonetheless support the President's policy precisely when it is a strong one. But Moscow, Peking, and Hanoi exploited the movement to the best of their abilities—expecting, or at least hoping, that it, together with a minority of Congressional voices also raised in opposition to the President, would force him to back-track on his policy.

That this has not happened is clear from his news conferences throughout 1966. The President has stood firm in his determination to find peace if possible but defend the independence of Viet Nam as long as may be necessary.

In most instances, the teach-ins and associated phenomena were a propaganda device to focus attention on dissatisfaction with United States policy in Viet Nam. There was little "teaching" associated with these ventures, and less learning. Any academician knows that a mass meeting conducted over many hours with audiences drifting in and out is hardly to be dignified as a teaching or learning opportunity. I have no quarrel with those who wish to air their opposition to any Administration policy, for on debate, democracy thrives. What is significant in these many months of shrill debate is the woeful ignorance concerning Viet Nam—its history, its peoples, its trials and tribulations—among so many of the protesters. The problem presented by the divided state of Viet Nam—divided de facto and de jure—is a vastly complicated one, as these pages have tried to make clear. The fact of war-making by one state against the other and the fact of a zealous attempt by a Communist minority to take over yet another state were largely lost in the heat of a debate that somehow found an object of attack in the Presidency. One may be forgiven, perhaps, for speculating that many of the academic and art communities that protested against President Johnson would not have done so against President Kennedy. They had accepted the latter and his policies as Senator and as President. They were shocked, as all were, by his assassination. They were perhaps incapable of transferring their loyalties to the new President even when he carried out policies the former had advocated but was unable to execute. President Johnson did not succeed in placating his critics—not for want of trying, as he so painfully confessed on numerous occasions, as in his address at Princeton University in May, 1966. But he did succeed in "pulling their teeth" in his steady march toward the objective he and his predecessors had defined: to guarantee the independence of the Republic of Viet Nam.

10. Conclusion: For a Free Viet Nam

What Price Wars of National Liberation?

A special kind of turbulence—a nice word for war—has marked the course of recent history. Until recently we have been unprepared for it. But this kind of turbulence has been planned and plotted, programmed and trained for, across the whole board of military, political, socio-economic, psychological, and cultural knowledge. It is basically a theory of warfare which the Communists have been developing since Lenin first outlined it at the Second Comintern Congress in 1920. Mao Tse-tung perfected it and applied it in China; Ho Chi Minh and Vo Nguyen Giap have ably, so far, extended its application in Viet Nam and to an extent in Laos.

This turbulence has been called by the Communists wars of national liberation—that is, warfare conducted at the lower end of the spectrum of military activity, accompanied by a full measure of political, socio-economic, and psychocultural activity. It is infinitely more complex than what is conventionally called guerrilla warfare, whose principles and operations have been known for centuries. Briefly, it is a form of revolutionary theory and practice through which disciplined, politically hardened, and militarily trained personnel can move into a social scene, especially where there is no organized, industrialized working class. Lenin said at the Comintern Congress that though class warfare (classical Marxist conflict between the capitalists and the workers) will continue; and though the capitalo-imperialist class will, because of rivalry for profits, engage in wars—wars the

206

working class, which has no fatherland, will seek to turn into class wars—there is another dimension to war. It is to enlist the "colonial and semi-independent" peoples—workers, petty bourgeoisie, and especially the rural masses, the peasants—under the leadership of the Communist Party in a revolutionary struggle. He expected this would succeed in what he, and later Mao and others, called a two-stage revolution.

This "front" for struggle would first achieve national "democratic" hegemony; it would then be converted into Communist hegemony. Since history is, according to the Communists, on the side of the Marxian dialectic, the imperialist powers will fight and fail; and since the Communists will inherit the future, their task is to midwife the future. They do this by analyzing the objective conditions and then using the weapons of revolutionary practice to hasten the day.

Wars of national liberation—a more recent Communist phrase—are the application of this theory to those states and territories of the world where according to Mao five basic conditions obtain. These are (1) political weakness of a government in power, particularly characteristic of the newly independent or otherwise febrile states of Asia, Africa, and Latin America; (2) prolonged external conflict or induced civil strife; (3) geographical nearness to an existing Communist or related state for support and sanctuary; (4) weakness and division in the Free World; and (5) reliance on the strategy of nuclear stalemate. Where all or most of these conditions prevail, the Communists should press history.

The recent (September 3, 1965) statement of Vice Premier and Defense Minister Lin Piao, made on the twentieth anniversary of V-J day, sets out Peking's view of the international significance and applicability of the revolutionary formula. "Long Live the Victory of People's War," as he calls it, is a paean of praise, with footnotes, to Mao's foresight and Peking's pre-eminence. But the fact that this document is hagiographical should not blind us to the fact that it is rooted in Marxist-Leninist-Stalinist-Khrushchevist doctrine. The seizure of power by armed force is the central task and highest form of revolution. The use of the "countryside" to surround the "city," that is, the employment of methods and programs to "win over" the bodies necessary to assault the citadel of the entrenched power—a kind of adaptation of the classic siege strategy and tactics—has been carefully worked out and at.

This is what we have been experiencing in Viet Nam, where the "citadel," the capital and other cities, has been reasonably well held, but where the "countryside" has been either neglected or poorly defended and handled.

In the course of this war, there arose to confound the United States and its allies five basic fallacies:

1. The Fallacy of the Sins of the Father. The United States had come to the support of French colonialism in Indochina. The French were there for a long time and were defeated. The United States would be defeated for similar reasons. This is the current French and Communist version.

Yes, we were there in misguided support of the French. *But* (a) we have no colonial ambitions, either political or economic; (b) we want the Vietnamese to win and to be sovereign in their own territory. Our task is to make this clear by word and deed.

2. The Fallacy of the "Wrong War, Wrong Place." This is a legacy of the Korean War—the frustration of having power to win but being unwilling to use it against the determined enemy, Communist China. But South Viet Nam is not Korea. It is another location where the Communists attempt their war of national liberation. And in this war we decided to accept the de facto partition as de jure. All that was and is required is to defend the partition line, not to destroy Hanoi or Peking. There is no "right" place for war; there is also no right or wrong war. War is the extension of politics when politics no longer solves the problem which the human condition produces. One's choices of the answers to the

problem may be right or wrong. In the case of Viet Nam, the argument favors South Viet Nam by all the rules we know and the values we cherish.

3. The Fallacy of Duplicating the Past. This fallacy is to insist that the present requires what was "good" in the past. Communist insurgency had been defeated in Malaya by a combination of "strategic hamlets"—enforced relocation of many thousands of Chinese settlers who by relocation would not or could not give succor to the Malay Communist Party (primarily Chinese in membership)—and a ratio of 10 : 1 or 15 : 1. Therefore, the United States would be required, if it really tried to do the job, to increase American forces to ten to fifteen times the number of hard-core Viet Cong and paramilitary Viet Cong forces. This, of course, would require 1 million or 2 million troops, or an astronomical figure that no reasonable person could accept.

Not until more thorough analysis punctured this ballon of the past were we over the hump—though more United States forces have been needed than were originally contemplated.

4. The Fallacy of Time and Distance. The United States is a long way from Viet Nam, the Chinese Communists are close. Fact. But a less material fact. Our ability to move, supply, and otherwise communicate are factors of our advanced technology. China has none or few of these. What is more, its industrial North is separated from North Viet Nam by more "time-*facility*" than South Viet Nam is distanced from the United States.

5. The Fallacy of Irreplaceable Communist Appeal. According to this argument, only the Communists can give land to the landless—without taxes; only they can supply better health, education, credit, housing, schooling—all of which the peasantry yearn for. We can do no better here than to quote again the words of President Kennedy, that the United States must offer the Vietnamese "a political, economic, and social revolution far superior to anything the Communists can

offer—far more peaceful, far more democratic and far more locally controlled." Nothing need prevent us from translating this promise into action.

These fallacies are in part understood; in part paralyzing. The answers to them are contained in the diagnosis. All one had to do is to do it—that is, carry out the correct prescription.

The Honolulu Meeting

After many starts and stops, the Johnson Administration decided to "do it." This was the significance of the Lodge-Lansdale-Westmoreland team even though some secondary members of that team might have been strengthened. For any knowledgeable Vietnamese or American specialist could have—and some did—write the prescription years ago. This prescription is contained in the Declaration and Joint Communiqué issued after the meeting of President Johnson and the South Vietnamese Chief of State, Lieutenant General Nguyen Van Thieu, and Premier Nguyen Cao Ky in Honolulu in February, 1966.*

Why should these two documents encourage optimism where previous and not dissimilar ones have failed?

It is at this point that one must look to the crystal ball. In my view, these propositions are essentially true:

1. President Johnson's own genius for the practical has at long last seized upon the elements which flesh out the military, political, socio-economic, and psycho-cultural aspects of improvement for the *masses* of Viet Nam.

2. President Johnson's advisers—Secretary of State Dean Rusk and Secretary of Defense Robert S. McNamara—agree on the theoretical and practical meaning of "wars of national liberation." This is different from mere antagonism to Communism, which all highly placed Americans share; it is a determination and a capacity to shed illusions about the need to

---

* For the text of these two documents, see Appendix.

study it—*as it has not been studied before.* In this context "wars of national liberation" come to the top of the list, whatever impatience President Johnson may have with "studying" in contrast to "operating." The American pragmatist—to use this word in a simple context—is necessary. But without fundamental knowledge he can be egregiously at a loss.

3. In this case President Johnson, the political leader of the allies in Viet Nam, has determined to fulfill the terms of the Declaration cited above. Since he commands the power to produce what is needed, all that he requires—admittedly a big "all"—is the personnel to carry out the manifold tasks of conflict management in Viet Nam. That mistakes will be made is to be expected. That the over-all balance will favor a free and independent Viet Nam is also predictable.

The Stakes in Viet Nam: Freedom for the Republic of Viet Nam

I submit that the following propositions sum up the argument:

1. The State of Viet Nam—South Viet Nam—became independent after a worthy struggle against the colonial power of France. This happened in 1954. It became a republic under President Ngo Dinh Diem in 1955.

2. This state did not, as the United States did not, become a signatory of the Geneva Accords of 1954. It is not bound by them.

3. The anticolonial struggle in Viet Nam included many elements, among them bona fide nationalists, Communists, and others. In the North, above the 17th parallel, the Communists won out. They successfully defeated the French and liquidated nationalists and others whom they could not control.

4. In the South, the nationalists won out, but they were *immediately* subjected—in violation, be it said, of the Geneva Accords—to attack from the Communists, who refused to abide by the legal forms of the new state. These Communists

were members of the same party as their Communist colleagues of the North, popularly called Viet Minh. They formed an "army of national liberation" in 1955 to contend by arms against the legitimate government of South Viet Nam.

5. This "army of national liberation" has, under various names since 1955, conducted the armed rebellion in South Viet Nam. From Hanoi, and at second remove from Peking and Moscow, it has received (a) open political and military direction; (b) arms and resupply of men; and (c) training facilities for more than a decade.

6. The United States under bilateral and multilateral agreements came to the aid of South Viet Nam. Some thirty other countries—including Asian ones—have similarly, if belatedly, come to the aid of the Republic of Viet Nam. Correlatively, the Sino-Soviet bloc and satellites have aided Hanoi.

7. Not until February, 1965, did the United States and South Viet Nam mount a campaign to interdict the enemy on his soil. For ten years the enemy had enjoyed the unique-in-warfare luxury of striking but not being "struck."

8. In the final analysis, United States policy in South Viet Nam rests on two fundamental objectives: (a) to deny its territory and people to the Communist enemy; (b) to help the South Vietnamese create the kind of secure and stable society *they* want when they have at long last crushed the Communist uprising within and blocked Communist aggression against their land. This is the meaning of February 7, 1965, and February 8, 1966.

In pursuit of these two objectives, President Johnson and the overwhelming majority of the Congress have pledged United States support. May that support not falter now that it appears to be turning the tide.

To turn the tide is not simple. The United States must be prepared to assist its allies and friends in remote areas of the globe in the same way that it decided to assist its allies and friends in World War II. The risks of escalation in Southeast Asia are real, but they can be confined provided the United

States adheres to its declared objective: the defense and security of the Republic of Viet Nam, not (unless endlessly provoked) the destruction of the Communist North Viet Nam. The R.V.N. must continue to receive military and other aid until it can restore political and economic stability and viability to its life as a small, responsible sovereign nation. Neither the "essentials" nor the "specifics" (whatever these be) of the 1954 Geneva Agreements, nor the coalition-with-Communist policy applied as the almost-fatal "solution" in the Geneva Agreements of 1962 for Laos, offers guides to the future security of the Republic of Viet Nam. Its land and sea borders must be guaranteed and defended by powerful friends and allies while it seeks to establish domestic peace.

A successful outcome to the defense of the Republic of Viet Nam will have an immediate and salutary effect on the policies of neighboring Southeast Asian states. It will free them from fear—fear of that form of contemporary warfare at the lower end of the spectrum which today is the hallmark of Communist aggression. We call it Communist insurgency; the Communists call it wars of national liberation.

Only in the context of national security for each Southeast Asian state can there be expected to grow in Southeast Asia the genuine forms of Asian and United Nations cooperation that President Johnson has proposed. A massive aid program (the current Mekong Basin is one example), a Free Asian Common Market, the varied programs of the U.N. Economic Commission for Asia and the Far East (ECAFE), the new Asian Development Bank, and the Honolulu program itself are ready for action. But their endorsement and advocacy are meaningful only in the context of security from Communist and other aggression. In that context, improvement in the conditions of living and the encouragement and spread of representative institutions of government will become the best counter-defense to the enemy's strategy and tactics. In that context, he will be denied his target: the Himalayan rimlands, the Irrawaddy and Mekong basins, the Southeast Asian rice bowl—he will be denied the power to subjugate people like the Vietnamese, who, like ourselves, want to be secure—and free.

Perhaps, because I began my teaching career at Johns Hopkins long ago, I may be permitted to close this book with the words of President Johnson's April 7, 1965, speech at that university. He said:

This war, like most wars, is filled with terrible irony. For what do the people of North Viet Nam want? They want what their neighbors also desire—food for their hunger, health for their bodies, a chance to learn, progress for their country, and an end to the bondage of material misery. And they would find all these things far more readily in peaceful association with others than in the endless course of battle.

These countries of Southeast Asia are homes for millions of impoverished people. Each day these people rise at dawn and struggle through until the night to wrest existence from the soil. They are often wracked by diseases, plagued by hunger, and death comes at the early age of forty.

Stability and peace do not come easily in such a land. Neither independence nor human dignity will ever be won through by arms alone. It also requires the works of peace. The American people have helped generously in times past in these works, and now there must be a much more massive effort to improve the life of man in that conflict-torn corner of our world.

The first step is for the countries of Southeast Asia to associate themselves in a greatly expanded cooperative effort for development. We would hope that North Viet Nam would take its place in the common effort just as soon as peaceful cooperation is possible.

The United Nations is already actively engaged in development in this area, and as far back as 1961 I conferred with our authorities in Viet Nam in connection with their work there. And I would hope tonight that the Secretary General of the United Nations could use the prestige of his great office and his deep knowledge of Asia to initiate, as soon as possible, with the countries of that area, a plan for cooperation in increased development.

For our part I will ask the Congress to join in a billion-dollar American investment in this effort as soon as it is underway.

And I would hope that all other industrialized countries, including the Soviet Union, will join in this effort to replace despair with hope and terror with progress.

The task is nothing less than to enrich the hopes and existence of more than a hundred million people. And there is much to be done.

The vast Mekong River can provide food and water and power on a scale to dwarf even our own TVA.

The wonders of modern medicine can be spread through villages where thousands die every year from lack of care. Schools can be established to train people in the skills needed to manage the process of development. And these objectives, and more, are within the reach of a cooperative and determined effort.

I also intend to expand and speed up a program to make available our farm surpluses to assist in feeding and clothing the needy in Asia. We should not allow people to go hungry and wear rags while our own warehouses overflow with an abundance of wheat and corn and rice and cotton.

So I will very shortly name a special team of outstanding, patriotic, and distinguished Americans to inaugurate our participation in these programs. This team will be headed by Mr. Eugene Black, the very able former President of the World Bank.

This will be a disorderly planet for a long time. In Asia, and elsewhere, the forces of the modern world are shaking old ways and uprooting ancient civilizations. There will be turbulence and struggle and even violence. Great social change—as we see in our own country—does not always come without conflict.

We must also expect that nations will on occasion be in dispute with us. It may be because we are rich, or powerful, or because we have made some mistakes, or because they honestly fear our intentions. However, no nation need ever fear that we desire their land, or to impose our will, or to dictate their institutions.

But we will always oppose the effort of one nation to conquer another nation.

We will do this because our own security is at stake.

But there is more to it than that. For our generation has a dream. It is a very old dream. But we have the power, and now we have the opportunity to make that dream come true.

For centuries nations have struggled among each other. But we dream of a world where disputes are settled by law and reason. And we will try to make it so.

For most of history men have hated and killed one another in battle. But we dream of an end to war. And we will try to make it so.

For all existence most men have lived in poverty, threatened by hunger. But we dream of a world where all are fed and charged with hope. And we will help to make it so.

The ordinary men and women of North Viet Nam and South Viet Nam, of China and India, of Russia and America, are brave people. They are filled with the same proportions of hate and fear, of love and hope. Most of them want the same things for themselves and their families. Most of them do not want their sons to ever die in battle, or to see their homes, or the homes of others, destroyed.

Well, this can be their world yet. Man now has the knowledge —always before denied—to make this planet serve the real needs of the people who live on it.

I know this will not be easy. I know how difficult it is for reason to guide passion, and love to master hate. The complexities of this world do not bow easily to pure and consistent answers. . . .

But the simple truths are there just the same. We must all try to follow them as best we can.

Epilogue

There is no "end" to a book of this character. It was originally planned to allow three major events to serve as the "conclusion": President Johnson's decision of February, 1965, to attack the attackers; his outstanding presentation of the rewards of peace at Johns Hopkins University in April, 1965; and the basis for future U.S.–South Vietnamese relations as affirmed in the Declaration of Honolulu of February, 1966. I deliberately omitted the not widely reported mid-1965 elections for provincial councils held in every province of the Republic of Viet Nam. More than half of the 9 million South Vietnamese who were eligible, registered to vote. Of these, 73 per cent in fact voted, in proportions ranging from 90 per cent in the more secure provinces to a low of 53 per cent in one province. The Communists tried to discourage the elections everywhere but succeeded nowhere. I welcomed this event, but omitted it from the text because I thought that these elections could not yet serve as a *continuing* experience for the Vietnamese, who so quietly demonstrate that they want security *and* freedom of choice. Two related events, both occurring in 1966, indicate that, at long last, there may come, sooner than expected, such a continuing experience.

The first of these happened on March 10, when Premier Nguyen Cao Ky dismissed his military and political rival in the ruling group. Lieutenant General Nguyen Chanh Thi, boss of the five northern provinces, including the cities of Danang and Hué, was ousted. General Thi, as long ago as June-July 1965, had been expected to succeed Premier Ky. His dismissal, following the Honolulu meeting of President Johnson and Marshal Ky, seemed at first a sign of strength for the latter. In fact, it led to yet another "Buddhist crisis" which kept South Viet Nam on edge during the spring of 1966. The Unified Buddhist Church, a well-organized Buddhist political minority headed by Thich Tri Quang, appeared in 1966 to be capable of bringing down the Ky government, as it had, in major part, the Diem government. In this it failed.

Premier Ky not only survived, he surmounted. Political Buddhist dissidence was put down in Saigon, Danang, and Hué. And though the individual case of General Thi remains to be clarified, his military supporters—five generals who aided him and the Buddhist-led anti-government campaign—were dismissed from the army and punished with light sentences of detention.

Out of this turmoil there came a dividend. In April, Marshal Ky agreed to new national elections for a constitution-drafting convention which, as in 1955–56, may become the herald of a new start at democratic political life in the Republic of Viet Nam. These elections were scheduled for September, 1966.

The second event came in the closing days of June, 1966, and continued thereafter. The United States and its Vietnamese allies launched a series of air-strikes against the oil reserves and stocks stored near the North Vietnamese cities of Hanoi and Haiphong. These strikes were not like the strategic area bombing in World War II; they did not hit the cities and civilian populations as military targets. As Secretary of Defense McNamara put it, these strikes "were initiated to counter a mounting reliance by North Viet Nam on the use of trucks and powered junks to facilitate the infiltration of men and arms into South Viet Nam." They were part of the campaign of interdiction begun in February, 1965, a campaign not to destroy Hanoi and its government but to make its prosecution of the war more difficult and more costly.

To raise "the price on those who wage war against the freedom of their neighbors" was the way President Johnson expressed it in a speech at Omaha on June 30. But he also indicated, once again, that he was prepared for peace talks anywhere with "the leaders of North Viet Nam . . . in a matter of hours." Clearly the air strikes on oil stocks and storage facilities were intended to alert Hanoi to the fact that the United States was determined to stay in the conflict for as long as it would take to finish it; they also indicated that the self-imposed restraints on U.S. power would not last forever. Our armed forces in Viet Nam have grown to about 300,000 men and will be increased if needed. Popular opinion was revealed as more, not less, responsive to the President's position as a result of the air strikes in the vicinity of Hanoi and Haiphong.

In sum, the first half of 1966 demonstrated that the South Vietnamese, after three years of domestic infelicity, may be on the threshold of a better life; and that the United States was still very much determined to give them a chance to have some domestic peace and security and improvement in the conditions of living.

F.N.T.

August 1, 1966

Appendix

The Declaration of Honolulu

February 8, 1966

PART I

The Republic of Viet Nam and the United States of America jointly declare:

Their determination in defense against aggression,

Their dedication to the hopes of all the people of South Viet Nam,

And their commitment to the search for just and stable peace.

In pursuit of these objectives the leaders of their Governments have agreed upon this Declaration, which sets forth:

The purposes of the Government of Viet Nam,

The purposes of the Government of the United States,

And the common commitment of both Governments.

PART II

THE PURPOSES OF THE GOVERNMENT OF VIET NAM

Here in the mid-Pacific, halfway between Asia and North America, we take the opportunity to state again the aims of our Government.

We are a Government—indeed a generation—of revolutionary transformation. Our people are caught up in a mortal struggle.

This struggle has four sides.

1. *We must defeat the Viet Cong and those illegally fighting with them on our soil.* We are the victims of an aggression directed and supported from Hanoi. That aggression—that so-called "war of national liberation"—is part of the Communist plan for the conquest of all of southeast Asia. The defeat of that aggression is vital for the future of our people of South Viet Nam.

2. *We are dedicated to the eradication of social injustice among our people.* We must bring about a true social revolution and construct a

221

modern society in which every man can know that he has a future; that he has respect and dignity; that he has the opportunity for himself and for his children to live in an environment where all is not disappointment, despair and dejection; that the opportunities exist for the full expression of his talents and his hopes.

3. *We must establish and maintain a stable, viable economy and build a better material life for our people.* In spite of the war, which creates many unusual and unpredictable economic situations, we are determined to continue with a policy of austerity; to make the best possible use of the assistance granted us from abroad; and to help our people achieve regular economic growth and improved material welfare.

4. *We must build true democracy for our land and for our people.* In this effort we shall continue to imbue the people with a sense of national unity, a stronger commitment to civic responsibility. We shall encourage a widened and more active participation in and contribution to the building of a free, independent, strong and peaceful Viet Nam. In particular, we pledge again:

To formulate a democratic constitution in the months ahead, including an electoral law;

To take that constitution to our people for discussion and modification;

To seek its ratification by secret ballot;

To create, on the basis of elections rooted in that constitution, an elected government.

These things shall be accomplished mainly with the blood, intelligence, and dedication of the Vietnamese people themselves. But in this interdependent world we shall need the help of others: to win the war of independence; to build while we fight; to reconstruct and develop our nation when terror ceases.

To those future citizens of a free, democratic South Viet Nam now fighting with the Viet Cong, we take this occasion to say come and join in this national revolutionary adventure:

Come safely to join us through the Open Arms Program

Stop killing your brothers, sisters, their elders and their children

Come and work through constitutional democracy to build together that life of dignity, freedom and peace those in the North would deny the people of Viet Nam.

Thus, we are fighting this war. It is a military war, a war for the hearts of our people. We cannot win one without winning the other. But the war for the hearts of the people is more than a military tactic.

It is a moral principle. For this we shall strive as we fight to bring about a true social revolution.

PART III

THE PURPOSES OF THE GOVERNMENT OF THE UNITED STATES

1. The United States of America is joined with the people and Government of Viet Nam to prevent aggression. This is the purpose of the determined effort of the American armed forces now engaged in Viet Nam. The United States seeks no bases. It seeks no colonial presence. It seeks to impose no alliance or alignment. It seeks only to prevent aggression, and its pledge to that purpose is firm. It aims simply to help a people and Government who are determined to help themselves.

2. The United States is pledged to the principles of the self-determination of peoples, and of government by the consent of the governed. It therefore gives its full support to the purpose of free elections proclaimed by the Government of South Viet Nam and to the principle of open arms and amnesty for all who turn from terror toward peace and rural construction. The United States will give its full support to measures of social revolution including land reform based upon the principle of building upward from the hopes and purposes of all the people of Viet Nam.

3. Just as the United States is pledged to play its full part in the worldwide attack upon hunger, ignorance, and disease, so in Viet Nam it will give special support to the work of the people of that country to build even while they fight. We have helped and we will help them —to stabilize the economy—to increase the production of food—to spread the light of education—to stamp out disease.

4. The purpose of the United States remains a purpose of peace. The United States Government and the Government of Viet Nam will continue in the future, as they have in the past, to press the quest for a peaceful settlement in every forum. The world knows the harsh and negative response these efforts have thus far received. But the world should know, too, that the United States Government and the Government of Viet Nam remain determined that no path to peace shall be unexplored. Within the framework of their international commitments, the United States and Viet Nam aim to create with others a stable peace in southeast Asia which will permit the governments and peoples of the region to devote themselves to lifting the condition of man. With the understanding and support of the Government of Viet

Nam the peace offensive of the United States Government and the Government of South Viet Nam will continue until peace is secured.

PART IV

THE COMMON COMMITMENT

The President of the United States and the Chief of State and Prime Minister of the Republic of Viet Nam are thus pledged again:
To defense against aggression,
To the work of social revolution,
To the goal of free self-government,
To the attack on hunger, ignorance, and disease,
And to the unending quest for peace.

Joint Statement Following Discussions Between President Johnson, General Thieu, and Prime Minister Ky in Honolulu on February 7 and 8

February 8, 1966

1. The President of the United States and the Chief of State and Prime Minister of the Republic of Viet Nam have concluded three days of the most intense and friendly discussion, and their fundamental concord of purpose and policy is stated in the Declaration of Honolulu which they are issuing together today. In addition there has been opportunity for extended review of many urgent specific questions, both at the level of the Chiefs of Government and at the level of Cabinet Ministers. The results of this immediate discussion are reported in the remaining paragraphs of this communique.

2. The leaders of the two Governments, with their advisers, reviewed the intense efforts for peace undertaken by the Government of the United States between Christmas and the end of January. Both Governments noted with regret the total absence of a present interest in peace on the part of the Government of North Viet Nam. They reviewed the present diplomatic situation in the United Nations and elsewhere, and they agreed upon continued diplomatic efforts for peace.

3. The economic advisers of the two Governments had a thorough discussion of their cooperative programs for maintaining economic stability and controlling the cost of living in a war-torn country. On the basis of their reports, the President and the Chief of State and Prime Minister have agreed that their two Governments will take further concrete steps to combat inflation in Viet Nam.

4. The leaders of the two Governments received comprehensive reports on the intensified program of rural construction. The Government of Viet Nam set forth a plan for efforts of particular strength and intensity in areas of high priority, and the President gave directions to ensure full and prompt support by all agencies of the United States Government.

5. In the construction program three particular points were agreed on as essential for rapid progress:

(1) Continued emphasis by both Vietnamese and Allied forces on the effort to build democracy in the rural areas—an effort as important as the military battle itself.

(2) Continued emphasis on the design of rural construction work to meet the people's needs for larger output, more efficient production, improved credit, handicrafts and light industry, and rural electrification.

(3) Concentration of resources—both Vietnamese and American—in selected priority areas which are properly related to military plans so that the work of rural construction can be protected against disruption by the enemy.

6. Cabinet members of both Governments had thorough discussions of special needs of the people of South Viet Nam in the fields of agriculture, health, and education. In agriculture it was agreed that special effort would be made to move agricultural know-how—particularly new species of highly productive rice and corn and vegetable seed—from the experimental station to the farmer in the fields. Steps for more rapid land reform were carefully reviewed. It was agreed that Secretary of Agriculture Freeman and a team of agricultural experts would proceed at once to Viet Nam for the purpose of developing enlarged programs of agricultural cooperation.

7. It was also agreed that programs in health and education would be intensified. The President pledged that he would soon dispatch teams of experts in those fields to Viet Nam under the direction of Secretary Gardner. Both Governments agreed to make increased efforts in the training of health personnel, in providing teams for medical care, and creating a stronger medical logistics system. They also agreed to strengthen their cooperation in building elementary schools, in training teachers, in reinforcing vocational and technical education, and in supplying textbooks.

8. It was agreed that the refugees who have of their own free will come over from the enemy side must be adequately cared for and prepared to resume a useful role in society. The Government of Viet Nam described its plans to meet this problem and the President as-

sured them of full American support. It was agreed that a special effort will be made to provide good schools for refugee children.

9. There was a full discussion of the military situation and of military plans and programs. The leaders of the two Governments reached full agreement upon a policy of growing military effectiveness and of still closer cooperation between the military forces of Viet Nam and those of the United States. They reaffirmed their determination to act with all possible regard for the rights of innocent civilians, to adhere to the Geneva Convention of 1949 on the treatment of prisoners of war, and to act with full respect for the independence and territorial integrity of neighboring countries which wish to live in peace.

10. Finally, it was agreed that the leaders of the two Governments will have further meetings like this one in the future for the continued execution of the policies and purposes of the Declaration of Honolulu.

Notes

Chapter 1. The Viet People: Who, When, and Where

1. Gerald C. Hickey, *Village in Viet Nam* (New Haven, Conn.: Yale University Press, 1964), p. 5.
2. See Pierre Huard and Maurice Durand, *Connaissance du Viet-Nam* (Paris: Imprimerie Nationale, 1954), p. 33, for a map that dates the southward progress of the Viets from the northern point of their country to the tip of the Camau peninsula.
3. Abbé Adrien Launay, *Histoire Generale de la Société des Missions Etrangeres* (Paris, 1894), I, 186.
4. John F. Cady, *The Roots of French Imperialism in Eastern Asia* (Ithaca, N.Y.: Cornell University Press, 1954), p. 17.
5. *Le Viet-Nam* (Paris: Les Editions de Minuit, 1955), p. 324.
6. *Ibid.*, pp. 339–40.
7. Quoted in Launay, *op. cit*, Vol. III, p. 337.
8. Georges Taboulet, *La Geste Française en Indochine* (Paris: Adrien-Maisonneuve, 1955), a fine, two-volume collection of original documents by contemporaries of the events, traces the course of the French conquest of Indochina from its beginnings to 1914.

Chapter 2. Viet Nam Fights for Independence Against the French

1. See T. E. Ennis, *French Policy and Developments in Indochina* (Chicago: University of Chicago Press, 1936), pp. 72–77, for an outline of this complicated system.
2. As quoted in *Asia* (Saigon), Vol. I, No. 1 (March, 1951), p. 59.
3. *French Indochina* (New York: Macmillan, 1937), p. 399.
4. J. S. Furnivall, *Colonial Policy and Practice* (Cambridge: Cambridge University Press, 1948), pp. 214–16 and *passim*.
5. See Le Thanh Koi, *Le Viet-Nam*, p. 391.
6. Reprinted in *Bulletin d l'Ecole Française de l'Extrême-Orient*, June, 1907.
7. This section has been culled largely from the pages of *Asie Française*. Its contribution to an understanding of the nationalist movement should not be evaluated in terms of the extent to which it turned up all the facts modern historical study has revealed. Viet Nam had the most primitive communication facilities at the beginning of the century, which made reporting difficult. More importantly, it is obvious that a contemporary reporter in an alien culture cannot possibly uncover all the facts about an illegal underground movement.

French censorship prevented the appearance of a free, local newspaper

—or other publication—that could adequately express indigenous opinion. The Indochinese press, run by French colonials, was ultraconservative and uniformly denounced anything that smacked of local self-improvement or independent activity. In view of the paucity and unavailability of articulate Vietnamese writings for the period or relatively unbiased news accounts, *Asie Française* appears a useful original source of moderate French outlook.

Many of its accounts have not turned up in any other literature and add a sense of color which makes the period much more alive than the few pages devoted to it in most histories would indicate. Its analysis of the shortcomings of the early nationalist leadership, and its ability to place the nationalist movement in the historical perspective of European-Asian tensions have been borne out by the work of subsequent students. It is clear to this writer that Le Thanh Khoi, who has written the best—and Marxist-oriented—single-volume history of Viet Nam, has carefully used its pages in preparing his text.

Asie Française was generally just in its criticism of the French administration and fairly perspicacious in pointing out danger signals. In relation to the security of the colony, the journal in retrospect seemed to have an exaggerated fear of Chinese potential, as shown by the preponderance of articles on developments in that country. This is understandable in light of the fact that the French held Indochina for many years before they ceased thinking of their colony primarily in terms of an entry into the south of China. But this was a preoccupation which they shared with their nineteenth-century rival England for control of the whole peninsula. Only later did they begin to plan for Indochina's own development.

The picture of the early nationalist movement that emerges from *Asie Française* is relatively complete in that it transmits the currents of ideas, the basic personalities, and significance of the movement. I must conclude that if French policy-makers had conscientiously read it, and followed its suggestions, the political and social history of Viet Nam would have been considerably different. But then, so would colonial history elsewhere.

8. Frank N. Trager (ed.), *Marxism in Southeast Asia: A Study of Four Countries* (Stanford, Calif.: Stanford University Press, 1959).

9. For fuller details of the vicissitudes of the various parties, see I. Milton Sacks, "Marxism in Viet Nam," in Trager (ed.), *Marxism in Southeast Asia.*

10. For a Viet Minh account, see Truong Chinh, *Premier for Revolt* (New York: Frederick A. Praeger, 1963), pp. 9–53. Truong Chinh's account was first published in 1946.

11. *History of French Colonial Policy (1870–1925)* (London: King and Son, 1929), p. 478.

12. *Ibid.*, p. 429.

CHAPTER 3. THE WAR AGAINST THE FRENCH: TO DIEN BIEN PHU

1. *Primer for Revolt*, pp. 28–29.

2. For various views by Viet Minh leaders on the application of Communist revolutionary theory and practices, see Truong Chinh, *Primer for Revolt;* Vo Nguyen Giap, *People's War, People's Army* (Hanoi: Foreign Languages Publishing House, 1960–62), a collection of General Giap's papers;

and Ho Chi Minh, *Selected Works* (Hanoi: Foreign Languages Publishing House, 1961), in four volumes.

3. Robert Shaplen, *The Lost Revolution* (New York: Harper & Row, 1965), pp. 58–59.

4. In an address before the Pakistan Institute of International Affairs, December, 1954; reprinted in *Pakistan Horizon*, Vol. VII, No. 4 (1954), pp. 171–88.

5. *People's War, People's Army*, p. 22.

6. Henri Navarre, *Agonie de l'Indochine* (Paris, 1956), p. 46, n. 20.

7. *Ibid.*, pp. 46–47.

CHAPTER 4. THE GENEVA CONFERENCE OF 1954—AND ITS RESULTS

1. From Dwight D. Eisenhower, *Mandate for Change, 1953–1956* (New York: Doubleday, 1963); extracted in *Why Vietnam* (Washington, D.C.: Government Printing Office, 1965).

2. This is supported by the authoritative annual surveys of both the British Royal Institute of International Affairs and the American Council on Foreign Affairs. See *Survey of International Affairs 1954* (London: Oxford University Press, 1957), pp. 31–35; and *The United States in World Affairs 1954* (New York: Harper, 1956), pp. 222–25.

3. *Documents on International Affairs, 1954* (London: Oxford University Press, 1957), pp. 124–25, 135–37.

4. Quoted in *Survey of International Affairs 1954*, p. 47.

5. The documents were published in *Documents Relating to the Discussion of Korea and Indo-China at the Geneva Conference*, Cmd. 9186 (London: HMSO, 1954); and *Further Documents Relating to the Discussion of Korea and Indo-China at the Geneva Conference*, Cmd. 9239 (London: HMSO, 1954). The latter omits the full statement by the Representative of the State of Viet Nam, dated July 21, 1954. This will be found in *Documents on American Foreign Relations 1954* (New York: Harper, 1956), pp. 282–317, esp. pp. 315–17.

6. See *Documents on American Foreign Relations 1954*, pp. 315–16.

7. Senator J. W. Fulbright, address on Viet Nam, reported in *The New York Times*, June 16, 1965.

8. This and subsequent references are to the section "Viet Nam," from *Further Documents* . . . Cmd. 9239.

9. P. 67.

10. See Richard W. Lindholm (ed.), *Vietnam: The First Five Years* (East Lansing, Mich.: Michigan State University Press, 1959), pp. 48–103.

11. See *Documents Relating* . . . , Cmd. 9186, pp. 123–24.

CHAPTER 5. THE WAR BETWEEN THE STATES BEGINS

1. New York: Harper & Row, n.d. [1965], pp. 113–32.

2. Paul Devinat, *Politique Etrangère*, Vol. XXI (July–August, 1956), p. 431.

3. For an amusing account, see Hoang Van Chi, *From Colonialism to Communism: A Case History of North Viet Nam* (with an introduction by P. J. Honey) (New York: Frederick A. Praeger, 1964), pp. 59, 70–71.

4. Reprinted in Allen B. Cole (ed.), *Conflict in Indo-China and International Repercussions: A Documentary History, 1945–1955* (Ithaca, N.Y.: Cornell University Press, 1956), pp. 106–10.

5. "The Foreign Policy of North Viet Nam" (mimeo.; May, 1965), pp. 12–13, 16. This will be a chapter in a forthcoming book.

6. Cole (ed.), *op. cit.*, pp. 226–28.

7. John T. Dorsey, Jr., "South Viet Nam in Perspective," *Far Eastern Survey*, Vol. XXVII (December, 1958), p. 180. Professor Dorsey worked in South Viet Nam between July, 1955, and May, 1956, and again from July, 1957, almost until the time of publication of the article.

8. The complaints were faithfully reproduced in the ICC's *First Interim Report* (London: HMSO, 1955), and in subsequent Interim Reports.

9. "South Viet Nam's Internal Problems," *Pacific Affairs*, Vol. XXXI (September, 1958), p. 255.

CHAPTER 6. THE SEARCH FOR SECURITY, STABILITY, AND IMPROVEMENT IN THE CONDITIONS OF LIVING, 1955–63

1. Department of State *Bulletin*, June 11, 1956, pp. 972–74.

2. "The 1954 Geneva Conference: An Assessment," *America's Stake in Viet Nam* (New York: American Friends of Viet Nam, 1956), p. 68.

3. *Le Monde*, December 25, 1957.

4. Vol. XXXI (September, 1958), pp. 241–60.

5. See Roy Jumper, "Mandarin Bureaucracy and Politics in South Viet Nam," *Pacific Affairs*, Vol. XXX (March, 1957), pp. 47–58.

6. See Francis J. Corley, "Viet-Nam Since Geneva," *Thought*, Vol. XXXIII (Winter, 1958–59), pp. 515–68.

7. Published in *Why Vietnam* (Washington, D.C.: Government Printing Office, 1965), p. 2. There is some confusion as to the date of this letter. Prepared on October 1, it was not sent until October 23. Press reports appeared in *The New York Times* of October 25 and October 27, 1954.

8. "Progress Report on Southern Viet Nam," *Pacific Affairs*, Vol. XXX (September, 1957), pp. 224–25. This writer had occasion to see Ladejinsky's work during three visits to Viet Nam in 1956, 1958, and 1962.

9. As listed in the *Times of Viet Nam*, July 7, 1956. This was an English-language weekly which became, essentially, the voice of Diem's family.

10. See *The Constitution of the Republic of Viet Nam* (Saigon: Secretariat of State for Information, October 26, 1956). See also Ngo Dinh Diem, *On Democracy, Addresses Relative to the Constitution* (Saigon: Press Office, October, 1957).

11. Robert Scigliano, *South Vietnam: Nation Under Stress* (Boston: Houghton Mifflin, 1963), p. 99.

12. In addition to several titles suggested above, the reader may wish to review three critical appraisals of this period written by informed observers of the Vietnamese scene at that time: Brian Crozier, "The International Situation in Indochina," *Pacific Affairs*, Vol. XIX (December, 1956); William Henderson, "South Viet Nam Finds Itself," *Foreign Affairs*, Vol. XXXV, No. 2 (1957); and John Osborne, "The Tough Miracle Man of Viet Nam," *Life*, May 13, 1957.

CHAPTER 7. THE UNITED STATES AND THE DIEM REGIME

1. From a letter to Ngo Dinh Diem, October, 1954. See above, Chapter 6, pp. 129–30.

2. Reprinted in *Why Vietnam*, pp. 2–3.

3. *Ibid.*, p. 3.

4. *Ibid.*, p. 5.

5. The table is from Richard W. Lindhold (ed.), *Viet-Nam: The First Five Years* (East Lansing, Mich.: Michigan State University Press, 1959), pp. 318–19.

6. *Ibid.*, p. 336.

7. *Aid to Viet Nam—An American Success Story* (New York: American Friends of Viet Nam, 1959), pp. 36–37.

8. His most comprehensive article on the Vietnamese program is "Agrarian Reform in the Republic of Viet Nam," published in Wesley R. Fishel (ed.), *Problems of Freedom* (East Lansing, Mich.: Michigan State University Press, 1961), chap. ix.

9. See William Henderson, "Viet Nam's Land Development Program," *ibid.*, chap. vii.

10. (New York: Frederick A. Praeger, 1964), chaps. xiii–xvii.

11. Reported in *Nhan Dan* (Hanoi), October 31, 1956.

12. (Canberra: Department of External Affairs), October, 1959.

13. 86th Cong., 2d sess.

14. "Political Parties in South Viet Nam Under the Republic," *Public Affairs*, Vol. XXXIII (December, 1960), pp. 327–46.

15. For friendly criticism of Diem, see Lindholm (ed.), *op. cit.*, the articles by William Henderson (p. 343) and John Mecklin (pp. 354–55).

16. Full text in Bernard B. Fall, *The Two Viet-Nams* (rev. ed.; New York: Frederick A. Praeger, 1964), pp. 442–48.

17. From an article in *The Reporter*, December 24, 1959.

18. Quoted in *The New York Times*, February 13, 1955.

CHAPTER 8. THE PROTRACTED CONFLICT, OR LONG WAR, SHORT CAMPAIGN

1. A translation of the captured report, covering twenty-six pages, was made available to this author by the United States Information Agency. It was used by the experienced Australian journalist Denis Warner as a basis for the chapter "A Village Goes Wrong," in his *The Last Confucian* (New York: Macmillan, 1963).

2. Quoted by Warner, *op. cit.*, pp. 136–37.

3. The quotations from the speeches at the congress from *Hoc Tap;* these and other quotations from the manifestos appear in *A Threat to the Peace: North Viet Nam's Effort to Conquer South Viet-Nam* (Washington, D.C.: Department of State, December, 1961), Parts I and II.

4. "The National Liberation Front," *Viet Nam Perspectives*, August, 1965. A companion article to this one, presenting the Front from the viewpoint of a knowledgeable reporter who interviewed defectors, deserves study. It is Tukahashi Oka's "The Other Regime in South Vietnam," which appeared in *The New York Times Magazine*, July 31, 1966. This Far Eastern correspondent for the *Christian Science Monitor* in 1959–64 has just completed a two-year fellowship study in Viet Nam, sponsored by the Institute for Current World Affairs.

5. *Mission in Torment* (New York: Doubleday, 1965), p. 305.

6. See Frank N. Trager, "Laos and the Defense of Southeast Asia," *Orbis*, Fall, 1963, pp. 550–82.

7. See Frank N. Trager, "Viet Nam: The Military Requirements for Victory," *Orbis*, Fall, 1964, pp. 565–83.

8. John Mecklin, who was the head of USIS in Saigon at the time, has given a valuable firsthand account in *Mission in Torment*. Robert Shaplen, in *The Lost Revolution*, has done the best job of reconstructing the events leading to the 1963 coup and the aftermath of intrigue, coup, and counter-coup until the summer of 1965, when Air Marshal Nguyen Cao Ky became premier.

9. Trager, "Viet Nam: The Military Requirements for Victory," pp. 577–78. See also the author's chapter "The Far East," in David M. Abshire and Richard V. Allen (eds.), *National Security: Political, Military, and Economic Strategies in the Decade Ahead* (New York: Frederick A. Praeger, 1963).

CHAPTER 9. TO GUARANTEE THE INDEPENDENCE OF THE REPUBLIC OF VIET NAM

1. *Spectator*, December 17, 1965.

2. See their article, "The United States in Viet Nam," *Bulletin of the Atomic Scientists*, Vol. XXI (June, 1965).

3. *Viet Nam and the United States* (Washington, D.C.: Public Affairs Press, 1965), pp. 63–65, 80.

Index

Abdul Rahman, Tungku, 10
Acheson, Dean, 13
Afghanistan, 189
Africa, 7, 207
Alexander VI (Pope), 24
Algeria, 59, 189
American Friends of Viet Nam, 110–11, 115, 130n., 149
Annam, 19, 25, 34, 52, 59, 60, 62, 73, 74, 118
Army of the Republic of Viet Nam, 140, 161, 164, 172, 174, 179
Asian Development Bank, 213
Association of Southeast Asia, 5
Auriol, Vincent, 74
Australia, 3, 13, 146, 180, 193

Ba Cut (General), 127, 128
Bandung Conference of 1955, 5, 13, 106
Bao Dai (Emperor), 52, 56, 57, 58, 73–74, 75, 87, 107, 108, 126, 127, 128, 131, 132, 133, 138, 158
Barrows, Leland, 149–50
Bay Vien (General), 127
Beau, Paul, 38, 40, 42–43, 49
Bert, Paul, 36
Bidault, Georges, 82, 83, 84–85, 87, 100
Binh Xuyen, 107, 108, 109, 126, 127, 128, 131, 132, 159, 161, 201
Black, Eugene, 215
Blaizot (General), 75
Bollaert, Emile, 73
Brazzaville Conference of 1944, 67
Brunei, 3
Buddhism, 3–4, 8, 22, 23, 28; Mahayana, 5, 18, 22; Theravada, 5
Buddhists, 23, 108, 131, 217
Bui Quang Chieu, 51

Bui Van Long, 152
Bulganin, Nikolai, 13
Burma, 5, 8, 11, 13, 14, 21, 39, 40, 55, 76, 112, 150, 151, 175
Buu Loc (Prince), 86, 107

Cambodia, 3, 13, 20, 21, 25, 29, 32, 33, 34, 59, 69, 74, 81, 86, 88, 89, 90, 91, 93, 94, 96, 101, 105, 112, 116, 117, 119, 140, 150, 152, 161, 170, 176
Canada, 100, 102, 146, 201
Cao Dai sect, 22, 52, 73, 108, 126, 127, 128, 201
Carpentier (General), 75–76
Casey, R. G., 148
Catholicism, 28, 157
Catholics, 23–27, 108, 131
Ceylon, 3, 5, 12, 189
Chiang Kai-shek, 58
China, 3, 7, 12–13, 16–32 *passim*, 45, 47, 51, 52, 54, 56, 58, 62, 63, 68
China, Communist, 5, 6, 7, 14, 15, 70, 71, 77, 79, 82–83, 85, 86, 87, 88, 90, 91, 94, 96, 98, 101, 106, 112, 165, 182, 188, 189, 195, 196, 200, 202, 204, 208, 212
China, Nationalist, 13, 146, 151, 153
Chou En-lai, 13, 85, 106
Christians, 4, 29, 30, 31
Chu Luc (army), 73, 76, 77
Churchill, Sir Winston, 84, 85, 86
Citizens Assembly (Tap Doan Cong Dan), 135
Clausewitz, Karl von, 181
Cochinchina, 25, 32, 34, 51, 54, 55, 59, 60, 62, 108, 110, 118
Collins, Lawton (General), 108, 128
Cominform, 5
Comintern, 8, 53, 70, 206
Comité de l'Asie Française, 45

Communist bloc, 13–14, 15, 79, 90
Compagnie des Indes Orientales, 25
Confucianism, 18, 23, 38, 41, 108, 157
Constituent Assembly of South Viet Nam, 134–35, 138; *see also* National Assembly of South Viet Nam
Coste-Floret, Paul, 70
Cuong De (Prince), 44, 48, 49, 50, 56
Cyprus, 111, 189
Czechoslovakia, 77, 100

Dai Viet [Greater Viet Nam] Progressive Party (Dai Viet Cap Tien), 135
Dang Nahn Dan Cach Mang (People's Revolutionary Party), 171
D'Argenlieu, Georges Thierry (Admiral), 73
Decoux, Jean (Admiral), 56
De Gaulle, Charles, 67
De la Motte, Pierre, 25
De Lanessan (Governor-General), 62
De Lattre de Tassigny, Jean (General), 76, 79
De Montigny, Louis Charles, 31
De Rhodes, Alexander (Father), 24, 25
De Tham, 34, 44, 45, 49
Dien Bien Phu, 12, 77, 79, 80, 81, 82, 83, 84, 86
Doan Quan Tan, 35–36
Doumer, Paul, 36–38
Dulles, John Foster, 82, 83, 84, 85, 86, 87, 123
Duong Van Giao, 52
Duy Tan (King), 50

Eden, Sir Anthony, 82, 84, 85, 86, 88, 90
Eisenhower, Dwight D., 12, 84, 86, 123, 128, 129, 130, 141–44, 183, 193, 194n.
Ely, Paul (General), 76, 84, 127
Ethiopia, 189
Etienne, Eugene, 45
European Defense Community (EDC), 12, 83, 93

Fall, Bernard B., 120–21, 125–26

Fatherland Front (To Quoc), 116, 117, 119, 120, 145, 199; *see also* Viet Minh
Fishel, Wesley R., 170–71
France, 5, 8, 12, 14, 23, 24, 25, 27, 28, 29, 30, 32, 33–80 *passim*, 81–102 *passim*, 105, 106, 107, 112, 118, 125, 126, 128, 129, 133, 140, 146, 151, 157, 159, 188, 199, 200, 201, 202, 208, 211
France, Free, 58, 67, 69
France, Vichy, 55, 56, 57, 58
Francis Xavier, St., 24
Franco, Francisco, 198
Freeman, Orville, 221
French Expeditionary Corps, 72, 78, 79, 97
French Foreign Legion, 62, 72, 78
French Union, 59, 69, 74, 81, 87, 88
Furnivall, J. S., 40

Gagelin, Francis Isadore (Father), 29
Gardner, John W., 221
General Association of Vietnamese Buddhists, 22
General Council of Burmese Associations, 8
Geneva Agreements of 1954, 14, 39, 80, 89–90, 91, 92, 94–102, 105, 107, 114, 118, 122, 125, 143, 174, 188, 191, 192, 196, 197, 198, 199, 201, 202, 211, 213
Geneva Agreements of 1962, 90, 96, 187, 191, 192, 196, 213
Geneva Conference of 1954, 12, 81–102 *passim*, 105, 115, 118, 125, 129, 130, 164
Geneva Conference of 1962, 14, 176
Geneva Convention of 1949, 222
Germany, 50
Germany, West, 146
Ghana, 189
Gia Long (Emperor), *see* Nguyen Anh
Gracey, Douglas (General), 69
Great Britain, 5, 12, 26, 28, 30, 31, 55, 58, 69, 75, 82, 85, 88, 89, 90, 93, 94, 96–97, 102, 105, 106, 118, 146, 151, 175, 188
Gromyko, Andrei, 118
Guatemala, 111

Guillain, Robert, 125, 126
Guinea, 189
Gulf of Tonkin, 180, 181, 195

Haiphong, 54, 59, 70, 72, 97, 118, 218
Ham Nghi (Emperor), 33, 41
Hammer, Ellen J., 133
Hanoi, 28, 40, 44, 54, 58, 70, 72, 76, 94, 97, 101, 106, 118, 218
Harkins, Paul D. (General), 176
Heath, Donald, 108
Hinduism, 4, 22
Ho Chi Minh, 44, 53, 54, 56, 57, 69, 70, 72, 73, 74, 87, 95, 115, 116, 145, 161, 164, 168, 199, 200, 201, 206
Ho Chi Minh Trail, 176
Hoa Hao sect, 22, 73, 108, 126, 127, 128, 201
Hoang Van Chi, 154
Honey, P. J., 117, 199–200
Hong Kong, 54, 73
Honolulu Conference of February, 1966, 193, 194, 210–11, 213, 217
Huc Xuyen (General), 170
Hué, 19, 72, 108, 155, 178
Hungary, 203
Huynh Tan Phat, 170

India, 3, 4, 5, 6, 7, 12, 21, 28, 69, 75, 87, 88, 100, 101, 112, 189, 201, 202, 216
Indochina, 14, 21, 23, 32, 34, 38, 39, 46, 48, 55, 59, 67, 70, 81, 82, 83, 86, 87, 88, 93, 100, 106, 111, 112, 116, 208
Indochinese Communist Party, 53, 54, 56, 67, 117
Indochinese Federation, 69
Indonesia, 3, 5, 6, 8, 11, 12, 13
Indonesian Communist Party, 8, 57
International Control Commission (Cambodia), 101
International Control Commission (Laos), 14, 90, 101
International Control Commission (Viet Nam), 97, 100, 101–2, 120, 201, 202
Iraq, 189
Irrawaddy basin, 213
Islam, 4, 8; Sarekat, 8
Italy, 151

Japan, 6, 8, 13, 24, 40, 42, 43, 44, 46,
47, 48, 50, 51, 55, 56, 57, 58, 63, 68, 69, 72, 112, 146
Java, 4
Jesuits, 24–27
Johnson, Lyndon B., 141, 144, 172–74, 179, 180, 181, 182, 183, 187, 189–90, 191, 192, 193, 194, 195, 204–5, 210, 211, 212, 213, 214–16, 217–18
Johnson, Samuel, 102

Kadar, Janos, 203
Kahin, George McT., 200
Kennedy, John F., 111–15, 123, 141, 142–43, 144, 165, 172, 174, 176, 177, 178, 179, 183, 193, 205, 209–10
Kenya, 189
Khai Dinh, 50, 52
Khmer Issarak (Free Cambodian) movement, 90, 91, 94
Khrushchev, Nikita S., 13, 207
Korea, South, 12, 13, 82, 83, 146, 180, 193
Korean War, 77, 208
Kublai Khan, 17
Kuomintang, 53, 56, 62, 69, 71, 72

Ladejinsky, Wolf, 151, 159–60
Laniel, Joseph, 81, 83, 85, 86–87
Lansdale, Edward T. (General), 126, 130, 193, 210
Lao Dong (Communist Party of North Viet Nam), 116, 119, 167–68, 169, 170, 171, 174, 199
Laos, 11, 14, 15, 21, 29, 32, 33, 34, 59, 69, 74, 79, 81, 86, 88, 89, 90, 91, 93, 96, 98, 101, 105, 107, 112, 116, 117, 118, 119, 140, 152, 161, 170, 176, 206, 213
Latin America, 207
Le Duan, 168, 169, 199–200
Le Thanh Khoi, 30
League of East Asians, 42
Leclerc, Philippe de H. (General), 69, 75
Lenin, V. I., 70, 71, 206–7
Lewis, John W., 200
Lien Viet (Vietnamese Alliance), 116, 117, 119; *see also* Viet Minh
Lin Piao, 207
Lodge, Henry Cabot, 178, 193, 210
Louis XIV (King), 25
Louis XVIII (King), 28

La Lutte, 54–55
Ly Bon (Ly Bi), 17
Ly Nam De, 17

MacArthur, Douglas (General), 151
McNamara, Robert S., 210, 218
Magsaysay, Ramon, 175
Malaya, 4, 5, 10, 12, 55, 106, 175, 179, 209
Malaysia, 3, 6, 10
Manila Pact of 1954, 13, 86, 105–6, 176, 181, 183; see also Southeast Asia Treaty Organization
Mansfield, Mike, 155
Mao Tse-tung, 57, 71, 72, 206–7
Maphilindo, 6
Mecklin, John, 175
Mekong delta, 6, 21, 22, 39, 55, 74, 119, 131, 140, 213, 215
Mendès-France, Pierre, 82, 83, 85, 87, 92, 93, 94, 99
Menon, Krishna, 88
Merlin, Martial, 50
Messimy (Minister), 49
Ming Mang (Emperor), 28, 29, 30
Molotov, V. M., 82, 85, 90, 93
Montagnards, 152, 201
Morgenthau, Hans J., 125, 200
Mountbatten, Lord Louis, 3
Movement for National Revolution (Phong Trao Cach Mang Quoc Gia), 135, 138
Movement to Win and Preserve Freedom (Phong Trao Tranh Thu Tu Do), 135
Muoi Cuc, 170
Mus, Paul, 73
Muslims, 5

Nagy, Imre, 203
Napoleon I, 28, 29
Napoleon III, 31–32
National Assembly of South Viet Nam, 135–36, 137, 139, 156, 157, 178–79, 198
National Liberation Front (NLF, NLFVN), 117, 145, 161, 166, 168, 169, 170–71, 174, 188
National Reunification Front (Thong Nhat Quoc Gia), 116; see also Viet Minh
Navarre, Henri (General), 76, 79

Nehru, Jawaharlal, 5, 13, 87, 88, 106
Nepal, 189
Netherlands, 5, 12
New Guinea, 3
New Zealand, 13, 146, 180, 193
Ngo Dinh Can, 179
Ngo Dinh Diem, 52, 56, 74–75, 99, 107, 108–9, 110, 111, 113, 115, 118, 119, 121, 122, 123, 124, 125, 127, 128, 129, 131, 132–34, 135n., 137, 138, 139, 140–62 passim, 166, 168, 174, 176, 177–78, 179, 192, 194, 199, 200, 211
Ngo Dinh Nhu, 135n., 138, 178, 179
Ngo Dinh Nhu, Mme. (Tran Le Xuan), 135n., 138, 178
Nguyen Anh (Emperor Gia Long), 26, 27, 28
Nguyen Binh, 73
Nguyen Cao Ky (Marshal), 192, 210, 217
Nguyen Chanh Thi (General), 217
Nguyen Cuong De, 42
Nguyen Don, 170
Nguyen Huu Tho, 170
Nguyen Phan Long, 52
Nguyen Thai Hoc, 53–54
Nguyen Van Hieu, 170
Nguyen Van Hinh, 108, 127
Nguyen Van Thieu, 192, 210, 220
Nguyen Van Vy, 127, 128
Nham Dien, 18
Nolting, Frederick E., Jr., 176
Norodom Sihanouk (Prince), 90
Nu, U, 13, 106

O'Daniel, John W. (General), 130, 161, 163
Operation Brotherhood, 120

Pakistan, 5, 12, 75, 100, 109
Pallu, François, 25
Pathet Lao, 11, 14, 15, 90, 91, 94, 101, 118
Paul VI (Pope), 191
People's Army of Viet Nam, 120, 169, 170, 180, 199
Pham Cong Tac, 127
Pham Van Dong, 57, 170, 188
Phan Boi Chau, 41–42, 44, 48, 49, 51, 52
Phan Chau Trinh, 42, 43, 44, 49, 51

Phan Dinh Phung, 41
Phan Quang Dan, 75
Phan Van Hum, 55
Philippines, 3, 4, 5, 11–12, 13, 47, 112, 120, 146
Pigneau de Béhaine (Monsignor), 26, 27
Pliny the Elder, 21
Poland, 100, 101, 201
Portugal, 24, 25
Portuguese Society for the Propagation of the Faith, 24
Potsdam Conference, 58

Radford, Arthur W. (Admiral), 84
Radio Hanoi, 154, 167
Red River delta, 4, 21, 22, 74, 77, 89, 97
Revolutionary Labor Party (Can Lao Nhan Vi), 135
Rigault de Genouilly (Captain), 31
Roberts, Stephen H., 59–60, 61
Robertson, Walter S., 123–24
Roosevelt, Franklin D., 69, 198
Rousseau, Jean-Jacques, 47
Rusk, Dean, 105, 210

Saigon, 28, 40, 54, 55, 58, 69, 72, 101, 107, 108, 109, 116, 126, 128, 147, 155, 158, 159, 172, 176, 192
Salan, Raoul (General), 76, 79
Sananikone (Premier), 101
Sarraut, Albert, 49
Scigliano, Robert, 156
Shaplen, Robert, 109, 128
Shih Huang-ti (Emperor), 16
Si Vattha (Prince), 33
Siam, 33
Sieu Heng, 90
Singapore, 12
Société des Missions Etrangères, 25, 27, 31
Souphanouvong (Prince), 14
Southeast Asia, 3–15 *passim*, 18, 38, 53, 84, 105, 123, 150, 179, 181, 189, 191, 213, 214, 217
Southeast Asia Treaty Organization (SEATO), 6, 13, 105, 113, 146, 161, 176
Souvanna Phouma (Prince), 14, 15, 101
Soviet Union, 7, 52, 53, 63, 77, 83,
86, 90, 93, 98, 99, 101, 102, 106, 118, 165, 182, 188, 195, 198, 200, 203, 204, 212, 215, 216
Spain, 11, 24, 32, 151, 198
Stalin, Joseph, 13, 68, 207
Stevenson, Adlai, 187–88
Strait of Formosa, 111
Suez Canal, 38
Sun Yat-sen, 40, 48
Syria, 189

Ta Thu Thau, 55
Taoism, 18
Tay Son Hué, 26, 27, 28
Tay Son Lu, 26, 27
Tay Son Nhac, 26, 27
Taylor, Maxwell D., 174
Thailand, 4, 5, 9, 11, 14, 21, 39, 112, 146, 150, 176, 203
Thanat Khoman, 203–4
Thanh Thai, 43
Thant, U, 188–89, 190
Thieu Tri (Emperor), 29, 31
Thompson, Viriginia, 37
Tibet, 12, 87, 189
Tich Quang, 18
Timor, 3, 7
Tito (Marshal), 200, 201
Tonkin, 19, 25, 28, 32, 34, 39, 54, 55, 60, 62, 73, 77, 78, 79, 118
Tran Chanh Thanh, 119
Tran Luong, 170
Tran Van Chuong, 114
Tran Van Do, 89
Tran Van Giau, 54, 55, 58, 73
Tran Van Soai, 73, 127
Tran Van Thach, 55
Tri Quang, Thich, 217
Trieu-Da (General), 16
Trinh Minh The, 126, 128
Truman, Harry S., 12
Trung Nhi, 17
Trung Trac, 17
Truong Chinh, 67–68, 154, 168
T'sing (Emperor), 27
Tu Duc (Emperor), 29, 31
Tunisia, 59, 189

Uganda, 189
United Arab Republic, 189
United Nations, 6, 7, 99, 100, 101,

106, 181, 187, 188, 189, 190, 196, 213, 214

United Nations Economic Commission for Asia and the Far East (ECAFE), 5, 213

United States, 5, 6, 11–12, 14, 15, 47, 57, 69, 72, 75, 77, 81, 82, 83, 84, 87, 88, 89, 90, 91, 92, 93, 94, 96, 98, 99, 105, 106, 109, 110, 112, 113, 114, 115, 122, 123, 129, 130, 140–62 *passim*, 164, 165, 168, 172–74, 175, 176, 179, 180–81, 182–83, 187–205 *passim*, 206–16 *passim*, 217–18

United States Military Assistance Advisory Group (MAAG), 163, 164, 174

United States Operations Mission (USOM), 149, 152

Valluy (General), 72, 75

Vatican, 24

Viet Cong, 98, 116, 122, 145, 152, 164, 165, 166, 167, 169, 170, 171, 172, 174, 175, 176, 177, 179, 180, 182, 187, 188, 192, 193, 195, 197, 199, 200, 204, 209, 217, 218

Viet Minh, 14, 56, 57, 59, 67, 68, 70, 72, 73, 75, 76, 77, 78, 79, 80, 81, 89, 90, 91, 95, 96, 97, 98, 100, 101, 106, 108, 114, 116, 118, 119, 122, 124, 131, 140, 164, 199, 200, 201, 212

Viet Nam Cach Menh Dong Minh

Hoi (Viet Nam Revolutionary League), 53, 56–57

Viet Nam Duy Tan Hoi, 42

Viet Nam Liberation Army (People's Army), 68, 71, 95, 97; *see also* Viet Minh

Viet Nam Nationalist Party (Viet Nam Quoc Dan Dang, VNQDD), 53, 54, 56

Viet Nam Quang Phuc Hoi (Viet Nam Restoration League), 48, 56

Viet people, 16–32 *passim*, 152–53

Vo Nguyen Giap (General), 57, 68, 70, 71, 73, 76, 77, 78, 79, 81, 145, 154–55, 170, 206

Voltaire, 47

Westmoreland, William C. (General), 193, 210

Williams, Samuel (General), 163

World Council of Churches, 196

World War I, 50

World War II, 3, 4, 10, 11, 12, 34, 39, 52, 62, 69, 116, 175, 190

Wu-ti (Emperor), 16

Young Men's Buddhist Association, 8

Young Men's Christian Association, 8

Yugoslavia, 189, 200

Zambia, 189